Three Decades
of
Fertility

**Ten Ordinary Women Surrender to the Creator
and Embrace Life**

A Visionary Womanhood Publication
www.visionarywomanhood.com

Visionary Womanhood
13605 Harwell Path, St. Paul, MN 55124
www.visionarywomanhood.com

ISBN-10: 0615800750
ISBN-13: 978-0615800752

Unless otherwise indicted, all Scripture quotations are from The Holy Bible, English Standard Version® (ESV®), copyright © 2001 by Crossway, a publishing ministry of Good News Publishers. Used by permission. All rights reserved.

The medical information in this book is provided as an information resource only, and is not to be used or relied on for any diagnostic or treatment purposes. This information is not intended to be patient education and should not be used as a substitute for professional diagnosis and treatment. Please consult your health care provider before making any healthcare decisions or for guidance about a specific medical condition.

Any Internet addresses (websites, blogs, etc.) printed in this book are offered as a resource. They are not intended to imply an endorsement by Visionary Womanhood, nor does Visionary Womanhood vouch for the content of these sites for the life of this book.

Cover and interior design by Design by Insight,
www.designbyinsight.net.

Printed in the United States of America

"Worthy are you, our Lord and God, to receive glory and honor and power, for you created all things, and by your will they existed and were created."

Revelation 4:11

Contents

Foreword

I t's easy to find out "what to expect when you're expecting" as the bookstores are flooded with the answers to every new mom's questions. But there is a growing number of women who, after discovering God's heart toward children, have surrendered their fertility to Him, bearing children well into their 40s by the Creator's design. These are ordinary women, full of faith and still with questions, fears, and a longing for companionship on this often-lonely journey.

It should be no surprise to us that our culture is grossly self-seeking, using human wisdom for its guide, rejecting the mooring of truth found in Scripture. Tragically, the church has largely followed the culture, retreating from God's Word when it comes to the way we treat children and fertility. Once recognized as a gift and an inheritance given by the One who gives and takes away, children are now often treated as a hindrance to our plans, and so we severely limit them and call it "wisdom," seldom even asking God His opinion.

Many families, however, are getting a larger vision for marriage and family, embracing the reality that God opens and closes the womb, in His perfect time, to fulfill His perfect plan. Natalie Klejwa, a woman familiar with this exciting yet culturally uncharted territory, is a woman of vision. That vision has not only impacted her personal life profoundly as she seeks to glorify God in the prosaic of life, but it extends into a passion for coming alongside other women, helping them see God's plan for their lives and families from His vantage point.

Three Decades of Fertility was born from that passionate vision. Inviting you into the intimate stories of ten ordinary women serving an extraordinary God, discover the trials and triumphs, the weak-turned-strong, and the sweet peace that comes when a woman begins to see children as God sees them, becoming a willing vessel for ushering immortal souls into His Kingdom. In addition to catching a glimpse of this vision or simply being encouraged as you walk the road of God-designed fertility, there are practical questions and answers at the end of each chapter making this book an *excellent* resource for small group studies.

As a mother of 10 just entering my 40th year, I can't begin to express how encouraged I was to read *Three Decades of Fertility* and how thrilled I am about the vision and hope it will project for so many women, impacting not only our generation but, by its nature, the generations to come!

Kelly Crawford
Generation Cedar

Introduction

Through the pages of this book you will travel on 10 different journeys through the fertile years of 10 ordinary women. Women with the same hopes, weaknesses, fears, and challenges you have. While they have lived routine lives in average places under common circumstances, they have put their hopes in an **extraordinary God**: their own Creator Who also, incidentally, created the entire universe. This joyful surrender to that all-wise and sovereign Creator gives their lives a distinct twist, and a considerably adventuresome one at that.

Twenty years ago I knew very few large families, and the ones I did know were, for the most part, secretly looked down on by us *normal* folks. But we hit a wave somewhere along the way that carried us to the heights of a new discovery: God likes big families and even *wants* a lot of people to have them. Though our pastors were telling us that sterilization was the only way to really dig in and accomplish the Great Commission (kids tend to get in the way of the important work), the Spirit of God through His Word was saying the opposite. And some Christians started listening. I'm glad they did, and so are a lot of people who were born to those folks during the course of the last three decades—including grandbabies, some of whom are playing in their sandboxes as I write.

Yes, Christians started catching God's vision, and because of that, it isn't quite so uncommon to see a large family at the grocery store anymore. We can go to church now, and instead of being the odd man out, we are part of a family of God that includes *families of all sizes.* That's a marvelous work of God. But it has introduced uncharted territory for the ones who have chosen to walk that counter-cultural path.

I remember having a conversation with a nurse when I was 35 years old and at the beginning of my fifth pregnancy. She looked at me sternly and chided, "Do you realize that if you don't use birth control, you could have a baby every two years until you are FIFTY?!" I stared blankly at her, feeling like a 6-year-old, unsure of how to respond to this visibly upset adult.

I managed a weak, "Really? Fifty? Doesn't menopause hit before then?" She assured me that there were no guarantees if I were going to leave pregnancy "to chance."

It was like being at the peak of a rollercoaster ride just before the cars start falling. I was scared and excited all at once. Scared because I wasn't sure how my body would hold out (or my sanity, for that matter), and excited because it sounded like a bigger adventure than I had bargained for, and I knew it would take a Big God to get me to the other side.

Here I am, 11 years and four babies later, and it's almost over. It's been the ride of a lifetime, and I'm glad I stayed on board. I'm going to be sad when the cars round that final corner and come to a stop.

And I guess that's why I wanted to put this book together.

Here I am, with a body that shows and feels the wear and tear of multiple pregnancies. Here I am, on the edge of saying goodbye to two red lines on a white stick, rolling movement inside a baby bump, lips pressed against a soft, downy head with that special baby scent, warm life drinking in warm life in the wee hours of the morning, and itty-bitty t-shirts. Here I am, looking around to see if anyone else with grey hair wishes they were pregnant—just one last time. Here I am, looking online to see if anyone is writing about this. Here I am. Feeling a bit odd. And alone.

Feeling the same? This book was written to let you know that you are not odd, and you are not alone. Part of a minority? Yes. But there's no shame in that. R.J. Rushdooney writes:

> *"History has never been dominated by majorities, but only by dedicated minorities who stand unconditionally on their faith."*

God is writing history today, as always, and you play a small, but significant role.

This book was also written to that woman who stands wide-eyed in the line, waiting to board the rollercoaster cars, wondering if she is making a big mistake, or if she is in on the brink of fulfilling the purpose for which God created her. Is your life messy? Is your faith weak? Feel like a fool? If so, you are the perfect candidate for this adventure!

> *But God chose what is foolish in the world to shame the wise; God chose what is weak in the world to shame the strong; God chose what is low and despised in the world, even things that are not, to bring to nothing things that are, so that no human being might boast in the presence of God.* (1 Corinthians 1:27-29)

What this book will **not** do is chart your course for you. This book isn't going to tell you what to do with your own fertility. That's God's job. This is, very simply, a humble collection of testimonies to God's faithfulness in the lives of 10 women. Some had five children. Some had a dozen. Some birthed at home in a tub of water, and some enjoyed epidurals in a hospital bed. Some spaced their children naturally, and some didn't space at all. They all made mistakes. They all had human "issues." They all stepped out into the unknown with fears and problems, not knowing how it would all turn out. Just hoping and trusting that if they let go— God would catch them.

He did.

I appeal to you therefore, brothers, by the mercies of God, to present your bodies as a living sacrifice, holy and acceptable to God, which is your spiritual worship. Do not be conformed to this world, but be transformed by the renewal of your mind, that by testing you may discern what is the will of God, what is good and acceptable and perfect. (Romans 12:1-2)

Natalie Klejwa
www.visionarywomanhood.com
June 2013

Progressive Revelation

By Carmon Friedrich

A bit of blue sky, a thread of a cloud, the tip of a pine tree. That's all I could see as I hungrily gazed out the window while confined to my bed. A hawk that soared above a tree brought a flash of jealousy for the freedom it enjoyed to fly freely and wander where it wished, while I was stuck in my house and unable to stray far from my nest. It was my ninth time to be on bed rest in 10 pregnancies, over two years of my life spent that way.

When my husband proposed to me overlooking the Pacific ocean on a cold January day in 1980, amid the joy of discussing our future life together, he asked me a question that I'm sure every engaged couple eventually broaches: "How many children would you like to have?" Each of us was the oldest of two children. Each of us had just one sister, and our mothers bore their children in their late teens and early 20s. By the time they were in their 40s, both our mothers were "empty nesters."

How many children would I like to have?

I didn't hesitate when I gave my answer, "Four." But Steve's eyes widened as I said it.

"Four? That's a lot!" he replied, but we continued to build castles in the sky and bask in the newness of the commitment we

13

had made to build a life together, hoping that children would be an important part of that future.

We laugh and tell others that story of our discussion of having a "big" family, because the punch line is that we ended up with 10 children. *That's* a lot! Though I imagine it's all a matter of perspective, as once I had the privilege of meeting Michelle Duggar, who has twice as many living children as I do. It was the only time I've ever said to anyone, "I ONLY have 10 children."

Following the standard counsel from well-meaning folks who love to give newlyweds advice, we decided to wait for a while before starting a family. I got a prescription for birth control pills (which we later regretted as we learned about the abortive possibilities of hormonal birth control), and we plunged into married life, an adventure, but also a steep learning curve for me at 19, with divorced parents and an immature faith. My husband says he was a late bloomer, and at 25 he was still figuring out his career path, while I was learning to stretch our tiny income and simultaneously teach myself to cook. Feeding two people seemed daunting at times, let alone adding other little mouths to feed.

There was no aha! moment when we decided to have a baby, but there was some job stability when I became pregnant almost two years after our wedding. Steve teased me that if I WAS pregnant, I wouldn't be able to keep a secret. A challenge! So on a trip to visit my mom in Oregon, I went to the doctor who had cared for our family since I was a girl to have blood drawn for a pregnancy test. Those were the days before the miracle of home pregnancy tests, and I had to wait for a day or so to get the lab results. When the call came, I was, amazingly, pregnant. Though it's happened to billions of people before, when it happens to you, it IS amazing.

Remembering the challenge (well, I took it as one), I kept the news to myself, intending to give my husband a big surprise on my return home. I found a cute congratulations card with a picture of a baby and bought a cigar, and when I got off the train I presented my "announcement" to Steve at the train station. I couldn't wait till we got home.

Here's a bit of advice my husband likes to give young married couples: waiting to have children until you are "ready" may sound like a good idea but in reality does not stand the test. In reality, a man responds to the heat of the crucible by growing in his ability to meet responsibility. It is not by avoiding the pressure of responsibility that growth occurs. The time of most intense testing is the exercise that strengthens our souls, and learning to sacrifice our time, energy, and desires to care for helpless human beings is definitely a time of testing.

A woman's first pregnancy is probably her most indelible memory. I was 22 and had a lot of growing up to do. Being a mother was an exciting prospect, and being pregnant was a new and unknown experience. I had never been around other pregnant women, and I did not have any older women to give me a head's up about what to expect while I was expecting. I didn't even have the plethora of pregnancy books now easily available. I relied on my obstetrician and any literature he gave me to bone up on what was happening to my body. It wasn't much to go on. But I loved the tiny flutters at 16 weeks that turned into bumps and kicks. When I got married I had to have my size two wedding dress altered to be smaller. Now, after gaining 28 pounds, which mostly gathered into a big ball on the front of my small frame, I worried about ever fitting into normal clothing. Maternity clothes were ugly, tent-like, expensive, uncomfortable, polyester tops with gaudy stripes or plaid, and typically included "cute" touches like giant bows at the neck. Looking back, I wish I had known some hippies to get tips on where to find organic cotton and simple flowing skirts with more natural patterns.

We lived in a rural California community in the Sierra foothills, so rural that there wasn't even a traffic signal in the entire county. Every month we faithfully made the one-and-a-half hour trek to Stockton to visit the obstetrician, where I peed in a cup, got weighed, listened to the baby's heartbeat, and chatted for about five minutes with the nurse-practitioner, Maria. There wasn't much talk about nutrition, just an admonition about too much weight gain and avoiding salt so I didn't get high blood pressure. I would get a couple of minutes of the ob-gyn's time as he stepped into the examining room, glanced at my chart, and asked if I had any questions. I sat on the end of the examining table with a paper cover over my bare legs, feeling exposed and vulnerable. I didn't have many questions.

My baby was due the day after Christmas, but New Year's Day came and went with no baby yet. Now my appointments were weekly, and we drove to the city for my check-up. It was about a week past my due date, and the doctor told me that since it was taking so long for this baby to be born, we should help things along with an induction. So he put me on the schedule for that Friday morning, choosing for me the day my baby would arrive, 11 days after my due date.

It was a cold, foggy morning as we drove to the hospital, so early that not many cars were on the country roads. I had read enough that I knew some of the interventions to expect when they were prepping me for my labor, and I somehow figured out that I could express an opinion about whether or not I wanted them to do certain things. So after we checked into a labor room, I donned the hospital gown and climbed into the bed. I declined having my pubic hair shaved, but I conceded, after the nurse insisted that I would be glad I did, to having an enema. Then she hooked me up to an IV with Pitocin, and I waited for labor to start.

If I was not well prepared for experiencing childbirth, my husband was even less so. But he was a pro at being a comforting and cheerful companion that day. We had taken a Lamaze class at the county hospital, so we knew a little about breathing through contractions. Steve later joked that we used the "LeMans" method of birth, where the woman screams like a Ferrari. My contractions took a few hours to begin, and when they did, it was scary as I had no idea what they would feel like, and the breathing and relaxation I had practiced in theory did not help me much in reality. I have since learned that Pitocin can cause contractions that are much stronger than normal. When my labor began to pick up, the intensity of those contractions was a big surprise, and I got panicky. Nobody knows how long her labor will be, but a woman's first birth is especially unpredictable. Once my labor started, it only took three hours until our son was born. About an hour before his birth, I was struggling so much with the fear of the contractions that the doctor, who had come to do his rounds that afternoon and check on me, told them to give me a pudendal block, a shot of pain medication on each side of my cervix, which numbed me from the waist down. I could still tell I was having contractions, and I could see them on the fetal monitor, but I didn't feel much. The nurse had to keep checking to see how dilated I was. When I was fully dilated, they had to lift me onto a gurney and roll me to the delivery room.

My obstetrician liked something called the LeBoyer bath for the babies he delivered, so he made sure the lights in the delivery room were dimmed and that there was a warm bath ready for the new baby right after birth. They lifted me onto the delivery table, positioning my feet into stirrups and strapping them in. Then, whenever I had a contraction, which I couldn't feel, they commanded me to "push!" And I pushed, groaning and yelling as the pressure of the baby coming down frightened me, and I was fearful that I was going to turn inside out. I was embarrassed for yelling. Nobody seemed to mind though, and everyone kept reassuring me and telling me when to push. Finally, I pushed that baby out with a sense of great relief, and they put him on my chest. *"When a woman is giving birth, she has sorrow because her hour has come, but when she has delivered the baby, she no longer remembers*

the anguish, for joy that a human being has been born into the world,"
says John 16:21. We laughed over the funny little red, wrinkled
person who had just been evicted. But I didn't get to admire him
for very long. As they checked him over, his temperature was not
to their liking, so he missed his Leboyer bath and was placed in
an incubator until he was warmer, while the doctor stitched the
episiotomy he had cut. I didn't feel a thing.

Though I needed the nurses to teach me how to give my baby
a bath before I took him home, I quickly learned how to take care
of that helpless little being. I had never been a "baby person," but
now that I had my own baby, I was smitten. At 7 pounds 8 ounces,
he was average in weight, but I knew he was above average in every
other way. Sleepless nights, sore nipples from nursing, learning to
distinguish various cries, and daily laying down my life to keep my
baby alive; everything was a new experience but not unwelcome. I
was not prepared for this, but I knew I had no choice, so I learned
as I lived with my little guinea pig. And I started to become an
experienced mom.

It was a year before we got pregnant again. We had been using
birth control, helpfully provided by the ob-gyn at my six-week
checkup, but we weren't too worried about getting pregnant again,
so we were happy when we found we were going to have another
baby. Still no older women (other than the sweet ladies at church
who expressed happiness that we were going to have another
baby), still no books to give me much information, though we had
decided we were going to homeschool our children after hearing
Raymond Moore on the radio and reading his book *Homegrown
Kids*. Our thinking about children and family was starting to be
shaped outside of the box. We went back to the same ob-gyn,
upon whom we had lavished profuse thanks for his role in catching
our first baby after scheduling that Friday induction. Same old,
same old at the monthly visits, until there was something new. At
around seven months I noticed that my uterus was contracting a

18

lot. There was no pain, but I was having regular, strong tightening, and my growing stomach felt like a rock when I touched it. At my next doctor visit, I mentioned it, causing some alarm bells to go off, changing my status from normal to risky as the nurse observed those contractions in the office and called in the doctor. His prescription: bed rest.

When you have a toddler under the age of two and a husband who works long hours, "bed rest" is not what you want to hear. But my husband was calm and calmed me down, too, and my mom flew out to help us until I was declared safe to go into labor. Many women think that being told to have a time of forced rest would be a dream come true. But after a couple of days of inactivity, I know most women would find themselves getting antsy and ready to tackle the laundry or cook dinner again. It's not as much fun being chained to the sofa or bed as you might think. I am a big reader, but the dreariness and loneliness of week after week of little activity turned my brain to mush, and I couldn't even concentrate on a book for very long. I found myself getting depressed with some guilt thrown in for not being able to care for my baby, my husband, or my home. I felt isolated and didn't hear much from anyone while I was away from the bustle of church activity. I resolved then that when I was on my feet again, I would make sure to help others who were in a similar situation.

Finally though, the days were getting shorter as we headed into fall and closer to my October due date, the bed rest restriction was removed, and it seemed like the sunshine had come back to my life. I had gained less than 20 pounds because the inactivity caused muscles to atrophy and my bladder to work overtime. My nesting instinct was in overdrive. Because of all the pre-term labor, I expected that once I was off bed rest, real labor would soon start. But I waited and waited, and it wasn't until four days before my due date, in the middle of the night, that my labor began. It just happened to be my birthday.

I woke up my husband, and after a friend came to stay with our sleeping toddler, we began our drive down the winding highway in the dark, experiencing for the first time a trip to the hospital with a woman IN labor. As we wound our way toward the valley from the foothills, my contractions were really intense. I had nothing to compare it with, except my Pitocin-induced, medicated labor, but I began to sense that I was not going to make it all the way to the city. "I'm not going to make it," I told Steve, who was intently concentrating on the dark road. Thankfully, the small county hospital was on the way, and we decided to stop there and get checked.

It was around 3 a.m. with chilly, fall weather. We found the dimly lighted sign for the emergency room and parked as close to the door as we could. Steve managed to get me to the entrance, but the door was locked. We knocked. Soon, a nurse opened the door, and we told her I was having a baby, and it might be soon. She calmly led us to an examining room where she moved in excruciatingly slow motion while I had a contraction that doubled me over. Gloved, she did an internal exam to assess the situation. She quickly discovered that, yes, it might be soon, like in a minute or two! Her previous lethargy was gone, and she was energized. I don't know if she actually used the word "stat," but she called for back-up, and again I was on a gurney, being whisked to the emergency room. This time the lights were not dimmed, and I had to hoist myself from the gurney to the table, where I was not numb and could feel every sensation. Nobody had to tell me to push. I don't remember if I yelled this baby out, but within a few minutes we had another son. The emergency room doctor caught him. Happy birthday to me.

There was no problem finding a room this time as I was the only woman that day to have delivered a baby, and we were fussed over, especially because of the novelty of having a baby on my birthday. I was pretty proud of the fact that my delivery had been so easy and "natural." When going through Lamaze with my first pregnancy, I wondered if I could do it without medication, and though the teacher of the class wasn't pushing for that, I got the impression it was "better" somehow. This time my labor from the first contraction that woke me up until the baby was born was only one-and-a-half hours. A natural birth was sovereignly thrust upon me, but I survived and quickly recovered my strength.

We liked being country mice, but my husband's work as a software engineer led to a job change that turned us into city mice for a season. It was the only time a moving company packed our household and moved our belongings, a welcome help with two small boys and a cat to move, too. One of my favorite parts of living in an urban area was easy access to parks, bookstores, and libraries. My self-education and homeschooling journey began, and though my little boys were still years away from reading for themselves, reading to them became just as essential as breakfast, lunch, and dinner.

I hunted down the homeschooling moms at our large, urban, evangelical church, and I asked question after question. I collected resources they recommended, and somehow I obtained Mary Pride's book *The Way Home*, which was newly published and quite controversial. Pride details her transformation away from feminism and toward a biblical view of marriage and family. The controversy for most people arose when she went from "preachin' to meddlin'" by making a very strong case for foregoing birth control and considering welcoming any children God may choose to create. In the chapter titled "Who's Afraid of the Big Bad Baby?" she says:

> The real reason that couples are so attracted to family planning has nothing to do with the Bible. It has to do with fear. We're afraid that we can't afford a large family. We're afraid that we wouldn't be able to control so many children. Some of us

fear that without family planning we would have
to give up cherished parts of our present lifestyle
(page 46).

Ouch.

Some have portrayed Pride's arguments as extreme, but we
found them compelling enough to make a dramatic change, and
we stopped using birth control out of a conviction that God should
choose our family for us.

We were still on baby number two, and we hadn't yet arrived
at that number pulled from a hat on our engagement day, but
we now believed we should be open to having a "big" family that
might even exceed that arbitrary goal. We saw our new resolve as
not so much throwing caution to the wind but throwing in our lot
with God's wise goals for us, goals that we, in our mortal frailty,
did not have the ability to determine alone. So, we got pregnant
again.

When we got to that seven-month mark, the contractions
began again, too regular and very intense. My doctor this time was
a laid-back and funny fellow who was a general practitioner, which
meant he could be our children's pediatrician as well as my doctor.
With my history, of course, he had to prescribe the dreaded bed
rest. Our church was large and still new to us, and it wasn't easy to
get to know people, which meant we didn't have a slew of friends
offering help. To make this work, we had to get creative. We hired
some responsible teenagers (which isn't always an oxymoron) from
our church to be mother's helpers. After my husband left for work,
I spent my day on the sofa, doing only the most minimal things to
take care of the boys, and I saved housework for the young people
who came to help in the afternoons.

The day of my release from captivity arrived, and my return to
"real life" triggered labor; 16 days before my due date I "popped." I
woke up that morning with strong contractions. We didn't dawdle.
We raced to the hospital, so quickly in fact, that when we came to

a stop light, my husband looked both ways. The coast was clear, so he gunned it and kept going. Then we heard the siren and saw the flashing lights. Steve contemplated making the police car follow us all the way to the hospital, but he decided it would be better to comply, so he slowed down and pulled over to the curb. It was like a scene from a movie when the officer walks up to the window and the anxious husband points to his laboring wife. The policeman waved us on, not even offering an escort with lights and siren to hasten us on our way.

We made it to the hospital with about half an hour to spare, in time to welcome another boy into the world. This was before routine ultrasounds and the ability to find out the baby's sex, but we loved the moment when everyone asked, "Is it a boy?" or "Is it a girl?" so we never found out ahead of time which we were expecting.

With three boys, 4, 2, and newborn, life settled into a routine: work, housework, naps, reading, walks and park outings, shopping, and church. It was busy but not overwhelming. Then I noticed that I was feeling really tired and emotional, my face was breaking out, and I was losing hair. Could it be? I hadn't had a period since my baby was born, and I was still nursing him at 9 months old. I could now get a pregnancy test from the drug store and do it in the privacy of my bathroom. Yep. I was pregnant. After two and a half years between the last two births, this time it felt like having twins. The news was received in different ways by different people. It was as if we had crossed over an imaginary line, like the equator, by having another baby, and so soon after the last.

One night in my sixth month of pregnancy, my husband came home from work and announced he was taking us out to eat. I never got really sick in pregnancy, but I sure got tired! We strapped the two youngest in their car seats, and we all went to Hobie's for some down-home organic cooking. While we were munching, I started to feel icky. I thought it was just that tired feeling overwhelming me again, so we finished our food, but by the end of the meal I asked my husband to get me home quickly. We put the boys to bed; by then I was having some pretty heavy-duty contractions. I was 26 weeks pregnant. Steve ran across the street to the neighbors and asked them to come stay with the boys while he took me to the hospital.

I was in real labor, and once we arrived at the hospital they hooked me up to an IV filled with magnesium sulfate to try to stop it. I had contracted a stomach virus, and my persnickety uterus was contracting in response. Thankfully, the drug did its job, and my labor slowed and stopped. I had to spend the next three days in the hospital alone, and Steve stayed home with the boys, who had all gotten sick too. This was not the happy scenario I imagined when we decided to be open to lots of children. One of my favorite poets, Anne Bradstreet, wrote, "If we had no winter, the spring would not be so pleasant; if we did not sometimes taste of adversity, prosperity would not be so welcome."

Because my pregnancy was now high risk, my jovial GP had to hand over the reins to an official OB. I was hooked up to a home fetal monitor which sent a record of each day's contractions via phone to the doctor. I also was given a medication called Terbutaline which made me jumpy, emotional, and depressed. According to WebMD.com:

> Terbutaline should not be used to prevent or treat early labor, since it has risks to the mother that are greater than the benefits. Serious (sometimes fatal) side effects have infrequently occurred in mothers taking terbutaline during labor, such as chest pain, fast/irregular heartbeats, and trouble breathing. If you are pregnant or become pregnant and are taking terbutaline for another medical condition (such as asthma), talk to your

doctor or pharmacist about whether terbutaline
is still right for you.

At 36 weeks, after 10 weeks of bed rest, I was free. It wasn't
until close to my due date that I woke up after dreaming I had wet
the bed to find my water had broken. Another race to the hospital,
but this time too soon out of the starting gate. No contractions,
or very intermittent. This was new. I was told that if I didn't go
into labor by the end of the day, it was induction for me. All the
interventions I had endured up to this point had been difficult,
and if I could get my labor started on my own, you bet I was going
to try!

My muscles were weak. I walked for hours up and down the
hospital halls. Late in the afternoon, the contractions that had
once been my enemy were now a welcome pain. Refusing any pain
medication after all the drugs I had taken, I discovered that the
end of the hospital bed could be removed, and I had the nurse put
the back of the bed in an upright position so I could be sitting on
a slight incline to deliver my baby. No stirrups. It was my easiest
birth, though not the shortest, with the hours of walking and
about two-and-a-half hours of active labor. Our little girl was 6
pounds 10 ounces.

We finally had that "big family" spoken of as we dreamed
about our future. Four didn't seem like so many now; it just
seemed normal.

With all my reading and trying out my newfangled/old-
fashioned ideas of mothering on my hapless subjects, I was feeling
pretty confident about my calling. Easy babies and a chorus of
"Yes, Mommy" trained into my children contributed to the pride I
took in my abilities. I was on a roll, and another baby on the way
was taken in stride, except for the concern about the possibility
of again having pre-term labor. We found a midwife who had an
office and a professional manner that gave us confidence in making
the transition from hospital to home for this baby's birth.

She encouraged me to be proactive, not waiting for an emergency, but preparing for the possibility of pre-term labor by putting myself on bed rest before it became a crisis. So around six months we did that. Lining up mother's helpers, organizing our schedule and lives to have Mommy lie low and still keep the household running, I managed to keep this baby in the maternal incubator until close to my due date.

I had an appointment with my midwife a few days before D-day. Her only caveat was to tell me not to have the baby that night, as she was going to be out of town. My husband jokes that you should never tell me not to do something. That night, sure enough, I started having contractions that were different than usual.

We had planned a home birth, so there was no bag packed and nothing ready for having a baby elsewhere. I had to dig up the number for the back-up doctor and get directions for the birth center next to Stanford hospital. He didn't do home births. A neighbor stayed with the children, and I clutched the directions in my fist, running to the car in my bare feet. We arrived at the birth center, met at the door by the nurses. I ripped off my clothes, climbed on the bed, and within 20 minutes, our little girl was born. It was 10 p.m., only an hour or so of labor to get her on the outside.

The midwife stopped by on her way home to check on me. She had been at the San Francisco Symphony and was dressed in a glittering evening gown. I was not dressed at all and felt a bit intimidated by her glorious appearance while I was in such a disheveled state. She released us to go home, and we got there before midnight with our precious bundle, our sleeping children unaware that we had left and returned with a little sister.

Baby number five, though she now boasts that being the middle child means she is the most well-adjusted, had a bona fide case of colic. Every evening, from dinnertime to 11 p.m., she screamed and screamed, while I walked the floor with her and prayed and prayed for strength to get through to the other side. The first four children had all been born on Friday. This grumpy little girl broke the pattern by arriving on a Wednesday. I couldn't help thinking about that old nursery rhyme as I tried to calm her: "Wednesday's child is full of woe." God brought me down a notch or two as I had been pretty proud of my mothering abilities to this point.

We were living in a big house with a big mortgage, bought at the top of the market shortly before a recession sent house prices plummeting. At the same time, my husband's business had a downturn, and we were unable to pay or mortgage or sell our house. While this personal financial crisis was coming to a head, I was pregnant with baby number six. It was finally evident that we were going to lose our house and would need to move. Where to go? After five years of being city mice, we decided to move back to the country, so we looked for a place to rent in the rural foothills of the Gold Country.

At six months, I still hadn't found a midwife, and I had pushed myself pretty hard to pack up our household and move the few hours' drive away. My contractions were starting again, and it was time to stop the activity and wait patiently for the baby to grow big enough to be born safely. I asked about midwives in our new homeschool group. Eureka! (We were in the Gold Country, now.) I got a name of a Christian, homeschooling mama who delivered babies at home. Though I was back on the sofa, I was hoping to have my first home birth.

Kimberly had delivered several hundred babies; she and I had a lot in common, and we struck up a friendship, enjoying discussions about our family and theology. Not fazed by my pregnancy history, she encouraged me to keep a food diary and make sure my protein intake was sufficient. She also recommended drinking a nasty infusion of nettles and raspberry leaf, a quart each day, which I was glad I could make more palatable with some cinnamon-flavored Good Earth tea. I settled into the routine of managing our household from the couch. This was becoming easier with my oldest being a mature 9-year-old helper, though a bit more difficult with my husband working in the Bay Area part of the week.

Kimberly lived an hour away, so we decided to induce my labor a little early, but not with Pitocin. With herbs and stimulating my cervix, as well as breaking the amniotic sac, we were sure that it wouldn't be hard to get my labor to kick in. Kimberly arrived late on a Monday morning, as did a couple of friends I had invited to be there. My birth kit was ready, and there was a party-like atmosphere as we jumpstarted my labor. There was a bit of déjà vu as I walked up and down the long driveway with various companions helping my contractions turn into productive labor.

This time I wanted to labor in the big tub in our master bathroom. I entered more gradually into the different phases of labor, but that gave me too much time to think about what was happening, and I became frightened when I went into that shaky stage of transition. In spite of my strong desire to have a home birth, I also had some fear about whether it would have a good outcome. When I got in the tub I was unable to relax, enjoy the warm water, and ease into the contractions, so I asked to move to the bed. Labor progressed rapidly, but I had trouble relaxing, and my instinct was to pull my legs together rather than open them for the baby to be born. The midwife and my husband had to hold my legs apart (no stirrups, thankfully) and I pulled a muscle in my groin while pushing out my biggest baby yet: 8 pounds 6 ounces of chubby-cheeked girl. I tore a little and needed stitches, then I limped to the bathroom where the tub was my friend as I settled into the warm water again, floating my round little baby's body just under the water containing a soothing herbal concoction, healing my sore spots and causing the baby's umbilical cord to heal and fall quickly.

A young mother once asked me at what point in having children I felt overwhelmed. As I have mentioned, I felt pretty confident up to this point about my supermom powers, though the colic had shaken my resolve for a bit. Baby number six was my tipping point.

Our new baby was easier than her older sister, but with my husband commuting to the Bay Area, my older boys beginning to develop their own personalities and ideas that didn't always agree with mine, and with so many little people to diaper, discipline, teach, feed, clothe, and endure, my perfectionistic tendencies were thwarted at every turn, praise God. It is not uncommon for people blessed with children to make the transition from control to chaos at some point, but it is uncommon, I'm afraid, for parents to realize that the latter state is preferable to the former. It is where the blessings are found.

God tells us that if we are faithful in little, He can trust us to be faithful in much. We were learning this as we had many small trials to test our faith and our confidence, such as the family's month-long bout with chicken pox beginning at Thanksgiving and lasting through Christmas, with baby and Mommy coming down with it at the same time. Enduring those small trials trained us to have faith during larger ones to come. We also had a major car accident with all six children in our white 15-passenger van, Moby Dick, and our oldest son needed major surgery at 10 years old. These are the times that try moms' souls.

The injuries from the accident healed, and we settled back into normal, for us. This meant we were expecting another baby. And like normal, I didn't have bad morning sickness, just extreme weariness. I needed naps almost every day, and I was not happy if I didn't get one. Having routines and the help of the older children kept us all on track without mother's helpers this time.

Another routine we settled into was Mommy's bed rest, taking care to head off contractions at the pass. The last two pregnancies

Luke 16:10

had gone well with this policy, and it became the new normal. Life on the sofa was boring as ever. Occasionally friends would bring a meal or come to visit, but most of the families we knew were just as busy with their own little ones, and self-imposed pregnancy confinement is not a crisis of the same caliber as a car accident or a serious illness, though one insurance carrier informed us that pregnancy would be treated "like any other illness."

Kimberly had moved out of state, so we hired another midwife, Sheila, an apple-cheeked grandmotherly lady with lots of experience. We grew to love her and looked forward to her visits.

In the latter months of pregnancy I began having vivid dreams and couldn't get into a deep sleep. I told Sheila I felt like I had been run over by a truck every morning when I woke up. She recommended I take Valerian, a smelly herb that one person told me smelled like "stinky gym socks." That helped me relax enough to sleep more deeply so I could cope better with the busy days that still revolved around my sofa. Sheila also recommended that when I began to have strong and regular contractions, I should drink a glass of red wine to calm things down. It worked.

One hot August night (we were in a rut with birthdays piling up in summer, from June till September), I was awakened by a contraction that really hurt, feeling strong vaginal pressure. I woke Steve up and told him to call the midwife. He was groggy, but he came to alertness quickly— my contractions were stacking up and double-peaked, and I began to shake. It wasn't long before I realized this baby was not waiting for the midwife, and I told Steve he was *it*. He stayed calm and caught our baby. Sheila arrived nine minutes after he was born, and not one of the children woke up from all the commotion. Three boys, three girls, and now another boy.

I nursed my first six babies, no problem. I was (and still am) a big believer in the benefits of breastfeeding for both mother and baby. I confess that I used to look askance at women who gave their babies bottles of formula. I assumed that I would just be able to nurse this baby like all the others, but I had trouble from the beginning with sore and cracked nipples. The little guy was gnawing on me, and I realized later it was because he wasn't getting enough to eat. Sheila sent me to the lactation consultant who told me something I didn't want to hear: I needed to feed my baby formula. I cried, but I knew that feeding that baby was more important than my wounded pride. Using a breast pump and supplementing with the bottle, I was able to nurse my baby for an entire year, about the time I had weaned my other babies. This taught me a hard lesson about not condemning others, especially when I don't know their stories and struggles.

When I was 36, past the point when worldly wisdom tells you that you are gambling with your fertility and need to have an amniocentesis in case you have a problem pregnancy, I was expecting baby number eight. I struggled for the first time with being joyful at the news that we were having another baby. The problems nursing the last baby and the difficulty of having Steve gone each week for work and leaving me to run the household were among some of the challenges causing these ambivalent feelings. This time in the wilderness was part of God continuing to grow me up.

In her book *A Mom Just Like You*, Vickie Farris tells of her struggles to be willing to stop using birth control and trust God to give whatever children He planned for their family. Vickie quotes Oswald Chambers as she recounts her own turmoil:

> There are times in spiritual life when there is confusion, and it is no way out to say that there ought not to be confusion. It is not a question of right and wrong, but a question of God taking you by a way which in the meantime you do not understand, and it is only by going through the confusion that you will get at what God wants. (*My Utmost for His Highest*, September 12 entry)

We again used Sheila as a midwife, looking forward to her cheerful visits. I was on self-imposed bed rest from six months onward. We had another summer due date, and our July wedding anniversary was celebrated quietly in our room with dinner and a movie as I couldn't go anywhere for a date with my hubby. Later that month, in the wee hours of the morning, our wee baby boy was born in our bed. The midwife made it on time.

As the old ditty goes, "second verse, same as the first," not much was different with pregnancy number nine, except that there was a little more space between babies, and everyone was worried about Y2K. My children were also getting older and helping in the running of the household enough to make it easier to take a nap or do the shopping. Gone were the days of mother duck waddling along with all her ducklings lined up behind her. Well, the waddling wasn't gone. I continued to gain around 20-25 pounds each pregnancy, was faithful to take my prenatal vitamins, and semi-faithful about drinking the red raspberry tea in the latter part of pregnancy (there is some dispute about whether this makes uterine contractions worse in situations like mine). I felt extremely sluggish and had a hard time getting through the afternoon, even with a nap.

Sheila was like part of the family by now, and she took a couple of false alarms in stride, one of the pitfalls of having such fast labors and not wanting to wait too long to call. But one spring day it was the real deal, and she didn't have to leave until the baby arrived. We decided to try for a water birth this time. Our ninth baby and sixth boy was born in the tub, with little fuss and less muss. He was named after my paternal grandfather and my father, to make up for scaring my father a few weeks before with a practical joke: I had sent him an email announcing the birth of "twins named Jack and Jill" when our goat had babies. I think he was disappointed that we didn't actually have twins.

I still had the same nursing problems with the last two babies, though I had been hopeful with each one that it would somehow be resolved. We wondered if the seatbelt injuries I had from our car accident could have damaged milk ducts in my breasts. I followed the same protocol as before with nursing, pumping, and bottles for a year each. If you're keeping score, we are up to nine children 16 and under. Our older boys were involved with pro-life and political activism, so we spent more quality time as a family driving around in Moby Pickle (the green 15-passenger van), having car picnics, listening to educational CDs, and reading from a portable library I kept in a box in the back. A year went by, then another, and just when I began to wonder, and people began to ask if we were going to have any more babies, I was expecting baby number 10. The birthdays between this baby and the last would be almost three years apart. I was relieved I could have another child.

I was much more conscious about eating healthy this pregnancy as this baby would be born halfway between my 40th and 41st birthdays. After having problems losing baby fat from the last pregnancy, I had been eating low-carb and was exercising, and I was proud that I didn't look like I had borne nine babies. Now I thought it would be good to reintroduce "healthy" whole grains and lots of fruit into my diet. At first, I assumed my extreme sluggishness and queasiness was due to pregnancy morning sickness. I also knew that my age meant more difficulty with the "normal" symptoms of pregnancy. I was frustrated that there were no books written for women who had several children! I was getting bad headaches too, and over Thanksgiving I cried every night with extreme arthritic pains that began in my left hip and radiated down my femur.

Kimberly, the midwife at our first home birth nine years earlier, had moved back to the area, so we hired her again. When my symptoms were not abating after the first trimester, she ordered a blood test. My fasting blood sugar showed I was close to having gestational diabetes. Kimberly told me to go back to my low-carb regimen with minimal grains and fruit in my diet. Within a few days I felt great, better than I had in any of my previous pregnancies. Glancing back at pictures, I can tell I had less water retention evident in my face, and I looked healthier.

When I was about five months pregnant, we were hit with a family crisis, that was more emotionally wrenching than anything we had yet experienced, involving close relatives and broken relationships. This was a big trial that those smaller trials had been training us to handle. When the time for my "confinement" arrived, I felt like I was cut off from society yet again. With emotional turmoil in our family, I fought against depression and frustration with myself as I seemed to be unlearning all those hard-learned lessons from before. By now I thought I should have been a spiritual giant able to weather this small irritation, but I stared out the window and just wanted to escape.

A friend gave me a poem I tucked in my Bible, "Prayer Answered by Crosses," by John Newton. The poet first says,

> I ask'd the Lord, that I might grow
>
> In faith, and love, and ev'ry grace,
>
> Might more of his salvation know,
>
> And seek more earnestly his face.

After this earnest prayer, the petitioner is given hardships in answer and cries out to God asking, "Why?" This was the answer:

> These inward trials I employ,
>
> From self and pride to set thee free;
>
> And break thy schemes of earthly joy,
>
> That thou mayst seek thy all in me.

Those words were a great comfort to me.

A friend, who had used Kimberly for her midwife with her first baby and asked me to coach her through her labor, had moved away and wanted to hear my birth story. I wrote it out for her shortly after the baby was born, another planned "induction":

Kimberly arrived around 10 a.m. on Monday with Kris, who was her assistant at your birth. After the commotion from all the children died down, they started to set up all their equipment in my bedroom. Then Kimberly checked to see how dilated I was...3 cm, then while she was checking I went to 4 cm. She waited for a contraction (that didn't take long) then ruptured my membranes with her amniohook.

Kimberly suggested that she and I go for another walk, so off again. This time we went down the driveway toward the main road. We had a nice talk, and I started to slow down a little as my contractions felt a bit stronger. I had a fleeting moment where I wondered what Kimberly would do if the baby started coming really fast while we were so far up the road with nobody around. But we made it home safe and sound.

I needed to go to the bathroom and, while there, started to have those funny feelings that things were really starting. I came out and sat in the rocking chair, and everyone looked at me, and it got really quiet. I started having some really hard contractions where I needed to breathe, so I sat in the chair with my eyes closed and concentrated on relaxing. That was about 2:45 p.m. Steve made sure the kids stayed out, then he helped me through the contractions as they were coming quite frequently, every 3-4 minutes. (Something funny: Samuel had been following me around with his hands together to "catch" the baby in case it popped out. Jojo kept wanting me to get in the tub so the baby could come out.)

At first I was able to just breathe through my contractions like before. I worked very hard to relax. (Does that make sense?) I had put a quote from George Macdonald's *Lilith* on the wall: "Inhabit the trembling, yet be brave." It refers to someone who needed to face death in order to live. I tried to think about that quote plus look at a picture of our family, which we had on the edge of the tub. As the contractions got stronger, I remembered your birth and the low noises Kimberly had you make when you got panicky. I breathed in deeply as the contraction started, then I moaned out lowly with my breath until the contraction ended. Steve talked to me constantly and also helped me breathe. Kimberly didn't really do anything except wait as Steve and I were doing it all together.

I started trembling when I hit transition, and the contractions were really strong. I remember smiling when I started shaking because I knew the baby would be here soon. But it hurt! The contractions now had two peaks, so when I breathed out, I wasn't just moaning it out, I was groaning it out. I still worked on relaxing and not fighting against the labor. I could feel the baby moving downward each time. Suddenly I knew that it was time to push! I felt a little panicky, but

36

I didn't let that feeling overwhelm me. Kimberly saw that I was there, so she came over to the tub and gave me instructions (go slow!). I tucked my chin down and pushed, this time with a little yell, which I tried to keep low, not screeching! I pushed a couple of times, and his head popped out, then one more push and whoosh! Out came a little body. Kimberly scooped him up and put him on my stomach. I immediately started laughing. Sarah ran into the bathroom (she had been waiting in my bedroom) and asked, "Is it a boy or a girl?" I didn't want to know right away; I just wanted to enjoy holding the little body. Finally I peeked, and there was a little penis. We had a William!

At 6 pounds 3 ounces, William Wallace was our smallest baby and not as strapping as his namesake was reputed to be, but he was healthy and strong. That baby was the last one God gave us. While we were in the midst of building those stairs, step by step, it seemed like a job that would never end. But 10 years later, four of our children are married, and we have three grandbabies with two on the way. Moby Pickle has been retired, and we drive smaller cars now. I have coached our girls through three homebirths so far (two babies born in the water). Sharing with our daughters what God taught me, not just about childbirth but about life, has been a privilege I did not anticipate when I was overwhelmed with the dailiness of life. Lord willing, our youngest unborn grandbaby will be caught next fall by Sheila, the midwife who caught three of that baby's uncles.

His mercies are new every morning.

Carmon Answers the Survey Questions

1. How do you deal with the fear of increased miscarriage, infant loss, or birth defects? How can one handle that kind of pain, especially over and over again?

I never had a miscarriage, though I often thought of the possibility of having a baby with birth defects, especially as I got older. Our family has been involved in pro-life activism, and we felt we would welcome a child with health problems as a testimony to others that we truly loved any child God sovereignly gave to our family. We know many other families who have dealt with both the heartache of miscarriage and the difficulty of a child with disabilities, and observing their trust in God's providence in those circumstances has been a great encouragement to us, even though we have not personally experienced it. One thing we have learned though, is that everyone has trials (John 16:33), so even if they come through pregnancy and childbirth, those circumstances still come to us from our loving God's hand.

2. How do you balance life with older kids and babies? Do you feel this is unfair to the older children? How do they feel about having more brothers and sisters? Is it being greedy to want more babies at the risk of not being able to meet the needs of the rest of the family?

When we were on our way home from an ob-gyn appointment in my second pregnancy, I began to sob in the car. My husband pulled over to ask what was wrong – I was wondering if I could love our new baby as much as I did the first! Time showed that I could. I'm sure at times our older children did feel overwhelmed by so many little ones underfoot. I know I did. But we were very deliberate to teach them that we believed God had placed each eternal soul in our home, and we worked hard to show them love and remind them of how important they are to us. Even with many children, there should not be a problem meeting the real needs of each one if you refuse to let non-essentials encroach on what is truly important to keep family peace and unity a top priority.

3. What about the ethical issues of repeated miscarriages? Shouldn't I avoid conception if I know that the chances of that child living are minimal? Am I enabling death when I should be promoting life?

God is responsible for the conception of each eternal soul, planning that child from the beginning of time, and if a little one dies it is due to the eternal plan of God. When He takes that soul to live with Him, there is great comfort trusting in His eternal plan, and the responsibility for life and death are placed in proper perspective. Doug Phillips, whose wife Beall had two miscarriages, in his excellent talk called "A Hopeful Theology of Miscarriage" asks, "What if miscarriage was God's means of showing mercy and love on a human soul, and if He chose you to be the honored vehicle to usher that child into eternity?"

4. Do pregnancy, childbirth and recovery get harder in your 40s? I already feel like I'm coming apart at the seams! How will I hold out until menopause if I keep having babies? Am I acting responsibly when it comes to taking care of my health?

Yes, it can get harder. After our ninth baby, I was feeling sluggish and having trouble losing the extra padding, and I knew something had to change. I don't believe that pregnancy on its own "destroys" your body. It does have a profound effect on our bodies, but we do have choices we can make to minimize the extent of the wear and tear. I spent most of my childbearing years eating a lousy diet heavy on sugar and carbs. I said I had a "sweet tooth," but I was using sugar as a comfort food. My husband, also needing to lose some extra padding, suggested he and I go on a low-carb diet (in those days it was "Atkins") and exercise together, alternating between using weights, walking, and rebounding, just 20 minutes a day. The padding dissolved, and we had more energy than ever. We still eat this way, making sure to have lots of good fat and real food in our diet, and in our 50s we look and feel better than we did in our 30s.

5. How do I deal with extended family members, friends, and even the medical community who disapprove of our continuing to want more babies as we get older?

From my fourth pregnancy onward we heard, "This is the last one, isn't it?" A friend who had three boys the same ages as my first three, when I told her I was pregnant again, exclaimed, "I'm glad it's you and not me!" I felt like telling her, "Me too!" I never had anyone explicitly tell me that I was too old to have a baby. Having lots of friends who rejoice with you when you announce a new baby, no matter how many you already have, helps to get through the disapproving stares of others. We determined early on that instead of needing the approval of others, we would depend instead on the approval of God. If our feelings keep getting hurt by insensitive remarks, then we need to see it as an opportunity to grow into Christian maturity rather than allow bitterness to grow. A gracious response to disapproval (and by that, I don't mean a lecture about the blessing of children, but kind and gentle firmness) will disarm, and maybe even win over, those who don't "get it." As for the medical community, if you get flak from those you have hired to help you with your health care, *they* work for *you*, and you can fire them and look for someone who will work with you and not against you.

6. Will I have the energy I need to continue to raise children into my 50s if I have some in my 40s? Is it fair to the child to have older parents?

I already addressed the importance of diet and how it affects energy. But I also believe that our sovereign God ordains when a child will be born into a family, and the ages of the parents are perfect for each child God gives. Our older children were blessed with parents who had youth and energy, but they were cursed with parents who had less wisdom and little instruction about raising children. Our younger children have some great advantages the older ones missed out on, including more opportunities to do fun things because of all the adult siblings who are able to spend time with them, and the financial stability we have at this time of life means that we can do things as a family that were not possible in earlier years.

7. How do you explain miscarriage to older children, especially if you have repeated losses?

As I said, I have never had a miscarriage, but our children know a great deal about abortion, and they understand the grief of the loss of a life that has just begun. We had a friend whose baby died in her womb at 17 weeks, and she had to wait for a month before her child was miscarried from her body. We all prayed for her and spent time with her while she waited for this sad occurrence, crying often with our friends in their sadness. When the baby was born, this family buried the tiny body in their yard under a special tree, and our children gave a large donation to Cherish California's Children in memory of that little person who was now in Heaven. Children are very tenderhearted toward babies, and their grief is real and should be addressed in a direct and hopeful way. This can be part of their sanctification as well as our own.

41

8. How does having babies in your 40s affect your relationship with your husband? Don't I owe him some of my best years?

This is so important! Yes, your husband deserves your best years, but there is not an either/or choice involved: husband or children, which do I love more? Many women, being so busy with babies and children, neglect the man who is the head of the home and forget about their calling as his helpmeet. There are very few marriages of older couples we know who appear to be truly happy and loving toward one another. This is very sad and totally unnecessary. So many women think they have to find a balance between husband and children, but the real problem often lies in an improper view of self and family. Women sometimes think their "sacrifices" for the family are selfless when they are really being selfish: the problem comes not from too much attention directed to the children, but from women who find too much self-fulfillment from their children. Children *are* easier to control than a husband.

Too much focus on children is often too much focus on self. Yes, the daily trials of home and the expenditure of energy required for pregnancy and childbirth make it difficult to keep things in proper perspective. You must make a disciplined effort to honestly look at yourself, your emotions, your schedule, and the way you relate to your children compared to the way you relate to your husband. Be honest in your assessment of yourself and make changes if you must. It's easy to operate from fear and see your family as a reflection of YOU, worrying that their lives depend on Mommy being perfect. But *God* gives life, breath, and all things, and He gives us the privilege of being the means to being a *small* part of those things for our children. However, He gives us the greater privilege of being a picture, together with our husbands, of the intimate relationship between Christ and the Church. Don't forget it.

9. Do you have any practical tips for high mileage mamas dealing with fatigue, pelvic separation, joint pain, varicose veins, etc.? In other words, what kinds of pregnancy issues did you have to deal with, and how did you deal with them?

Fatigue was my biggest trial. Diet made a huge difference in my energy levels. But keeping a flexible schedule and not pushing the limits of my energy when I was pregnant helped a lot, too. When I was going through the long, long days of bed rest, I would be envious of mothers I saw who were busy, busy, busy right up till the day their babies were born. One mom I know was playing baseball and butchering pigs at nine months pregnant with her tenth baby! I felt like a wimp. But with some hindsight, I see a lot of women who pushed themselves too much and ended up with health issues later, such as adrenal fatigue. We were careful about doing too many outside activities, making frequent adjustments to schedules in order to avoid burnout. We kept order in our home with a daily routine, giving our day structure without being too fussy about the details:

Everyone got up around 7 a.m., and I made breakfast, or one of the older boys poured bowls of cereal. Then everyone was required to make their bed and pick up clothing and other detritus that had collected on the floor of their room. I would throw laundry into the washer when I would wander past the utility room, so that we didn't get overwhelmed by Laundry Mountain. Then we started school (beginning with Bible time), and kept going till noon. For many years I was either pregnant or nursing and always had a toddler to make life interesting. We expected reasonable obedience from our little ones, including no interrupting, but there were still lots of interruptions from them every day, which was frustrating at times, but we all learned to take it in stride and pick up right where we left off, whether reading aloud or working through a math problem. If anyone was prone to ADHD, having to deal with those interruptions gave them an ability to concentrate that could not be breached. After lunch, I looked around to see what chores needed attention: sweeping floors, emptying garbage, cleaning bathrooms, vacuuming carpets, and I matched chores to children until all was done. Laundry was a community effort, sorted into baskets while watching a movie together, and sent off to various rooms to be put into drawers and closets. There was another general cleaning of clutter before dinner, and bedtimes were early (some were allowed to read before turning out the lights) so Mommy and Daddy could have time to visit and recuperate for the next busy day.

10. Are there real statistics (not skewed to the cultural norm) available regarding having babies in one's 40s? How many mothers do you know who have had babies in their 40s? Share your thoughts regarding statistics and odds.

I am not aware of any official studies regarding older mothers, though it seems to be rather fashionable to be an older mother if the limited amount of exposure I have to the lives of celebrities is any indication. Women who are concerned about their "biological clocks" ticking away have demanded the right, because for modern women it's all about rights, to have children later in life after they have experienced the success of education and career. I'm not sure we should care too much about the cultural statistics and norms or even put too much trust in the culture of motherhood that our circles may represent. I do know many women who have had babies in their 40s. Some have, sadly, put their eggs (pun intended) all in the basket of peer pressure when it comes to family life and bearing children. As Jesus explained in the parable of the soils, when life inevitably gets hard, *"they are choked by the cares and riches and pleasures of life, and their fruit does not mature."* (Luke 8:14)

Though Mark Twain's quip about the reliability of statistics holds true, The Howard Center is a reliable source of statistics about the benefits of children and the importance of healthy family life for society (see http://www.profam.org/pub/archive_nr.htm).

11. Hind sight is 20/20. Do you have any regrets? Looking back, is there anything you would have done differently?

My husband says that if you wouldn't do things differently, then you haven't been paying attention. I had the honor of being a participant in two different panel discussions during Vision Forum's Baby Conference, one of which was a Ladies' Symposium on "Preserving and Promoting the Highest Ideals of Christian Motherhood." Beall Phillips was the moderator, and one of the last questions she asked in that two-hour discussion was, "If you could speak to your younger self, what would you tell her?"

How I wish I could time travel and give my younger self encouragement and counsel. My answer included telling myself not to be too harsh, not to take too seriously things that are not of great consequence. Our children are not pets or toys or extensions of ourselves. They are individuals created in the image of God with their own minds and their own personalities, and we cannot impose anything on them through force of will. That does not mean we should not discipline them or carefully teach them God's truth each day. But the Holy Spirit changes their hearts. We have the honor of being means God uses to bring them along, nurturing them in both love and truth, keeping the tension tight between those two crucial ideas. Too often, we err on one side or the other.

Carmon Friedrich *is a 51-year-old mother of ten, grandmother of five, and wife to one amazing man, Steve, for 31 years. She blogged at Buried Treasure Books before blogging was cool, and she now has a ministry counseling and encouraging Christian women face to face. Carmon appears in the film The Monstrous Regiment of Women, and she has edited several books including Passionate Housewives Desperate for God.*

Tracing God's Hand

By Jeannette Paulson

For as long as I can remember, I have loved dot-to-dot pictures. What initially looks like a bunch of random dots and numbers begins to take shape as you connect the dots. I have seen pictures made of 1,400 dots. Similarly, events in our life sometimes appear random, but they are not. The psalmist in Psalm 57:2 says, *"I cry out to God Most High, to God who fulfills his purpose for me."* Based on this verse, Puritan John Flavel encourages the believer to take note of God's hand in his life and to record it. He promises that in doing so we will be ravished by God's wisdom, tenderness, and protection.

I have not always traced God's hand in this way, but the writing of this chapter is my resolve to make amends. In it I trace God's providential kindness and help in my childbearing years. My story will not be your story, but I hope you will see the faithfulness of God to me and draw on that unchanging faithfulness for yourself.

Before I trace His kindness in my childbearing years, however, I need to step back and give some background. I was most comfortable as a scholar. Books are safe. When I was young I hoped I might write. That way I would be in charge of the story.

The world appeared a dangerous place with many things to fear. As a young teen I had vowed never to marry, and as a college student I had vowed never to let children interfere with my career. Nothing was going to put a crimp in my style. Nothing.

But I had not reckoned with God. He has a way of unsettling the best-laid plans. At a friend's house on a college break I randomly picked up a devotional by Martyn Lloyd-Jones. Some portions were on depression, and Lloyd-Jones understood it. Because I have struggled with depression, my hungry heart drove me to read more. I found *Spiritual Depression: Its Causes and Cure* in a used bookstore and later bought several volumes of Lloyd-Jones' sermons on Ephesians 2. On a summer break I set about to read and take notes.

I had grown up in the church but viewed sin mostly as dramatic things like hijacking airplanes and leaving your spouse. Yet God began to convict me of my love of honor and my lack of love for others. When Lloyd-Jones said that one has to be lost before he can be found, I suddenly saw with Job some of the "terrible majesty" of God and was deeply ashamed that I had loved my honor more than His. I felt His presence as never before. It was a sweet day. Finally I had someone bigger and more glorious to live for than myself, and I sensed that seeking His glory would be infinitely more satisfying than seeking my own. I gave God all of my dreams, put my hand in His, and resolved to follow. Now I knew I was part of a bigger story of which He was the author. I began my journey in learning to trust.

For the first time the Bible was living, and I wanted more of it. I enrolled in Reformed Bible College where I met the man I would later marry, although at this point I still saw my future in terms of singleness. But now, rather than some prestigious career, I was thinking of being a single missionary. Doors to go overseas closed decidedly, and I went home to Canada to learn to love my nearest neighbors—my family.

At a conference I attended, Elizabeth Elliot challenged the audience to read Mary Pride's *The Way Home* where children are viewed as a divine calling, and fertility is viewed as an integral part of Christian marriage. She exposed the bogus claims of overpopulation and the decided bent in our culture against children. Over against this, she set the biblical view of children as a gift and a privilege, a glorious calling by which we could glorify God. Nothing smaller could have induced me to put my fears behind and open my heart to being a mother at home. Shifting gears took time, thought, and prayer.

Unknown to me, Harlan, the man I had met at Bible College, was reading the same book. When we renewed contact, the book launched us into a discussion about marriage and children. We decided that we would marry with hearts open to children. This commitment I made by faith. From my youth I had dreamed of career—not children, and I did not feel confident. I felt weak, dependent, and afraid. It was a hard but good place to be. I hung on to Matthew Henry's words from his Concise Commentary, "Children are a heritage, and a reward and are so to be accounted blessings and not burdens; for he that sends mouths will send meat if we trust in him."

I was 28 when we married. Four months later we conceived. My husband had given me Robert Mendelson's *Male Practice* to read. Suspicious of medical intervention, we planned a homebirth and got some experienced midwives. For good measure we got a back-up doctor who assured us that not only would I be allowed to walk while in labor, I was also free to stand on my head if I wished—my kind of doctor.

The back-up doctor became more than a formality when my water broke four weeks too soon, and there was meconium staining in the water. The midwives came and said that the two complications together made it unwise to deliver at home. I had not even packed for the hospital because I was sure we would not go there. God had a different plan.

It was Christmas, and our doctor said we could go home and come back the next day for the baby to be induced. Under five pounds and his birth aided by Pitocin, David slipped into the world almost effortlessly. He was precious. He was small. And he had an infection. It was a mercy that he came early and that the midwives sent us to the hospital. With profound wisdom and infinite tenderness God spoiled our confident plan. What if David had stayed longer in the womb or had been born at home and the infection gone undetected? We came out less sure of our own plans and more dependent on the One who gives every breath. I have often reminded myself of Proverbs 16:9, "*The heart of man plans his way, but the Lord establishes his steps.*" Indeed, God's ways are higher than our ways, and His thoughts are higher than our thoughts.

When David was 4 months old, Joseph was conceived. David stopped nursing, and I was brokenhearted. A friend speculated that the taste of my milk had changed. I had set my heart on nursing David for as long as possible. My Father was asking me not to set my heart on things of this earth, however wholesome, but to set my heart on things above. He is a jealous God and wanted me to find satisfaction in Him first of all. He is the living water, a true oasis—all else is mirage. Though I did not see it then, I see now that I had committed myself to serve my first son hand and foot, catering to his every whim. God's cure for my indulgence was a brother for David.

As we began our family we had to deal with my husband being RH positive and me being RH negative. This required Rhogam shots during pregnancy and after the birth of an RH+ baby. Failure to do this would mean serious complications and the possible deaths of future children conceived. This was early in the AIDS crisis, and we were concerned that Rhogam, being a blood product, would be contaminated. Some careful research showed that this was no danger.

Joseph was born at home. There were no complications, and we were thrilled to welcome our very robust boy, 8 pounds 7 ounces, into the world. I was 30 years old. Looking back, it was my most difficult birth because of inexperience. David, being nearly four pounds lighter, required very little pushing. I did not understand what a friend later told me offhandedly, that the uterus is a huge muscle that actually does the major work. I took little rest in the pushing stage and therefore got very tired. I also felt rushed as another mother was also in labor waiting for the midwives. Yet God was present. He knew my exhaustion and graciously inclined my mother-in-law to stay two weeks to help rather than the few days she had at first planned. This was a sweet provision. And I discovered that each child has a special place in the heart of his mother.

Hannah came 19 months later—a beautiful little girl, very content and alert. A girl added a whole new flavor to the family, and we were thrilled and a little afraid. I sort of knew how to do boys—but what about girls? During the pregnancy I had slight blood pressure elevation but was carefully monitored. I was very excited for this birth, and a friend came over to encourage me and prepare soup, making the experience sweet. I have great memories of this home birth.

I had three very young children now and felt overwhelmed. At this point God provided an older friend from Canada (in her 70s) to stay for a few months to help. It was winter in Michigan, and she used to joke that by the time you got three little ones bundled up to go outside you had done a half-day's work.

Part of the reason that I was so stressed is because I ran a child-centered home—seeking to please my children in all things and to never cross them except in cases of great danger. This child rearing method makes motherhood a dismal affair. My child's naturally sinful heart, reinforced by my indulgence, made him demanding. I was tired of him, but thankfully God convicted me that this was not his fault but mine. I was being passive, unwilling to take responsibility. God used this misery to push me to grow up and take charge. It was also at this time that we read Henry Trumbull's *Hints on Child Training* in which he wisely said parents are not to break the will of their child by forced obedience but rather to train their will by giving consequences that will encourage obedience and discourage disobedience.

The physical intensity of these years is lessened in later years when older children share the labor. But those years were hard work. Later I hired help with housework, but I wish I had done so earlier. I remember talking with a Christian friend on the phone (how sweet Christian friends have been along the way), and we agreed we were not assuring ourselves that we could get through the next hour but rather the next five minutes! It is at this time, unfortunately, that some couples, with the exhaustion of the moment blinding them to the big picture, make emotional decisions about huge issues like permanent sterilization. I wonder if people are sufficiently aware of the spiritual warfare that goes on at this time.

I had always struggled with fear of man, and now it took the form of worrying about what people thought of us having this many babies—this fast. I aimed to please and was haunted by actual and imaginary criticism. God was going to deal with that area of sin in my life next with a big surprise.

Five months after dear Hannah was born, we conceived again. Fear of man crowded in. One morning, two months into that pregnancy, I felt cramping and lost a baby that day. Because of my fear of man I did not make the loss public, but I did go to the doctor, and she confirmed that my HCG levels were decreasing. I was surprised a couple of months later when someone commented that I had the pregnancy glow. I wondered. We did a pregnancy test. Positive. Back to the doctor.

While I sat in the office wondering what an ultrasound would tell us, the fear of man again crept up and threatened to choke me.

Then it came to me: I began to see that if people were unhappy with me being pregnant again, it was their problem and not mine. I was a married woman. This baby was my husband's and not that of another man. I was not in sin. Why should I feel like I needed to explain anything? Why should I feel ashamed? Fear relaxed its grip, and I said with Mary, "Behold I am the servant of the Lord." I threw myself upon the Lord; a very good place to be.

It is good we did not have a routine D and C after the miscarriage because I discovered that, though I had lost a baby, I was still carrying one, and she was four months along. The midwives had heard of this before and were not surprised. Harlan had read about miscarriages and the possibility of losing a fraternal twin, and it convinced us that a D and C should only be done if necessary.

Though I had come to peace about the pregnancy, I was weary. Harlan sent me home with Hannah to see my parents. We are not self-sufficient. We need others, and this break was a sweet rest. I had high blood pressures in the third trimester of this pregnancy but nothing critical.

About five months later our beautiful Ruth was born—full term and weighing 8 pounds 11 ounces. She gave a hardy cry and began nursing after a few minutes. It was another sweet home birth with tea, bagels, cream cheese, friends, and laughter to punctuate the hard work of labor.

I happened to marry a man with a wonderful library. In those early years I fed on the Puritans: *The Christian in Complete Armor* by William Gurnall, *Keeping the Heart* by John Flavel, *The Mute Christian Under the Rod* by Thomas Brooks, and *Precious Remedies Against Satan's Devices* also by Brooks. The Puritans aimed to do three things: inform the mind, stir the affections, and motivate the will to action. These books were like a hearth for the heart— they warmed my affections while exposing my sin, increasing my discernment and pushing me to obedience. Along with the

Scriptures, I still read the Puritans, usually a few paragraphs a day, taking notes in my journal.

All the while I was busy building a home library and researching home school curricula. Many people in our church were homeschooling, and though I was afraid, I was also intrigued. My perfectionism was a snare to me though, and I felt myself drawn to all of the most teacher-intensive curricula. Just to give a little snapshot into that period of my life, I can remember doing Winston Grammar with David when he was 5 or 6 years old while the breakfast table remained uncleared and the two girls ran with wild, uncombed curls through the house. God had more work to do in me.

Some people worried that I was taking on too much. On reflection, I think some of those concerns were legitimate. I was having babies, taking in boarders, beginning a teacher-intensive school curriculum (though we had a great Christian school in mind as a back-up option), keeping my home, and designing and sewing curtains. I was unrealistic about what I should commit to—too many good things—and the sense of always being behind was disheartening.

Sometime after Ruth we had an early miscarriage. We had a quiet burial service in the flowerbed at the front of our home.

Andrew was born about two years after Ruth on a beautiful, sunny day. I was 35 years old. I had some spotting with this pregnancy. Near the end of the pregnancy, he was pressing against my sciatica nerve causing great pain. I remember shuffling woodenly down the sidewalk much slower than my 89-year-old mother walks today. But God kept me through the difficulty, and his birth brought an end to the pain. He was 8 pounds 8 ounces—alert and with clear lungs. As I held him I knew he was well worth all the pain I had carrying him. After birth he proved to be a fussy baby, but again, the Lord, through friends, showed me that he was allergic to certain fatty foods that were affecting my milk. I cut out fats, which did no harm to my figure.

I have long loved a poem by Annie Johnson Flint called "A Red Sea Place." With God our difficulties are no more insoluble than Moses waiting with Israel at the shore of the Red Sea while Pharaoh thunders in pursuit. Did Moses imagine that God would open the Red Sea? The poem always encouraged me to trust that God would make a way in the situations that looked hopeless to me. Here is the first verse of Annie's poem:

> Have you come to the Red Sea place in your life,
> Where in spite of all you can do,
> There is no way out, there is no way back,
> There is no other way but through?
> Then wait on the Lord with a trust serene
> Till the night of your fear is gone;
> He will send the wind, He will heap the floods,
> When He says to your soul "Go on."

I had seen time after time how God had acted for me when I was in difficult situations. Though I was confused, God was not. Though I was weary, He was not. God always parted the waters. My part was to cry out to Him and then step forward. Testing and proving the faithfulness of God gave me faith and hope.

Seventeen months later Stephen was born—8 pounds 8 ounces and healthy. We gave thanks. I was 36 years old. At 6 months he literally would not stand in my lap but bounced up and down like he had his own inner soundtrack. I should have known he would love music. This made for two boys, two girls, and now two boys. When God later gave two more girls, we chuckled deeply at God's design.

Over two years later sweet Esther was born. She was 8 pounds 12 ounces and came with a vigorous cry and no complications. Her siblings warmly welcomed her. She soon had a head of curls, and we loved her.

Soon after Esther's birth we moved from Michigan to Spokane in Washington State. I had lived a total of 22 years in Michigan, and this was a huge uprooting. Some plants grow best when root bound; others thrive when they are dug up and transplanted. This move pushed us to grow in many ways.

I knew when I was fertile. My husband asked whether I would consider having another baby. He had always embraced every new baby with a warm heart and open arms. I was 41. I prayed about it and said yes. Abigail was conceived when Esther was about 18 months.

When we discovered that the work we had expected was not available, God provided part-time work with the post office in the western part of Washington. Maple Falls is a lovely little village in the Cascade Mountains on the road to Mount Baker, and that is where we moved.

As the pregnancy progressed, I was having severe back pain and was afraid of giving birth because of that. One night I had intense pain. Harlan prayed for me and reminded me of God's promise never to give us more than we can bear. The pain left and I slept. Four weeks later another sweet girl was born—an easy labor and birth. Shortly after her birth we discovered that my back pain was due to gallstones, and surgery was arranged.

In quiet Maple Falls we endured a storm. I had taken on the extra commitments of selling books for a publisher in Canada and teaching a writing class in a nearby city (neither of which God or my husband had asked of me). I was intensely homeschooling, and with a new little one, I found myself thoroughly exhausted and crying every day. I would wake up in the morning with a feeling of anxiety and dark clouds over my head. My husband said I should go to see the doctor. The doctor diagnosed me with depression and sent me home with a prescription for antidepressants. Before committing to medication, however, I resolved to look more carefully at my life to see if my priorities were in the right place.

Today I thank and bless God for this depression. It was His gift. It was the pain that woke me to a deep self-righteousness and resentment in my heart. C.S. Lewis said, "We can ignore even pleasure. But pain insists upon being attended to. God whispers to us in our pleasures, speaks in our conscience, but shouts in our pains: it is his megaphone to rouse a deaf world." This trial also exposed idolatry. I wanted my husband to solve all of my problems and make my life easy. Surprise. He failed me. My resentment stemmed from my idolatry. The pain helped to wean me from hoping in my husband and drove me to take refuge in God who alone is our help and strength. The crushing of the flower petal brings perfume.

I was exhausted. Our marriage was strained. We had sinned away the romance. Before I was married I would drop relationships when they got difficult. Impatience and unforgiveness disguised as restlessness would send me in search of new friends. But now I was married. I had made a vow before God and man that I would love, respect, and be faithful to this man. Vows are not hard to keep when you are in the "better," but they are tested when the "worse" comes. I bless God that He kept me those days.

One way that God kept me was my heritage. My parents had never even spoken the word *divorce*, and I had not spent even one minute of my childhood worrying about whether they would stay together. Their commitment was rock solid through the better and the worse. This is no small gift to give to children. This deeply shaped the seriousness with which I entered marriage. I did not intend to remain married only as long as it was personally satisfying. I had committed to something bigger than my own fulfillment, and that held me when the romance was gone.

The other great gift God gave me at the time was hope. Oh, dear reader, God is in all. He is in the book you pick up off the shelf. I picked up *Competent to Counsel* by Jay Adams. In this book Adams quotes Romans 15:13, *"May the God of hope fill you with all joy and peace in believing, so that by the power of the Holy Spirit you may abound in hope.*" God gave hope to me through those words.

There was nothing random about God reminding me from His Word "*First take the log out of your own eye and then you will see clearly to take out the speck that is in your brother's eye.*" (Luke 6:42) I was good at rehearsing what I saw as my husband's neglect of duties, but I saw now that I had a litany of excuses for my own neglect of duty. I began to pray daily for my husband.

The verse I prayed for myself was from Psalm 139:

> "*Search me O God and know my heart; Try me and know my anxious thoughts.*
>
> *See if there be any wicked way in me and lead me in the way everlasting.*"

Besides hope, this trial worked a new humility and repentance in me. This is undoubtedly the best way of wooing romance back.

When we lived in Washington State we were told that in the past the Nooksack River was dredged so that it would hold more water and not keep overflowing its banks. In a book on prayer I read Spurgeon's wonderful metaphor for suffering:

> "He is digging you out; you are like an old ditch, you cannot hold anymore, and God is digging you out to make more room for more grace. . .The spade will cut sharply and dig up sod after sod and throw it on one side. The very thing you would like to keep shall be cast away."

The sweetest thing was God bringing us to this lovely, quiet, mountain village to do this digging. I began to walk every day, and God walked with me in the smell of pine and amongst the white trillium and pink foxgloves.

We got an easier curriculum, and my husband, working part time, took on the lion's share of schooling the children.

A few years after Abigail's birth, we had another early miscarriage. My husband called all of the children together and we had a solemn little funeral service in the yard where we lived. This was a powerful testimony to life beginning at conception.

Then followed a move to Minnesota where we had two early miscarriages. My last pregnancy was when I was 46. Although I cannot remember all of the emotions, I am sure I was surprised and needed a few days to process it all. But soon I came to a place of deep rejoicing. I was deeply excited that God was giving another baby. So were the children. This was testimony that God had given me victory in this area from the fear of man. I had seen time after time how God had acted for me when I was in difficulty. When the baby died early in the womb everyone was sad. Some of us cried.

Walking with the Lord, a child born at 42 is a great blessing. I delight that at 55 I still have young teens at home. I feel very rich. I have a place; a calling for this season. There is rest in saying with the psalmist *"I cry out to God Most High, to God who fulfills his purpose for me."* (Psalm 57:2)

The tender care of the Father is clear when I trace His hand in my life. Under the joy, the busyness, the pain, the clarity, the confusion, and the delight, are His hands tenderly upholding me and working out His purposes for me. Study your life and see God's hand. Draw on his unchanging faithfulness today, tomorrow, and all the days he gives you.

Jeannette Answers the Survey Questions

1. How do you deal with the fear of increased miscarriage, infant loss, or birth defects? How can one handle that kind of pain, especially over and over again?

We fear many things. Fear is powerful. And fear is often worse than any actual pain we experience. We should resolve by God's grace not to live in fear but by faith.

In 1 Peter 3:6 Peter says to Christian women, *"And you are [Sarah's] children, if you do good and do not fear anything that is frightening."* And Paul says to Timothy in 2 Timothy 1:7 *"For God gave us a spirit not of fear but of power and love and self-control."* It is so easy to give way to fear in life. God understands this, and that's why He commands us so often in Scripture to trust Him. The life of faith is full of risk from our point of view, but faith is believing that God is orchestrating all for my good and for His glory.

Take specific fears and imagine the worst case scenario. For example, what if God gives you a baby with birth defects? John Knight, a father in our church, has a severely handicapped son and said that nothing had grown him like having a disabled son. He had met Christ and tasted His goodness as never before. Now there is a mystery of Providence.

Further, I can't help but think of a letter we recently received from a family whose 10th baby is a little girl with Down syndrome. They spoke of God gifting their Abigail with an extra chromosome. They said "gifting" because Scripture teaches every event in the universe is directed by the hand of the King of kings. Even those things that are the effect of the fall are used by God to bring honor to His name. Jesus spoke of a man born blind not due to the sin either of the man or his parents but "that the works of God should be revealed in him." If you could watch the video of their entire family cheering, laughing, giggling and pleading with little Abigail, at one month, to flip over, you would see that they believe God has given them a very special gift.

But knowing God is with us in the storm does not mean we feel no pain. Both of these families have felt the pain, but they have a theology of suffering. We all need that.

A theology of suffering shows us the root of suffering is in sin. But it also teaches us that alongside the deep sweet pleasure of knowing Christ, believers have been promised suffering. Suffering is an integral part of the Christian life, one of God's major tools for our sanctification. We do ourselves a great disservice to expect otherwise. John Calvin says, "For all whom the Lord has chosen and received into the society of his saints ought to prepare themselves for a life that is hard, difficult, laborious, and full of countless griefs." Calvin discusses how suffering, more than anything else, works faith, hope, humility, obedience, repentance, and joy in us, if we receive it from the gracious hand of God. "*He does not willingly afflict or grieve the children of men.*" (Lamentations 3:33) He does it for gracious purposes. Puritan Flavel said, "God's heart is full of love, whilst the face of providence is full of frowns." The proof of his love is his death on the cross.

To the godly, children are a heritage of the Lord and the fruit of the womb is His reward. Remember, nothing ventured, nothing gained.

2. How do you balance life with older kids and babies? Do you feel this is unfair to the older children? How do they feel about having more brothers and sisters? Is it being greedy to want more babies at the risk of not being able to meet the needs of the rest of the family?

We will all be helped if we look at God's law as our reference for what is right and wrong rather than our culture. There are many cultural taboos that are not violations of God's law so we should not be bound by them. God's law frees us to great ventures of obedience.

I would reframe that last question about greed this way: What are my duties to my children? How will having another baby keep me from doing those duties? It is slightly ironic to ask whether wanting another baby is greedy if we really understand the call to servanthood that motherhood is. Rachel Jankovic in *Fit to Burst* calls motherhood an opportunity to practice servanthood everyday—until, like practicing the piano, we do it well.

As parents we have clear and definite duties to our children. We sin when we neglect them. Joel Beeke has a lovely book called *Parenting by God's Promises* in which he talks about parents' duties to their children. Parents are not "consensus administrators," taking votes on decisions to be made for the household; neither are they "horns of plenty," breeding greed by indulging every desire of the child; and they are not "wishing wells," unpredictable because they rule by their feelings rather than principle. Rather a Christian father— helped by his wife—must be a prophet, the tool through whom God teaches children; a priest, praying for them and channeling God's blessing to them; and a governor through whom God rules over the children.

As far as balancing older children with babies, I actually never had that situation because I started late, and my batch of eight came in about a 12-year period. I can't see it being a problem, however. Babies make us laugh; they make us forget ourselves and set us on a grand mission. I thank God that our children welcomed each new baby that came along. In fact, after we had finished having our family, the children pleaded with us to adopt. That blessed my heart.

One father of a family of 12 talked of having antenna to pick up when a particular child is not doing well. I believe God gives that.

One child of ours was particularly naughty after the birth of a younger sibling. It was all uphill with her. But God gave wisdom. I began to see how she was feeling left out with all the fawning over the new baby. Repenting, I began saturating her in love, giving hugs and kisses, reading lots of stories and telling her how special she was to me. She adjusted well.

There are real benefits to a large family—practical and spiritual. Large families have many opportunities to serve each other and practice selflessness. Spiritually they can be of tremendous blessing to the church and state.

3. What about the ethical issues of repeated miscarriages? Shouldn't I avoid conception if I know that the chances of that child living are minimal? Am I enabling death when I should be promoting life?

Here the law of God is indispensable to distinguish real guilt from false guilt. Beware of the accuser. The sixth commandment calls us to protect and preserve life. This means we have a duty to care for our body and be as healthy as possible for pregnancy and the health and life of the baby. Anything that harms life is sin. Means to protect the life in the womb include delaying delivery, progesterone shots, Rhogam shots, or vitamins. We have a friend who, having lost two babies, found herself pregnant and with low progesterone. Her Christian doctor taught her husband how to give a progesterone shot twice a week, and today they are kissing a precious baby boy.

We must beware of a fatalism that purports to know the future. It is inconsistent with being a child of God. God says that the days of everyone's life are written in His book. *"Are not two sparrows sold for a penny? And not one of them will fall to the ground apart from your Father."* (Matthew 10:29) Nothing is by chance or random. One Puritan said that God does not leave His creation like a boat with no one to steer it, to be crashed by the waves and rocks. The future is in God's hands. And real life stories are full of surprises. Chances for Isaac being born were certainly laughable.

4. Do pregnancy, childbirth, and recovery get harder in your 40s? I already feel like I'm coming apart at the seams! How will I hold out until menopause if I keep having babies? Am I acting responsibly when it comes to taking care of my health?

Of course we should do whatever we can to take care of our health. And I don't mean just physical health, I mean spiritual and emotional as well. Mama needs to be cared for and should be given time and means to do so. Diet and exercise, rest and refreshment, supplements and medical care are all important. In most cases pregnancy is not a great risk, but sometimes it is. In those cases, I am not God, your husband, or your doctor to say what should be done. Ask for wisdom from God who gives generously without reproach.

In 1936 the Christian Reformed Church came out with a statement on birth control. It warned against a worldly attitude that looks as children as an incidental rather than a primary function of marriage and strongly encouraged that in instances of medical questions, a Christian doctor be sought who holds Christian morals.

Rebekah Jankovic in *Loving the Little Years* calls our bodies tools to be used, not treasures to be stored: "Scars and stretch marks and muffin tops are all part of your kingdom work . . . of joyfully giving your body to another." Of course, like tools, our bodies also need to be maintained. Read her book for more counter-cultural gems like that.

I guess what I want to say is do not live out of fear. Live in faith one day at a time. Do not borrow tomorrow's trouble. God is the God of the Red Sea.

5. How do I deal with extended family members, friends, and even the medical community who disapprove of our continuing to want more babies as we get older?

Get a Christian doctor and take his advice seriously. Know that many in the medical community have a worldly bias against children rather than the welcoming heart of the Lord Jesus.

If someone comes with concerns we should humbly listen to them and weigh what they say before God. It is important to guard your heart in all of this. Assume the best about these friends and family members. They care about you. But if they are suggesting that having more children is irresponsible, and your conscience is clear that it is not, do not give way to fear and man pleasing. This decision is ultimately between you, God, your husband, and your doctor.

6. Will I have the energy I need to continue to raise children into my 50s if I have some in my 40s? Is it fair to the child to have older parents?

You know, it is funny. I just turned 55, and I told my family that when I was young I thought 50 was old. But now that I am here, I do not feel old. Yes, my body needs more care in some ways, but isn't it an interesting providence that very few of us have toddlers to run after when we are this age? If we do, we usually have older children to help us. Also, the press of duties keeps us moving—one of the best ways to keep fit!

I am reading *Strong Women Stay Young*, a study done on older women. In the past it was assumed that losing bone mass, energy, strength, and muscle was inevitable as we get older. But they have discovered that a routine of simple strengthening exercises actually helps to reverse this decline.

If we are not all we were physically at 30, by God's grace we have grown in patience, wisdom, hope, prayer, affection, and humility. That is not a bad trade off in my opinion.

7. How do you explain miscarriage to older children, especially if you have repeated losses?

Tell them it is a call to suffer. Losing a baby in miscarriage is a teaching moment to give your children a theology of suffering. By God's grace, they won't be surprised and tempted to turn back from following the Lord when difficulty comes. Teach them that God is denying us certain pleasures in the present because He is working His eternal purposes for our good.

Tell them it is a call to faith. Talk to them about the sovereignty of God and the unspeakable mysteries of His providence. Tell and retell the story of Joseph who chose to trust and obey in the darkest night as God worked out His astonishing purposes. Model that trust in the storm. Though, as Puritan Flavel says, we see providence as the "disjointed wheels and scattered pins of a watch," yet in glory we will see the timepiece as a whole. This calls for the response of the writer of Psalm 131 who says, "*I do not occupy myself with things too great and too marvelous,*" but I will calm and quiet my soul like a weaned child with his mother.

Tell them that miscarriage demonstrates the fragility of life and the fact that we are not promised tomorrow. Press on them our need to use each day for God. I can't help but think of Temple Gairdner, brilliant and devoted missionary to the Muslims in Egypt, whose earnestness to follow God was born when his youngest brother suddenly died. Gairdner began to weigh his love of success and fame in the light of eternity and found it wanting. He gave himself for missions and mastered Arabic in six months, becoming, according to his Arabic teacher, "more Egyptian than the Egyptians."

8. How does having babies in your 40s affect your relationship with your husband? Don't I owe him some of my best years?

Let's define duty Biblically. Actually our husbands, after God, should always come before the children. This does not mean he always gets more time or attention, but his leadership should be honored and sought.

Rachel Jankovic wisely says that we should not consider time given to children as somehow stolen. My husband has always been very openhearted toward children. I like the big picture that the Puritans had on this. Joel Beeke in *Parenting by God's Promises* says:

> The Puritans viewed child rearing as a responsibility larger in scope than the interests of their own families. They viewed families as nurseries for church and society. Puritan parents thus did everything possible to make sure their children conformed to biblical norms and precepts so they would be well-trained, educated, self-disciplined, cultured and godly citizens of the commonwealth and stalwart members of Christ's church. Isn't that what we want today?

We are doing something very great together. Children are a huge venture of eternal significance.

9. Do you have any practical tips for high mileage mamas dealing with fatigue, pelvic separation, joint pain, varicose veins, etc.? In other words, what kinds of pregnancy issues did you have to deal with, and how did you deal with them?

Personally I have been blessed with very good health. Abigail's birth was excellent, and I felt well physically. I felt perfectly well even at 46. The incapacitating problems were treatable.

At one point after having a few children, I was very faint and dizzy. I could not clear the breakfast table without laying my head on the table. A friend had a great chiropractor who told her she needed B complex and calcium with magnesium. I took those and soon felt better.

I did have backaches that the chiropractor and a gallbladder operation took care of. I got plantar fascia and could not walk on my bare feet, but a trip to the podiatrist and $400 worth of shoes with proper arches and cushion put me back on my feet again.

I also had joint pain, especially knees, and severe lower back pain in my 50s which half crippled me. This combined with my sciatica acting up at times made it so that I could not sleep on my side. A visit to a good chiropractor showed me that I was not stretching properly, and tight muscles were pressing on sensitive areas. I began an exercise routine, and I feel 10 years younger than I did before.

On fatigue, I would say take daily naps, go early to bed when possible, and pick extras with great care. Focus. Focus. Ask God to help you discipline yourself to say **no**. Follow God and respect your husband's wishes. Do not allow others, including children, to dictate your schedule. God willing, there will be other seasons in your life to pursue further interests. If not, all of eternity awaits.

Get some help. Skip going out to eat and use the money to hire a housekeeper. At one point I also had some young ladies come to read to the children.

10. Are there real statistics (not skewed to the cultural norm) available regarding having babies in one's 40s? How many mothers do you know who have had babies in their 40s? Share your thoughts regarding statistics and odds.

I don't know much about statistics and odds. We have not researched that. As far as knowing anyone who has had babies in their 40s, I could name half a dozen without much thought.

11. Hind sight is 20/20. Do you have any regrets? Looking back, is there anything you would have done differently?

Let me say first that Lloyd-Jones would say that regrets are vain. They are the wasting of today over what you cannot change in the past.

But let me also say I believe parenting lays our sins bare as nothing else. And so, though regrets are vain, there is plenty of room for repentance. George Whitefield said the greatest burden of his life was his remaining sin. I understand that. I remember weeping over the phone seeking counsel from a godly woman. She said, "We suffer from the sins of our parents and our children suffer from ours. That is just the way it is." I was greatly comforted reading Puritan Thomas Brooks on reasons for God leaving us with remaining sin after conversion: It keeps us humble and reminds us of our ongoing desperate need of a Savior. The righteous man falls seven times and gets up again. That is the story of my life.

Early on, I cared more to have the obedience of my children than to have their heart. It was law without love more times than I care to remember.

Too many expectations for myself made me often feel a failure. My husband likes to quote St Francis of Assisi who apparently said, "Do few things and do them well." I remember being greatly impressed by Puritan Thomas Manton's analogy of a magnifying glass concentrating the beams of the sun so that a fire can start. Commenting in *Flowers from a Puritan Garden* Spurgeon goes on to say that many squander their energy on many pursuits whereas if they would concentrate their energies they would be able to accomplish something mighty.

I wish I had been more patient and joyful in the childbearing and childrearing season of my life. I have many interests and dreams—way more than could be accomplished in a lifetime—and it was hard for me to believe that this really was a season that would soon pass. Reading *The Rare Jewel of Christian Contentment* by Jeremiah Burroughs was a great help. So was Randy Alcorn's book *Heaven*. I was greatly relieved to learn that in heaven we will have eternity to pursue the work and interests we had not had time for on earth.

I also thought that the children's needs were more pressing than my husband's, and, I am sorry to say, I was inclined to honor their wishes first. But a child-centered home makes for angry and discontented children. God's counsel to obey your husband (rather than your children) is counterintuitive and countercultural., but wise and good. I continue to practice putting my husband first.

Psalm 65:3 in *The Complete Book of Psalms for Singing* goes, "*We're overwhelmed by many sins, but you've atoned for them.*" I am deeply thankful for a forgiving God who took the punishment I deserved and who is able to works all things together for good.

Jeannette Paulson *is beginning her 27th year of marriage and conversation with her husband, Harlan. She is the 55-year-old mother of eight and grandmother of one. She contributes to the Visionary Womanhood blog. Other favorite pursuits are homeschooling, cooking, reading, and teaching sewing.*

A favorite chapter.

Eternal Treasure

By Natalie Klejwa

While in college, when anyone asked me what I **really** wanted in life, my answer was always, "A husband and five children." My mom taught me that being a mother was the most rewarding job in the world, and I believed her.

I grew up the oldest in a family of three daughters. The only large family I knew was my aunt's, and she had seven children: four biological and three adopted. I loved visiting their home. There was always a comfortable ruckus going on. I thought if I had five children (seven was "over the top" to me), I would have the perfect family. Not too big and not too small.

The plan was to get a degree at a Christian college, meet my husband while there, get married upon graduation, and after having waited out the culturally obligatory period of one to three years of childlessness in order to "get to know" one another, begin having those five kids. It was all up to me. Whatever I wanted. I was in control of my destiny.

God had a lot to teach me.

After graduating from college with a degree in English education (which I pursued only because I loved literature, loved

71

teenagers, and wanted to home educate my own kids someday), I surveyed the landscape of my life and found it missing the husband part, and not for my lack of trying. At the age of 23 I went through my first crisis of faith, panicking, kicking, and weeping all the way.

Then, finally, I surrendered and experienced peace. I taught high school English for one year before going into full-time ministry on a university campus to work with young women doing Bible studies, counseling, and evangelism. During that time, I met my husband, Joe, who was also in full-time ministry. We became friends and married a year later in February 1992.

I asked Joe if we might forego the months of waiting to get pregnant and just go ahead and get started. I was 25, and he turned 30 two months after our wedding. I wanted a baby in the worst way. He said, "No." I asked if we could shorten the wait from one year (the norm in our particular church at the time) to six months. He said, "Maybe."

To while away the months, I began charting my cycles using the Natural Family Planning method of birth control. It was exciting to get to know my body and how it worked to prepare for new life. I imagined every month as a trial run, and anticipated the day when Joe would lift the baby ban.

Early that autumn, after realizing the "getting to know one another" period was going to take a lifetime anyway, Joe gave the thumbs up to having children, and by November I was pregnant. I remember taking the pregnancy test in the bathroom of our little apartment where we were caretakers and seeing the magical red line that meant there was a *living baby* inside of me. I burst into tears, literally skipped to the living room and collapsed on the floor, face in the carpet, weeping and repeatedly saying, "*Thank you, Jesus! Oh, Thank you Jesus!*" Next to my wedding day, it was the happiest moment of my life.

Within two weeks I was sick. I was exhausted. I whined. Is this what pregnancy means? Someone shoot me now. The hours, days, and weeks dragged by. And finally, relief slowly seeped into the cracks of never-ending agony, my belly began to swell, and I started to experience the miraculous flutters of life.

I was in heaven. We celebrated our first anniversary at a bed and breakfast, and I rejoiced to be given the gift of life after only one year of marriage.

However, a few days later my world collapsed in a million pieces. I woke up one Sunday to spotting. Spotting? How can that be? I could feel my baby moving. I was 19 weeks pregnant—long past the miscarriage stage. I just had an appointment with my midwife the week before and everything was fine.

When I called the nurse, I was told to stay off my feet and come in the next day. In the morning Joe took me to the clinic where a doctor did an internal exam and announced matter-of-factly, "I'm sorry to have to tell you this, but your pregnancy is ending. Your cervix is dilated to a three, the bag of waters is bulging into the birth canal, and you are going to lose the pregnancy soon. Here's a box of Kleenex. After you are done crying, we'll make arrangements for you to go to the hospital." No mention of a baby.

But there was a baby. *She was kicking me.*

He left the room. I began shaking and sobbing uncontrollably, thinking this **had** to be a bad dream. But I could not wake up.

My pregnancy did not end that day. I went into surgery where another doctor placed an emergency cerclage (a stitch that goes around the cervix to hold it together). After two weeks of bed rest and the drugs Terbutaline and magnesium sulfate to stop labor, my body went into labor anyway. At 21 weeks gestation, our daughter came into the world alive, 10 inches long, and weighing 12 ounces. She was beautiful, and I was devastated.

With her death, our fledgling marriage and my faith in God floundered. But I did get pregnant again within three months and began a new rollercoaster ride.

This second pregnancy was fraught with problems. From the beginning I spotted, cramped, went on extended bed rest, all the while struggling to be positive while my friends breezily sailed through problem-free pregnancies.

I remember Joe wheeling me through a shopping mall to get to a clinic (I was on strict bed rest and medication at this point), and we passed a maternity clothes shop. I gazed longingly at the lovely clothes. We were poor, and I couldn't go out anyway, so there was no point in spending money we didn't have on beautiful maternity clothes. All my dreams of proudly walking around sporting a cute baby bump underneath a pretty maternity top were just that. Dreams.

Almost every night I had nightmares about losing that baby. Then, one week before Christmas in 1993, when I was still only 29 weeks pregnant, I spiked a high fever and went into labor. Less than 24 hours later a healthy, three pound baby boy was born, whisked away, and intubated.

Samuel was in the NICU for seven weeks before coming home. There were many ups and downs related to his digestion and breathing, and the first year of his life was spent getting multiple CAT and MRI scans due to his rapidly growing head. God used this time to stretch my faith and teach me more about Himself.

Up until that time I believed that God blessed Christians who made all the right choices. As long as I obeyed Him, He would bless me with happiness. But I was learning that God was bigger than that. He was more dangerous than that. His ways were higher than my ways. He was sovereign over all things. Even over babies that languished in hospitals. Even over babies that died.

When Sam came home, a life long dream of mine came true. I loved every minute of tending to his needs. I loved the increase in laundry and the fact that my basket was now full of tiny little socks, shirts, and sleepers. While other young mothers moaned about how tired they were and how they hated nursing, I relished every minute I had a living child—wondering how long the bliss would last—fearing that I might love this little one too much, and God might decide to take him away.

I began to get continually weaker throughout that year, but I chalked it up to having been on bed rest and not fully recovering. I was sweating all the time, could hardly lift anything, and felt that even climbing the stairs took great effort. I couldn't sleep at night, and my heart was always racing. Because we spent so much time in hospitals due to Sam's health, I never thought to go in and get checked myself. When Sam was almost a year old, I collapsed one morning after getting out of bed with my heart racing and body shaking. We discovered in the emergency room that I had Graves Disease.

I was treated with radioactive iodine to kill off part of my thyroid and balance out my hormones. Looking back, I wish I would have known there were other options to explore. Now I realize this treatment puts me at high risk for thyroid cancer. I had to stop nursing Sam and go back to using birth control (Natural Family Planning) due to the radioactive residue in my body from the treatment.

After six months it was safe to get pregnant again, and God blessed us quickly with another son. Phillip was born in June of 1996 after six long, boring months on bed rest with daily medication and monitoring. We did not have Internet, so to pass the time I watched Sam, cross-stitched, read books, and watched TV. I gained 46 pounds.

God used some books during this time to completely transform how I viewed Him. How I viewed life. These included *Trusting God* by Jerry Bridges; *The Rare Jewel of Christian Contentment* by Jeremiah Burroughs; *Stepping Heavenward* by Elizabeth Prentiss;

The Christian's Secret of a Happy Life by Hannah Whitall Smith; and *Hind's Feet on High Places* by Hannah Hurnard. The time was a crucible, but when I came out on the other side, I was a new person. And God was bigger and nearer than ever.

The stitches in my cervix were removed at 37 weeks, and I fully expected to have a baby by the end of the day, but God wanted to bless me with three weeks of walking around like a "normal" pregnant person. Phillip was born the day before his due date. My water broke in the middle of the night, and he came four hours later after a normal, painful, but uneventful labor. He weighed 8 pounds 10 ounces—a shocker for me, who had only delivered little peanuts up until then.

I should have been done. I had two horrible pregnancies, a painful loss, and two beautiful sons. My eyebrows had all fallen out after Phillip was born, and they had finally grown back in again. I had shed the extra 46 pounds. Why not just move forward and leave all the "yuck" of being pregnant behind?

We didn't try—and we didn't try not to—and I didn't get pregnant for two years. Then, when Phillip turned two, I discovered I was pregnant. I was ready again, and we were excited. I really wanted a girl, but that pregnancy ended almost as soon as it began, and then I wasn't able to get pregnant again for another year, even though I was charting my cycles and we were actively trying. We learned that God really does make those ultimate decisions.

A year later, Y2K was around the corner, and while we weren't going *too* overboard with it, we did wonder if we should just hunker down and wait until it passed before we continued to try to get pregnant. After all, why run the risk of being pregnant and having a baby if the world as we knew it was going to collapse the following year? (You can read more about my thoughts on this crazy time here: http://www.visionarywomanhood.com/fruitful-multiply-why/)

After praying and talking it through, we came to the realization that **life** was eternal, not temporal, and that if God wanted to create a human being that would live and enjoy Him and fulfill an eternal destiny—why should we stop Him from doing that? *"… for God gave us a spirit not of fear but of power and love and self-control."* (II Timothy 1:7) So we let go, and the very next month we were pregnant with Aimee.

She was born in March 2000 on the birthday of our first baby girl that we lost. What an amazing God. He is tender and merciful—and He remembers. We are thrilled He had His way. I was on bed rest with that pregnancy as well, but I did not need monitoring or medication. While my body seemed to be figuring out how to do the whole pregnancy thing, my labor and delivery experience was not good this time. I had learned the Bradley method and was excited about trying it out, but the waves that I was supposed to "ride" slammed me repeatedly against a cliff. I bawled and screamed and swore my way through the whole thing; and after she was born, I hemorrhaged.

Maybe having three children was enough. I really did not relish going through another pregnancy, labor, and delivery. I had my boys—and now I had my girl. Life was good. But when Aimee was a year old, I went in for a routine pap smear, and they told me I was pregnant.

I was excited about another baby, but I dreaded the next nine months. The now-familiar routine commenced: three months of morning sickness that was more like 24 hour-a-day sickness, followed by one month of "normal," followed by four months of bed rest, followed by what I considered to be hell on earth: labor and delivery.

I whined. My sisters told me to get an epidural. An epidural? What a cop-out. I wanted to join Christ in His agonies. I wanted to be strong. I am woman; hear me ROAR (literally)! One of my epidural-loving friends told me that she and her husband played ***cards*** while she was in labor. I was appalled. She might as well have gotten her baby from a stork, for what that was worth. Where was the gumption and pluck? I was ***not*** going to be like ***that***.

Timothy was due January 1, 2002. I had my stitches taken out three weeks before that, and the New Year came and went uneventfully. In fact, nine more days came and went. It dawned on me that all that bed rest might not have been necessary, since here I was, nine days overdue with a very large baby pressing down on my cervix, which was not cooperating in the way a cervix should under the circumstances.

The day before a scheduled induction, I went into labor on my own in the middle of the night. By 7:00 a.m. I was in shockingly horrific back pain and still only dilated to a one. What was going on? Several doctors examined me, mystified as to why my cervix was so hard and rigid after being in active labor for so many hours. One doctor recommended that I have an epidural since it was obvious this was going to be a long and difficult labor. I consented, and sweet relief followed. Six hours later I had not dilated a bit. I had a cranky nurse who kept muttering that if I hadn't had the epidural, I would have had the baby by now. I knew she was wrong, but her comments played on all my insecurities.

They were getting ready to do a C-section, when the doctor who had originally taken out my stitch happened to come in to the hospital on her day off to pick up something. They told her what was going on, and she came in to examine me.

She discovered that the stitch had not come out completely and was holding my cervix together in spite of active labor! (I had suggested this possibility early on, but of course, what does a mother know?) She had to cut my cervix to get at the deeply embedded stitch, something they wouldn't have been able to do without giving me an epidural anyway, and in less than ten minutes Timothy was born sunny side up, which explained the back pain. I felt everything. I saw everything. It was the most glorious delivery, and I became an epidural aficionado. But the liberating thing was that **God did it!** And I learned a new lesson. God isn't any more pleased with us if we labor in agony than if we make use of modern medicine for pain relief. The bottom line is that there are risks no matter which way you slice it, and we need to ultimately trust HIM regardless of how our children come into the world. (Read more about this experience and the lessons I learned here: http:// www.visionarywomanhood.com/medical-vs-natural-childbirth-pendulum-series-post/

Four children put me over the top of what I could handle on my own. I was desperately reaching for God's help at this point as the sleep deprivation and added workload closed in on me. We were living in a very small house on the corner of two busy streets, which added to the stress. I had a hard time falling asleep after nursing in the middle of the night, and I wasn't able to take naps. Looking back, I believe that a mother in that season of life—with several small children, little money, and little help – is in the most difficult season physically, emotionally, and spiritually. Four walls can feel stifling at that point. No kudos. Nobody encouraging her or cheering her on. Dirty looks at the grocery store when she hauls her 3-4 little treasures along. No time to herself—even to use the bathroom.

Hard stuff

Mother, if you are in that season, rest in this hope: your labor is not in vain. You die to your own desires and pour your life out as an offering for the well being of your children and the glory of your God, and there will be a harvest one day. There will be a harvest either way. Let it be a satisfying one. The time seems to crawl by now, but it really is flying, and you are doing culture changing, eternally impacting work. Do not give up! *"And let us not grow weary of doing good, for in due season we will reap, if we do not give up."* (Galatians 6:9)

Joe and I had strong convictions by this time that children were a God-given treasure, and we decided to move forward in faith, trusting God with our fertility even though it made us both nervous. Besides, I had wanted five anyway, right? Once again, at my yearly Pap smear appointment, I discovered I was pregnant. Because of the circumstances of my previous pregnancy, my doctor and I decided I could be on my feet this time around, though he did keep a close eye on things. I still had a stitch placed in my cervix at 12 weeks gestation, and I also had internal checks every two weeks to make sure the stitch was holding. An ultrasound around 20 weeks revealed another baby girl. We were thrilled.

I bled heavily a couple of days before my scheduled surgery to have the cerclage placed. It turned out to be a tear in the placenta that ultimately healed over, but it did cause quite a scare. Otherwise the pregnancy went wonderfully. I only gained about 25 pounds this time and was active the entire time. In fact, we put our home on the market, sold it, bought a new one, and moved —all during the last three months. I gave birth to Stephanie (happily, with an epidural on board and no guilt about it) one week after we moved. The transition to our new home and to five children was smooth as silk. I was finally sleeping easily, the older children were becoming more help, and I finally (yes, it took four children to get there) found my "groove." I had never been happier!

When Stephanie was 1, we found out I was pregnant again. I was expecting another breezy pregnancy, but God brought a few surprises. By this time, I was 38 years old, and my body was starting to behave in new ways. Debilitating back pain, sciatica nerve pain, and varicose vein issues began to plague me around 26 weeks. My doctor prescribed support hose and a back brace, and while I wasn't put on bed rest, I began to spend most of the time lying down anyway just to get relief from the pain. I could hardly walk, and I chalked it all up to my age. I was an old lady having babies. What did I expect? I was never so happy for a pregnancy to end. When I was almost 39 years old, Katie came into the world, and I had to have my veins stripped a few weeks later to relieve extreme pain that crippled my mobility.

Now I was back to dreading the idea of getting pregnant. I could not imagine voluntarily going through all that pain again, but I loved having children and felt they were worth the temporary agony. I fully expected that we would find ourselves pregnant again by the time Katie was one, since that was our pattern for the last several babies. But this time would prove to be very different.

I turned 40.

I remember thinking that I had reached that age where you have climbed to the top of life's hill, and now all that was left was the climb back down the other side. The first side was sunny and happy and full of life. But the other side was overcast, sad, and full of watching loved ones die. This was the picture in my head, and I felt an impending doom close in over my spirit.

I did get pregnant when Katie was about 14 months, but we lost that baby around seven weeks. The feeling of doom increased. A few months later I was pregnant again. At seven weeks I had an ultrasound, but the baby wasn't measuring seven weeks, and the heartbeat was hovering right around 100. I knew something wasn't right. Normally I was very sick by this time, and instead I felt pretty good. Sure enough, when I was ten weeks along, I lost that baby. It came out intact, still in the sac. We all gathered around and examined the baby in awe. Fear began to overwhelm me as I contemplated a decade of getting pregnant and having miscarriages. Was God really calling me to that? From where I was standing, this was too difficult and not worth it.

But God was asking me to look at it from where HE was standing.

He wanted me to work through those fears from an *eternal* perspective. What was the worst thing that could happen? I could get pregnant and lose 42 babies. That's a lot of disappointment and pain. I knew I could not get used to that. But if life on earth was short, and life in eternity was long, and I'd get to spend eternity with all those precious humans—***that*** would be worth it. Ultimately.

This gave me courage to move forward, and God was able to bless us with Jennie Pearle when I was 41. While the pregnancy was painful toward the end (no sciatic pain this time, but I did get pubis-symphysis dysfunction toward the middle of this pregnancy), I had a problem-free, pain-free labor and delivery, and an easy recovery to boot.

I knew I was pressing the envelope with God, but I began to ask Him to give me one last child. A son. For seven years we had a name picked out for a boy: Peter. But God had given us three little girls in a row. I began dreaming of Peter and hoping that God would do one last miracle in my old age and give me this little boy.

I turned 42 and had another miscarriage. Then God blessed us with another pregnancy, and this one stuck. The big scare came at 18 weeks when I realized I had not felt the baby moving yet. I'm a fairly thin person, and with all of my other pregnancies I had felt movements right around 15 weeks. By the time my babies were 18 weeks, I was feeling them regularly, so this was very unusual. No matter how I tried—I felt nothing.

One morning I woke up with a sense of dread. I made an appointment to go in and have the heartbeat checked, fully expecting to discover that the baby was dead. I remember walking up to the door of the clinic with the verse God had given me for so many frightening experiences in my life: *"Fear not, for I am with you; be not dismayed, for I am your God; I will strengthen you, I will help you, I will uphold you with my righteous right hand."* (Isaiah 41:10)

When the nurse found the heartbeat I was ecstatic. And a couple of weeks later, an ultrasound revealed my little Peter—tucked behind a placenta that was lying over the front of my uterus, causing me not to be able to feel those early movements. ***Peter. Peter. Peter.*** God had answered my prayers. Once again, I had back, hip, and leg pain that was unbearable at times, but this time, I could have cared less. *Peter was in there.* I'd have gone to hell and back again just to have him. I was 43 when I delivered Peter, and he has been the most hilarious, charming, tender, and wild boy. I cannot imagine life without him.

About a month after his birth, I read a story about a 47 year old woman who had asked God for a ninth child, and God had given her a son. I decided to do the same. Before Peter turned 1, I was pregnant with David. Again, I was in a lot of pain, but God had amazingly given me another baby. I could not believe it. With that pregnancy, I got PUP, a somewhat common symptom of pregnancy that causes an excruciatingly itchy rash on your abdomen. I searched online and found out that Grandpa's Tar Soap does the trick of relieving the insane itching. It worked. I washed with that soap every morning and every night, applying organic jojoba to my belly afterward, and this took me to the end of that pregnancy.

[handwritten margin note: Tell belly?]

We had found out the sex of all our other babies up to this point, but we decided to let this one be a surprise. When David was born, we were so used to already knowing, that nobody asked what it was. They swaddled him up and laid him on my chest. Suddenly, one of the nurses exclaimed, "Do we know the sex?" I gasped and struggled to get that blanket off so I could see. A boy! Everyone laughed.

I must say that I bonded more with my other babies while they were in the womb when I knew their sex and could give them names prior to birth. But it was fun to experience that surprise too. If we had to do it over again, I would choose to know and begin that special pre-birth bonding I had with the others.

The other new trick I learned after so many pregnancies is how to put myself into labor naturally, effectively, and gently. It worked like a dream when I gave birth to David. (***Please note that it is not recommended for use before the due date. I was full term when I used it.***) If you'd like to read about that go here: http://www.visionarywomanhood.com/scripture-lullaby-giveaway-celebrate-arrival/

At the time of this writing I am 46 and David just turned 1. I am using FertilityFlower.com, a helpful online charting site, to keep track of my cycles. Charting provides clues about how my hormones are performing as I make the transition from fertility to perimenopause to menopause. I have always nursed my babies until they are about 12-15 months, and my cycles return at around 9-10 months. With the last two babies, the luteal phases of those initial cycles have been very short (3-5 days). This is the phase of a woman's cycle that comes after ovulation and before the onset of her period. An average luteal phase is between 12-14 days. It has to be at least 9 days for a fertilized egg to have the opportunity to implant. Short luteal phases indicate an issue with hormone levels, more specifically, progesterone levels. While it is normal to have shorter luteal phases in the first few cycles after childbirth, it is not a good sign if a woman consistently has short luteal phases.

If you want to learn more about how your body works and how to improve your cycles and optimize your fertility I highly recommend *Fertility, Cycles and Nutrition* by Marilyn M. Shannon. This is an excellent resource whether you are young and dealing with PMS, PCOS, or infertility, or whether you are older, heading into perimenopause and want to know what you can do to make the transition as smooth as possible.

I realize that my childbearing years may very well be over, and I am preparing myself for this reality; yet, I still pray that God may see fit to bless us again with another child. Why not? He is my Abba. I can ask. At the same time I am asking God for strength and humility to surrender to whatever He may have in store for my later years. I learned early on that having babies is temporary. In

Love this.

one short year those babies grow from little puddles in your arms to hefty toddlers in your cupboards. So before I close out my story, I'd like to talk briefly about raising a large family.

I've often heard people say, when they see our large family, "You must have *so much* patience! I could *never* do what you are doing!" *Heard that.* They assume that parents of many children are somehow more equipped to handle the challenges that come with raising a large family. The fact is, we are all selfish little Wemmicks. (Have you ever read Max Lucado's books for children about the Wemmicks? If not, you really should. They give a marvelous perspective of our foolishness and smallness and God's wisdom and greatness. The Visionary Womanhood blog loves Wemmicks and invites you to learn more about them as we seek to view all of life from the Creator's grand and lovely perspective rather than the Wemmicks' small and silly view: http://www.visionarywomanhood.com/ways-wemmicks/

On the one hand, God does give more grace when we are faced with greater difficulties. He is overwhelmingly generous that way. On the other hand, I have rough edges and besetting sins, too numerous to count, and it seems they all want to rear their ugly heads at various times of the day as I deal with the different relationships that are happening in our family. (Eleven people give us 65 relationship combinations. That's a set up for a lot of love *wow!* *and* a lot of conflict.) I have thrown my hands up in despair a few times and wondered *what* in the world I was doing—and *why* in *Been there.* the world I was doing it! That's normal for a Wemmick.

The missing piece is **VISION**. I see my little life and how my creature comforts are coming along. Am I happy? Am I fulfilled? Do I have what I want? I'm cross-eyed with shortness of vision. But when I open up God's Word and view my life from *His* vantage point, everything changes. I have to catch my breath, first of all, because the view is staggering. It goes on and on. Forever. And the way it meanders at first makes no sense; but then, as my vision adjusts, things begin to clear up, and it dawns on me that I get to play a small, but significant part in the drama of history (His story).

Like Christ Himself, I am called to *die* in order that I (and others) might find *life.*

> *"Truly, truly, I say to you, unless a grain of wheat falls into the earth and dies, it remains alone; but if it dies, it bears much fruit."* (John 12:24)

> *"For whoever would save his life will lose it, but whoever loses his life for my sake and the gospel's will save it."* (Mark 8:35)

> *"I appeal to you therefore, brothers, by the mercies of God, to present your bodies as a living sacrifice, holy and acceptable to God, which is your spiritual worship."* (Romans 12:1)

If you think these verses don't apply to raising children, then you either 1) haven't experienced children yet, or 2) haven't meditated on these verses long enough. The day I got married I gave up the rights to my own life, my own way, on my own terms (or at least, that was the idea). So did my husband. It's called partnership. Unity. Two becoming one. When we added children we watched the last trickle of autonomy slip away. Raising a family is a death to **self**-ness. But it is also a finding of our identity in something *greater* than self: God.

Like Christ, I am called to *love* unconditionally, bravely, freely, unreservedly, with longsuffering (don't miss that word, LONG).

> *"...with all humility and gentleness, with patience, bearing with one another in love,"* (Ephesians 4:2)

> *"...love one another earnestly from a pure heart,"* (1 Peter 1:22)

"Beloved, let us love one another, for love is from God, and whoever loves has been born of God and knows God." (1 John 4:7)

Like Christ, I am called to *disciple souls*. The souls of my children are my first priority, with other souls following as God leads and time allows. Jesus worked with twelve. I have nine. The number is irrelevant, but I need to be focused on that mission and courageous to *do it* regardless of what the rest of the world does or says. In fact, if I don't disciple them, the world is more than happy to do it for me. No thank you. ✱ Watch out.

This calling **to die, to love, and to disciple**, is the highest, and ultimately, the most rewarding calling of our lives. Will we take up the challenge and run the race God sets before us? Will we keep the prize in focus as we move forward with vision and purpose? Will we surrender our comfortable chair on the sidelines for the heat, the burn, the work of the race? Will we cross the finish line and be able to look back and know we truly lived our short lives to the fullest?

Having babies is one thing, but ultimately my deepest desire is to see them all saved by the blood of Jesus Christ. Since that day I found out I was pregnant for the first time, I have prayed almost daily:

"Father in Heaven, SAVE the souls of every single one of my children. Save them for eternity. Make them Yours. May you keep them in the palm of Your hand and never let them be plucked out. May each one seek to know and love You, the greatest Treasure in the universe, more than the plastic baubles of this world. May they truly see, with spiritual eyes, Your worth and beauty, and may they desire it more than anything else this world has to offer. Do not only save them, but save all of my posterity. Let there

not be one black sheep among them, but let them all belong to You eternally, fulfilling the purpose for which you created them."

It is my privilege and joy to pray this for them when I tuck them in at night as well as when I am drifting off to sleep in the privacy of my room. I cannot save my children, but He can. So I teach my children the Truth, and I ask Him to do the saving.

The key to a healthy family and healthy relationships, I'm convinced, is humility. It is the willingness to admit sin, repent of it, and ask for forgiveness. The families I know that practice this are just like every other family in that they sin against one another. But they maintain emotional and relational health because the individual members grieve over their sin, saying they are sorry and asking for forgiveness.

The families that struggle are the ones that have difficulty admitting sin. If the parents are prideful and refuse to admit wrongdoing, blaming other family members or making excuses for the ways they hurt others, the family as a whole will suffer in untold ways. So let me be clear. Healthy families are not sinless. **All families sin**, and they do it every day in numerous ways. We can make a difference for eternity by simply humbling ourselves before our family members and learning the art of saying sorry and asking forgiveness. (Just saying we're sorry, by the way, doesn't cut it. The key is to ask the person we've wronged for forgiveness.)

I'll never forget a testimony I read in which a young lady shared that her father would gather their family together once a week and ask if he had done anything to hurt any of them that week. If anyone shared a hurt, that father would immediately repent and ask forgiveness of that person. This young woman testified that because of his example, the hearts of the children and the parents were knit together in a special way.

88

I'll close by saying that I'm not having babies because I can handle it, I am a super mom, it has been easy, and it's loads of fun. I've had babies because I decided many years ago to trade my freedom for eternal dividends. I'm your run-of-the-mill selfish Wemmick, and I'm not doing this for nothing. ***I'm going for the gold***. My dream is to stand around the throne of the Living God one day, hand in hand in a huge circle with my children, children's children, and so forth, taking our marching orders (it's going to be fabulous) for our future productive, creative lives in eternity.

All of us together.

With Him.

Forever.

Natalie Answers the Survey Questions

1. How do you deal with the fear of increased miscarriage, infant loss, or birth defects? How can one handle that kind of pain, especially over and over again?

> *"For the righteous will never be moved; he will be remembered forever. He is not afraid of bad news; his heart is firm, trusting in the Lord."* (Psalm 112:6-7)

> *"...fear not, for I am with you; be not dismayed, for I am your God; I will strengthen you, I will help you, I will uphold you with my righteous right hand."* (Isaiah 41:10)

> *"Therefore do not be anxious about tomorrow, for tomorrow will be anxious for itself. Sufficient for the day is its own trouble."* (Matthew 6:34)

> *"...do not be anxious about anything, but in everything by prayer and supplication with thanksgiving let your requests be made known to God. And the peace of God, which surpasses all understanding, will guard your hearts and your minds in Christ Jesus."* (Philippians 4:6-7)

> *"Beloved, do not be surprised at the fiery trial when it comes upon you to test you, as though something strange were happening to you. But rejoice insofar as you share Christ's sufferings, that you may also rejoice and be glad when his glory is revealed."* (1 Peter 4:12-13)

I take strength and hope from these verses and others like them when I begin to allow fear of the future grip my heart. I've learned over the years, and through five losses so far, that God doesn't give me grace to face tomorrow's trials, but He abundantly pours out His comfort, strength, and peace in the middle of *today's* trials. He asks us to lean on Him *now* and trust the coming days to His wise plans.

When we take life one day at a time, *we can do it* in His strength. As soon as I start to entertain fearful thoughts, I work at replacing them with the truth. Let's say I start to think, "I can't go through another miscarriage. The disappointment is too much. It isn't normal to keep having babies anyway at my age. Why not just give myself the gift of closure and move on with life on my terms?" I stop and say, "No. This is not the truth. I *can* go through another loss if God allows that to happen to me." He will be there in the midst of that disappointment and sorrow, and He will bless me with more of Himself. All His promises will hold true for me—including added peace, inner joy in Him, renewed strength, and maturity in my faith.

I will also have had the privilege of being part of the creation of an eternal soul. I will choose to *"look not to the things that are seen but to the things that are unseen. For the things that are seen are transient, but the things that are unseen are eternal."* (2 Corinthians 4:18)

Something else to consider: there are many verses in Scripture that assure us humans that God is not a stingy, pinching God who takes and takes and rarely gives. This is what Satan would have us believe about God. Rather, the opposite is true. God's nature is benevolent, agape love. He gives freely and asks His children to do the same. Why? So He can exact some kind of payment from us? No. So He can open up the storehouses of BLESSING to us.

"Cast your bread upon the waters, for you will find it after many days." (Ecclesiastes 11:1)

"Whoever is generous to the poor lends to the LORD, and he will repay him for his deed." (Proverbs 19:17)

"In all things I have shown you that by working hard in this way we must help the weak and remember the words of the Lord Jesus, how he himself said, 'It is more blessed to give than to receive." (Acts 20:35)

The point is this: whoever sows sparingly will also reap sparingly, and whoever sows bountifully will also reap bountifully. Each one must give as he has decided in his heart, not reluctantly or under compulsion, for God loves a cheerful giver. And God is able to make all grace abound to you, so that having all sufficiency in all things at all times, you may abound in every good work. As it is written, 'He has distributed freely, he has given to the poor; his righteousness endures forever.' He who supplies seed to the sower and bread for food will supply and multiply your seed for sowing and increase the harvest of your righteousness. You will be enriched in every way to be generous in every way, which through us will produce thanksgiving to God. (2 Corinthians 9:6-11)

"One gives freely, yet grows all the richer; another withholds what he should give, and only suffers want." (Proverbs 11:24)

"Whoever brings blessing will be enriched, and one who waters will himself be watered." (Proverbs 11:25)

When I read these verses, I am encouraged that whatever I have given to the Lord, whether it be money, time, talents, children, or babies—I will never be able to out give Him. When I lose a baby or contemplate losing a baby, I view it the way God does—as a surrendering of that life back to Him. He gives and takes away, blessed be the name of the Lord, regardless of our feelings in the matter.

*"But I am not ashamed, for I know whom **I have believed**, and **I am convinced** that **he is able** to guard until that Day what has been entrusted to me."* (1 Timothy 1:12) I can trust Him to guard each one of these children, whether they live or die, for eternity. He loves them more than I do.

That said, I have struggled with fear my whole life. It isn't something that most people conquer once and for all. It is an exercise of faith to commit the future and the ones we love to His capable Hands.

2. How do you balance life with older kids and babies? Do you feel this is unfair to the older children? How do they feel about having more brothers and sisters? Is it being greedy to want more babies at the risk of not being able to meet the needs of the rest of the family?

My older children have all been overwhelmingly excited each time we announce a new pregnancy. Yes, including my two oldest boys, now 16 and 19. I asked them if they ever felt like their little brothers and sisters have ever stood in the way of their own objectives in life. They smiled and rolled their eyes as if I had asked a dumb question.

Of all the large families I know, I don't know a single one where the older kids don't adore having many little brothers and sisters to liven up their lives. My 13-year-old daughter is praying God would give us twins before we're done having children. I don't know if that will happen, but it does demonstrate the desires and hopes of an older sister. *She would say it was "unfair" if I decided I was done and didn't want any more!*

So far, God has efficiently and abundantly met all the needs of each family member. Perhaps we don't always know what we need, since we are little Wemmicks who know very little in the grand scheme of things. In our family, we've discovered that one of our most pressing needs is to grow in unselfishness. It's uncanny how adding people to the family gives us ample opportunities to practice kindness, long suffering, self-control and all the other fruits of the Spirit.

Unfair? Only if life is all about me and not about God.

3. What about the ethical issues of repeated miscarriages? Shouldn't I avoid conception if I know that the chances of that child living are minimal? Am I enabling death when I should be promoting life?

The answer to this question depends on who you believe ought to give and take life. If you believe it is the power and prerogative of human beings to give and take life, then yes, there might be ethical reasons to avoid pregnancy if you continue to miscarry. (Although there are no moral ethics when you take God out of the picture.) In addition, if you believe that this brief life on earth is all there is—then you'd be a fool not to do what it takes to avoid repeated miscarriages.

But. If there is a God, and if there is more to our lives than a short stint on earth, then the lives we conceive, whether they live for a day, a month, 5 years or 95 years, are lives that belong to that God to do as He pleases. If He sees fit to propagate eternity with a dozen of your children, can you live with that? I mean, can you live for an *eternity* with that? It is hard to live with that here on earth. But if our vision is so short sighted that we cannot see eternity, then we will make cross-eyed decisions that will have eternal consequences; some of which we may never fully comprehend. I know I don't want to mess with God's plans. I'm just a simple Wemmick.

I've got five babes in heaven right now, and while I sure don't relish the thought of losing more, I am confident that I will have the supreme joy and delight of knowing and loving every single one of those people *forever*. When I'm with them, I seriously doubt I'll ever look at them and say, "Jeepers, losing you on earth really wasn't worth it. I wish you had never been conceived. I sure would have been a lot happier down there."

4. Do pregnancy, childbirth and recovery get harder in your 40s? I already feel like I'm coming apart at the seams! How will I hold out until menopause if I keep having babies? Am I acting responsibly when it comes to taking care of my health?

Physically it has been more challenging. My varicose veins became a problem in my mid-30s. I have them running from my ankles up to my groin. I make sure to faithfully wear prescription strength compression hose as well as a support belt specifically designed to relieve the pain associated with vulvar varicosities. (I've used this belt for four pregnancies and could not live without it.) I have pubis-symphysis dysfunction as well as diastasis recti—a three-inch muscle separation in my abdomen due to repeated pregnancies. I can get back relief when I maintain a stretching and exercise regime as well as visit a chiropractor for necessary adjustments.

Actual childbirth and recovery have been much easier for me. I am familiar with the routine and better able to handle it as I take the time and rest necessary to prepare and recover. I have learned to listen to my body. The things that frightened me during the first couple of pregnancies are now familiar and "normal." I finally know what to expect when I'm expecting.

I believe that all women in their 40s, regardless of whether or not they continue to bear children, will need to take the necessary steps to maintain good health by eating better, exercising, and getting proper rest. Even those who are not having children can potentially "fall apart" if they are not vigilant with their health. In some ways, pregnancy and childbirth force one to pursue these things earlier rather than putting them off until one's 50s. I address this issue more here: http://www.visionarywomanhood.com/help-pregnancy-is-making-my-body-fall-apart

5. How do I deal with extended family members, friends, and even the medical community who disapprove of our continuing to want more babies as we get older?

This is something I struggled more with in my 20s and 30s. Once I hit my 40s my confidence grew dramatically. While others could choose to "move on" with life and leave childbearing behind, I could choose to happily continue to walk that path regardless of the opinions of others. The older I get, the bigger God gets and the smaller Wemmicks get. This is a freeing place to be.

When my mother-in-law groans each time I tell her we are expecting another baby, I just laugh and remind her how much she loves the other ones she groaned about in years past. I joke with the doctors, nurses, and medical staff at my OB clinic all the time about old ladies having babies. They have a hard time being critical when I'm laughing at myself. I get where they are coming from, and I know what they are thinking. I try to come at it from their angle so they are disarmed and even charmed. I did not have this kind of confidence when I was younger. I *love* being older!

6. Will I have the energy I need to continue to raise children into my 50s if I have some in my 40s? Is it fair to the child to have older parents?

Well now, you'd have to ask a few kids in their 20s and 30s if they feel it was unfair for them to exist and now have parents in their 70s. You might say, "Hey. I notice that your dad here looks like he's 85 years old. How tragic for you. How can you stand to be alive with such an old man for a father? How can your kids stand having such an old grandpa? What a fool he was to have you. I'll bet you regret his dumb choice every day of your sad, sorry existence."

Yeah. That would go over really well.

A woman I knew in college died in her 30s, leaving four young children behind. If she had known she was going to die young, would she have had children? Should she have? Do you think any of those kids wish they had never been born? What if you die when you are in your 50s? Then what will it matter whether or not you have any energy? How can one know what the future holds? Do we make eternal decisions based on our guesses about the energy levels we will maintain at certain ages?

My mom is in her late 60s and has more energy than some women my age. She takes good care of her health, and God has blessed her. How much energy does one need to love those around them? Can a paraplegic love his parents, friends, spouse, children? Do they need to be able to walk to love? Who made up the rule that in order to fully participate in a loving relationship with your children, you must have oodles of energy and be in perfect health? Who made up the idea that it is tragic for a person to have older parents? That's just silly Wemmick thinking.

My husband was 50 when our ninth child was born. I don't think David gives a rip that his dad is 50 now. And I don't think he's going to care much when he is 20 that his dad is 70. And when we are all enjoying eternity because Christ bought us with His blood, I think the relevance of this issue will be, well, non-existent.

If it won't matter then, why should it matter now?

7. How do you explain miscarriage to older children, especially if you have repeated losses?

Have you ever heard the saying, "grace grows best in winter?" Human beings who have experienced sorrows tend to be deeper, more compassionate, more understanding, kinder, sweeter, and more mature than those who have had sugar-coated lives. This doesn't mean we seek to bring sorrows into the lives of our children, but when our Heavenly Father chooses to do so, **we seize the opportunity** to help our children grasp eternal concepts. *"It is better to go to the house of mourning than to go to the house of feasting, for this is the end of all mankind, and the living will lay it to heart."* (Ecclesiastes 7:2)

8. How does having babies in your 40s affect your relationship with your husband? Don't I owe him some of my best years?

I guess if my husband was opposed to having them, it would affect our relationship negatively, and that wouldn't be good. But my husband likes growing our family just as much as I do. Yes, we do run into more relationship issues when I am pregnant and hormonal. This has not been easy, but this life is not a sprint. It is a marathon, and we're in it for the long haul. God uses these struggles to make us more like Christ (even though we often act more like Beelzebub at times), and it is this discipline that enables us to *"rejoice in hope of the glory of God. More than that, we rejoice in our sufferings, knowing that suffering produces endurance, and endurance produces character, and character produces hope, and hope does not put us to shame, because God's love has been poured into our hearts through the Holy Spirit who has been given to us.*" (Romans 5:2-5)

9. Do you have any practical tips for "high mileage mamas" dealing with fatigue, pelvic separation, joint pain, varicose veins, etc.? In other words, what kinds of pregnancy issues did you have to deal with, and how did you deal with them?

I've had my share of pregnancy related health issues, some of which are ongoing, and my doctors don't seem to be aware of many of the things I've dealt with. For example, I learned about the support belt that gives me relief from vulvar varicosities by researching it online. When I showed my doctor, he said he'd never seen one before. His response was, "Hey, if it works, use it!"

I've had pubis-symphysis dysfunction for over five years and didn't know what it was until recently when, again, I discovered it online. Neither my regular internal medicine doctor nor my OBGYN had any clue what I was talking about when I described my symptoms and asked for help. They brushed it off saying, "Sounds like your body is still recovering from pregnancy. It takes *a whole lot longer* the *older* you get." They didn't tell me what it was (I don't think they recognized it) or the fact that 7 percent of women will continue to have it even after they are finished having babies. It is a very painful condition to live with, one that causes some women to go into depression due to the daily pain.

The three-inch muscle separation in my abdomen makes me look four months pregnant. My legs have nasty purple veins running up and down. I have a weak lower back that goes out periodically, leaving me bedridden for days.

Practical tips? Discipline yourself to exercise. If you can see a chiropractor on a regular basis, that will help keep things in alignment. Eat healthy. Stretch out each morning.

Even doing all these things, you may still find yourself in my shoes—**living with the consequences of bearing and raising living souls.** As it turns out, every single one ended up being worth it—and BONUS: one day I'll trade in this old, rickety body for a brand new one. A day is coming—and it will be sooner than I can imagine—that I will step out of this heavy shell and be free. It will be glorious, and I won't have any regrets!

> *"But he said to me, 'My grace is sufficient for you, for my power is made perfect in weakness.' Therefore I will boast all the more gladly of my weaknesses, so that the power of Christ may rest upon me. For the sake of Christ, then, I am content with weaknesses, insults, hardships, persecutions, and calamities. For when I am weak, then I am strong . . . I will most gladly spend and be spent for your souls."* (II Corinthians 12:9-13, 15)

10. Are there real statistics (not skewed to the cultural norm) available regarding having babies in one's 40s? How many mothers do you know who have had babies in their 40s? Share your thoughts regarding statistics and odds.

My doctor once told me that it is rare for a woman to have a successful pregnancy after age 45. That said, I know several women who have, including me. From what I've read, 47 seems to be a major turning point in fertility even for those who have not had trouble previously. And for every woman I know who has had a baby in her mid-40s, I know a lot more who wish they could have, but never did.

I did find a study online that deals with this. It's taken from *Maturitas: The European Menopause Journal.* The study is called "Declining Fecundity and Ovarian Aging in Natural Fertility

Populations," by Kathleen A. O'Connor, Darryl J. Holman, James W. Wood. You can download the PDF file here: http://bit.ly/WamyQb

Keep in mind something crucial here, though. Statistics and odds only matter to us Wemmicks. God doesn't give a hoot about them. Think Sarah. Think Elizabeth. When God wants to make a baby, He makes one. Period.

Natalie Klejwa *is the wife of 21 years to Joe, and 46-year-old mother to 9 miracles ages 1-19. She is the creator of Apple Valley Natural Soap, founder and editress of the Visionary Womanhood blog, author of Visionary Womanhood Gatherings: A Family Strengthening Mentorship Tool for Women and Maidens, and a contributing author of The Heart of Simplicity: Foundations for Christian Homemaking and You Can Do It Too: 25 Homeschool Families Share Their Stories. You can hear her being interviewed on Kevin Swanson's Generations with Vision radio program.*

Just Another Mother in Love

By Stacy McDonald

When I was a girl, I recall being asked what I wanted to be when I grew up. I always answered that I wanted to be a housewife. However, I soon realized that a career sounded more impressive to most people, so I started adding, "Or I'll run a daycare"—as if taking care of someone else's child was somehow nobler than taking care of my own.

I was born with a form of spina bifida and severe scoliosis that resulted in multiple childhood surgeries and eventually a fused spine. In the back of my mind, I wondered what pregnancy and childbirth would be like for me. One uninformed doctor told me that if I ever had a child, I would probably need a C-section. I don't recall his specific reasons for saying such a thing, but until my first child was born, a quiet fear lurked in the back of my mind.

Interestingly enough, after numerous natural childbirths, and after having an eight-pound baby exit the birth canal in some sort of impossible position, my midwife marveled; she told me that because of the shape of my (deformed) pelvic bone, I could give birth to virtually any size child! I was humbled and grateful to the Lord for this "deformed body." In His grace, God used something I had always viewed as a curse to successfully bring forth children for His glory!

103

We know that for those who love God all things work together for good, for those who are called according to his purpose. (Romans 8:28)

I was 24 when my first child was born. I never knew such love existed! How amazing it was to gaze upon the face of someone I had never before met, but would suddenly die for without hesitation! Her scent, her sound, her warmth, her neediness... childbirth and nursing my baby were the most amazing things I had ever experienced.

I wondered how it was that all mothers weren't wandering about in a perpetual state of awe! This happens all the time? I wanted to ask every person I met, "Can you believe this miracle just happened?"

I had tasted motherhood and was hooked. I immersed myself in my new "job" and loved every moment of it. I found more satisfaction and joy in caring for my baby than anything I had ever done or dreamed of doing. In addition, as an adopted child who had trouble bonding, motherhood allowed me to experience a level of emotional closeness that I had never before known, and it was intoxicating.

However, in God's sovereignty, the next few years proved to be traumatizing. In the midst of some very painful circumstances, I wound up forced into the work place and cried many bitter tears over having to leave my precious little one in the care of others during the day. Thankfully, this didn't last long, but it was a difficult time, and it made me appreciate motherhood all the more.

To get to the heart of my story, I'll fast forward to 1995, the year of my first and only miscarriage. At this point, my husband, James, and I already had five children together and loved the idea of a large family, so we were thrilled to find out I was pregnant! However, the morning I announced to the lady's group at our church that we were expecting, I began to spot.

I was scared. I hoped that someone would tell me that this was all somehow normal (which can be the case sometimes), and that I wouldn't lose this baby. However, after a few weeks of watching, waiting, and blood tests, I miscarried. We were heartbroken.

The doctor told us we should wait at least six months before trying again. We ignored him, and I became pregnant shortly after my next period. In September 1996, we were blessed with our sixth child, Caleb. We had definitely crossed the line of what most people thought was a reasonable family size. When I took the children to the grocery store, people stared and cleared the way for our entourage of young ones. Strangers began to ask me if they were all mine or, ironically, if I was running a daycare.

When we visited a restaurant, the tension from other patrons was thick. You could almost read their minds, "Don't seat that herd of kids near me!" But, interestingly, by the end of the meal, we often received kind words from onlookers who were amazed by how well our children behaved (even though we didn't always agree with their definition of *behaved!*). In fact, on one occasion, two businessmen secretly paid for our entire dinner before leaving the restaurant.

Due to some challenging life details, the thought of getting pregnant again began to overwhelm me. At the church we attended, women often commiserated together about the stress of motherhood. Sadly, it was common for us ladies to swap stories and jokes that must have communicated to our children, and to others, that the little ones God had blessed us with were to us afflictions rather than gifts—burdens rather than blessings.

We casually chatted about birth control; one woman and I even joked about vasectomies and how handy it would be if our family doctors offered a "two-for-one special" to our husbands. I don't remember if our men shared the humor, but I still cringe over the crude ugliness of the jest.

Ironically, we discussed these matters while we rocked, nursed, and cuddled our little ones. We swapped stories of complaint while wiping noses and changing diapers. We bragged about our children in one breath while complaining about how difficult they were in the next. Of course, we all loved and cherished our little ones. The problem was that our words and attitude toward our children were often inconsistent with what was scripturally true:

> *Behold, children are a heritage from the Lord,*
> *the fruit of the womb a reward. Like arrows*
> *in the hand of a warrior are the children of*
> *one's youth. Blessed is the man who fills his*
> *quiver with them! He shall not be put to shame*
> *when he speaks with his enemies in the gate.*
> (Psalm 127:3–5)

By misrepresenting God's promise, and by our own foolish and idle words, we were in a very real way tearing down our own houses:

> *The wisest of women builds her house, but folly with*
> *her own hands tears it down.* (Proverbs 14:1)

But the weariness continued to drag me down. I had made a mental habit of complaining, which created an additional self-inflicted burden for me to carry. As I focused on how tired and overwhelmed I was, the days became longer. I couldn't imagine adding another child to my already physically and emotionally stressful load.

My youngest was very colicky and kept me awake night after night. To make matters worse, I had been told by a well-meaning older woman not to ever let my baby sleep or nurse in bed with me, since it would create a bad habit. So, every time my baby cried, I got up and nursed him on the couch, rather than cuddle beside him in the bed.

Since my husband had to be up early for work each morning, I stayed up alone, nursing and quieting the baby. I knew he needed to sleep so that he could provide for our family. I recall bursting into tears early one morning while nursing on the couch, because the sun was coming up, and I realized I hadn't actually fallen asleep yet. How in the world would I face another long day?

My husband was travelling a lot in those days, sometimes two to three weeks at a time, so I often felt alone and isolated. I wondered why God gave children so much energy, while mothers had less and less.

The lack of sleep began to weaken my strong will and wear down my independent spirit. The thought of doing this over and over again, with each new child, began to terrify me. I thought, "What if I lose it?" Though my thinking was still wrong, God was using my weakness to show me that I couldn't do it all. He wanted me to trust Him and to rely more on my husband, something I wasn't yet willing to do.

Admittedly, the idea of never having another child broke my heart, but the thought of *having* more children not only overwhelmed me, it also seemed like a selfish and irresponsible thing to do. If I can't handle the ones I have, who am I to consider having more?

Little did I realize it at the time, but even this line of thinking was evidence that I trusted in my own strength and ability more than I trusted in God's love and provision. It also revealed that I somehow viewed having children as an activity that was solely for the benefit (or detriment) of my husband and me, rather than for the service and glory of God.

After all, if it's all about me, why shouldn't I be the one to decide whether or not I want to be "blessed"? While I sang with Twila Paris, "God is in Control," I lived the lie that I was in control, even though the thought scared the daylights out of me!

Though I was indeed sleep deprived, I believe a larger part of my exhaustion was due to worry. I worried about finances. I worried about education. I worried about children when they were sick. I worried about something bad happening to my children. I worried about what I was able or not able to handle, and I worried about getting pregnant again.

You see, technically, we hadn't actually been using birth control. Instead, hoping for the best, we half-heartedly attempted to control conception by using the early withdrawal method.

Part of the problem was that we couldn't come up with a form of birth control that we felt comfortable with. We knew the pill and the intrauterine device (IUD) could cause a spontaneous abortion, so that was out of the question. For a short time, we attempted to use a condom, but it seemed like such a cold and dirty way to celebrate the holy gift of love-making.

We considered the diaphragm, but because of the twist in my spine, my doctor told me it wouldn't fit properly. I wasn't going to use the controversial Norplant, as it seemed so new and risky. So we just hoped for the best.

Then it happened, with Caleb just a year old and still nursing. I was pregnant again! Despite my fears, we were absolutely thrilled! I still recall our children running into the church building, joyfully announcing to all our friends that we were going to have another baby! Though congratulations were offered, the disapproving looks spoke louder than words. I recall actually feeling guilty for being pregnant—and for being happy about it. I wondered if we were being reckless or irresponsible.

This pregnancy proved more physically difficult for me. Though I didn't have morning sickness this time, I began to have a significant issue with hip pain, varicosities, and swelling in my right leg. These problems were related to my scoliosis and got worse with each pregnancy, as age and gravity shifted my organs.

So many issues that had been "no big deal" when I was younger soon became very big deals indeed. Pregnancy in my 30s proved to be much more difficult than pregnancy in my 20s!

Caleb was a voracious eater. He often nursed until he threw up, just so he could nurse some more! He was such a big baby that I had trouble toting him around the bigger we both became. I found myself feeling run down and having to force myself to eat enough to keep up with him and the baby growing inside me. Still, that summer, by God's grace, two weeks before moving out of our rental home into a new house, Abigail was born, happy and healthy!

We felt so blessed to finally be in a home that was all ours—a house that God had allowed us to build and customize ourselves! I was thankful to have plenty of space for the kids to run and play during the day, but Caleb, a typical toddler and "all boy," never stopped moving! Up the stairs. Down the stairs. In the toilet. Where did you get those scissors? Out the back door. Is that a bug in your mouth? Oops—Caleb locked himself in the bedroom again!

So, as usual, I continued to worry about everything.

To add to my anxiety, since becoming a Christian, I had always sworn that none of my children would ever attend government schools; however, we found we could no longer afford the tuition at the Christian school our church ran, even with the bartering/teaching agreement my husband had arranged.

Plus, with my husband's travel schedule, I was forced to fill in for him when he was out of town—with a toddler in tow and a baby on one hip. This couldn't go on.

We had contemplated homeschooling before, something we knew little about, but now that I was pregnant with a nursing baby, how would I handle such an enormous responsibility? The thought terrified me. More worry. More trusting in myself. I sank a little further into the abyss of self-reliance—a reliance that was actually causing the fear and worry that plagued me.

As God pricked my heart, I began to wonder if part of my problem was that I wanted to control my own life. Rather than have the godly resolve of Mary, and submit myself as a "maidservant of the Lord," I still struggled to maintain control.

> *Then Mary said, "Behold the maidservant of the Lord! Let it be to me according to your word…"*
> (Luke 1:38)

I had been through some pretty horrendous things in my past. However, rather than viewing them honestly as God's orchestrated plan for me (a plan that was meant for good and not for evil—Jeremiah 29:11), I somehow subconsciously viewed my trials as evidences of God's lack of protection.

Like a foolish child, I equated pain with a lack of love—a lack of care, not realizing that pain can sometimes be a great gift, especially when redeemed. Satan twisted in my mind the very evidence of God's love and sovereign care for me all those years, leaving me feeling fearful and anxious!

Somehow, though I didn't recognize it at the time for what it was, I struggled with accepting God's love for me. Maybe He would call me to some agonizing situation, and I'd suddenly discover I was all alone. Maybe He would ask me to do something I didn't think I could do, or that I didn't *want* to do! Maybe, now that things were going well, everything would suddenly come crashing down.

The reality was that I had not been trusting God. Ironically, God used my state of fear and anxiety to show me my own neediness—my own weakness. As much as I hated to admit it, I realized I couldn't trust myself either. I knew how weak I really was. And, if I couldn't rely on myself, there was only one place to turn. I had been choosing to walk in fear, the very opposite of faith. Once I realized what I had been doing, I repented and asked God to give me the faith I needed to trust Him.

> *"Lord I believe; help my unbelief!"* (Mark 9:24)

Slowly, I realized that if God had indeed called me to trust in His sovereignty, even His control over my womb, then I could also trust Him to provide for us and to equip me to physically and emotionally handle whatever He sent my way. That was sobering, but it was also very freeing.

I shared my concerns and contemplations with my husband who had already been having the same doubts about the inconsistencies of using birth control. Didn't God know what He was doing? Haven't we seen throughout Scripture that He is the One who opens and closes the womb? Looking back, God was very gracious to bring us to the same place at the same time. Together, by God's grace, we began a journey of trusting God in new ways.

We began to pray for God to give us the grace to handle another child. I imagined how old I might be by the time my body stopped having children. My husband reminded me that there wasn't any birth control in biblical times, and women did not *all* have 30 children! Some only had one or two children, and others begged God for even one little blessing!

Surprisingly, as we prayed for the faith that we needed to *accept* more children from His hand, God changed our hearts, and suddenly we began to beg Him to bless us again with another child!

Little did we know that this new level of trusting God would bring an avalanche of change into our lives: Homeschooling, faithful family worship, godly order in the home, modesty and discretion—my head was spinning. We began to live the Bible instead of just talk about it; and God began to bless us in enormous ways. I recall joking with my husband, "I'm afraid to wake up in the morning—what is He going to show us *tomorrow?*"

So it happened, during the summer of 2001, we discovered that God had indeed blessed us again with another child. It was wonderful to share the news with friends who truly rejoiced in our announcement—friends who agreed that our growing quiver was something worthy of celebration!

However, this pregnancy would prove to be a tough one. Just as a horrendous three months of morning sickness subsided, the unnatural swelling in my leg began again.

This time it was more than an inconvenience; my varicosities, along with the greyish purple color of my leg, concerned my doctor. I graduated from drug store support hose to $500, custom-fit, medical grade compression hose. However, even with the hose, I couldn't stay on my feet very long.

Everyday activities became more challenging. Cooking, laundry, cleaning, schooling, errands—simple tasks became major accomplishments. My older children, having learned the gift of mutual familial service somewhat unique to homeschool families, rose up and proved to be a blessing to our whole family. This precious fact would become especially vital during the next two pregnancies.

After our sweet Virginia Grace was born (in a whopping 20 minutes of labor!), she spent a long week in the hospital due to what should have been a minor medical issue. Because of this incident, James promised to pray about allowing me to have our next child at home. I was hopeful, but understood that he needed to be the one to make the final decision.

Another unexpected blessing came from our hospital experience with Grace. Because of being separated from her at birth (I wasn't allowed to nurse or hold her for her first three days of life), I attempted to make up for it by keeping her with me, wrapped in my arms, as much as possible. I also discovered that when she slept in bed with me, we both slept better. As a result, I enjoyed a new level of closeness with my little ones. It created in me a desire for my little ones to be as near me as possible—a mental habit of consistently living out the fact that they are blessings and not burdens.

Before Grace was a year old, and just as I was beginning to get my strength back, we discovered that God had blessed us again.

We were thrilled! However, this time, I was a little more fearful. I knew I was getting older; and with my last difficult pregnancy still fresh in my mind, my stubborn habit of imagining the worst began again.

During my first visit with the doctor, I showed him my seven-page birth plan: no IV, no drugs, no monitor during labor, privacy, baby never leaves my room, no shots, etc. I'm not sure if he was tired of us and considered our last birth too demanding or if he really wanted to see us satisfied; but my doctor actually *suggested* that perhaps we should consider having a home birth! This was a Catholic pro-life doctor who actively promoted birth control and thought we were nuts.

I rushed home and announced to my husband, "Honey, even the doctor thinks we should have a homebirth!" He laughed and scheduled an appointment with a midwife. I was elated, but I still vacillated back and forth between joy and fear over what was to come.

While I tried to put worst-case scenarios out of my mind, morning sickness (more like 24-hour sickness) hit me like a freight train. I couldn't stand even the thought of food, much less choking it down. I ate and drank as if I were taking a life-saving medicine— only because I had to. When I sipped water, I tried to distract myself with some profound thought, hoping to keep myself from throwing it all up. I woke up in the middle of the night in tears. "Couldn't I at least have relief at night?" I cried.

But, as usual, the season of sickness only lasted about three months. And, just as it ended, the swelling in my leg began. This time the hose were definitely not enough. I couldn't stand longer than a few moments before my leg was on fire, feeling like it would burst.

At this point my husband started to waver. He looked at my leg. "I think I'm changing my mind," he said. Worried that he was worried, I made another appointment with our ob-gyn and told him that, based on the odd swelling in my leg, we had changed our minds about the home birth.

Then I was told something amazing: "I'm sorry, but I don't take patients who are this far along." Not only that, he also told me that most doctors quit taking patients much earlier. I asked him what in the world I was supposed to do. He suggested that when I went into labor I should just go to the emergency room.

I was so angry! I cried on the phone and told him I couldn't believe that, as a Christian doctor, he had so little regard for the health of his patients. Even though this seemed like a bad thing at the time, it gave us the necessary push to pursue the home birth, which turned out to be such a blessing.

During my pregnancy with Emma, I was unable to stand longer than a few minutes at a time without experiencing extreme pain and swelling in my leg. Because of that, I eventually wound up needing a wheelchair. I share some of this humbling experience in the following excerpt from *Passionate Housewives Desperate for God*:

> When I was younger, pregnancy was a breeze. I remember being puzzled over why anyone would complain about something as exciting and effortless as pregnancy. My first baby didn't even bring morning sickness, so the few slight waves of nausea I supposedly "endured" gave me a mistaken sense of self-admiration. "What was everyone whining about anyway?" I thought, in my bubble of prenatal arrogance.
>
> However, as my body aged, and I continued to have children, each pregnancy became less and less fun. I still loved the end result (the babies), but I heard myself complaining about the very things I used to smugly misjudge in others.

As the pregnancies added up, so did the moments of nausea. No simple "morning" sickness for this "whiner"—24-hour sickness is more like it! And let's not leave off fatigue, sore muscles, aching hips, and a throbbing back. During the second half of my last few pregnancies, I was forced to be off my feet because the varicose veins in my right leg swelled so badly that I could hardly bear it. My skin felt like it was on fire and turned a ghastly shade of purple.

To keep myself from screaming out in pain, I was compelled to wear torturous medical-grade support hose that took me (with my husband's help) 15 minutes to get on each morning. And as for me and my "I can do it myself" attitude, I was resigned to go on outings riding in a wheelchair with an attachment that elevated my right leg. I assure you, it was a most humbling experience, especially the day I tried to regain a little control by using one of the electric numbers they provide in the stores now. Everything was fine until I knocked over an entire display of canned goods.

Worse than that, I was sure that everyone we passed in the grocery store was shaking their heads at me—the lazy pregnant woman who made her poor husband push her through the aisles. "Little do they know," I thought, "but, my husband loves it. I'm the one who hates it!" Normally, he doesn't care to grocery shop with me, because he says I take too long reading labels. He likes to get in and get out. This was his moment of victory;

just as I would begin to read "mono sodium glu…" off he went to the next aisle, with my hair blowing in the wind!

I was especially self-conscious when we passed young pregnant women. "She's rolling her 22-year-old eyes behind those trendy little sunglasses," I told myself. "She thinks I'm just riding in this wheelchair because I'm lazy and whiny." I continued my inner complaining, "Of course when she gets 'old' like me, she probably won't be having babies anymore."

I moaned and groaned inside, grumbling at the unfairness of it all. Then one day I snapped—I realized that because of my own sinful pride toward others in the past, I was making assumptions about what others must be thinking of me now. When I was young, and things were easier, I compared my circumstances to the circumstances of others and pridefully assumed their trials must be identical to mine—only I presumed my stamina was somehow superior to theirs.

Looking back, I cringed at my conceit. The irony of it was that when God humbled me and allowed me to finally go through the same trials I had wrongly judged in others, I once again made false assumptions—but this time I projected my past arrogance on them.

Two and one-half years after Emma was born, God blessed us with another baby boy, William Alexander. Although each pregnancy caused me to feel my age a little more keenly, my last two pregnancies (and birth experiences) hold some of the sweetest memories.

My pregnancies with William and Emma were very similar. Same morning sickness. Same aching hips. Same swollen leg. Same wheelchair. Same home birth. In fact, both William and Emma even weighed exactly the same—8 pounds even!

Though it's still possible that God could bless us with more children, William is nearly eight years old. If God were to bless my husband and I again, we would be amazed and grateful, but we will not obsess over whether or not it will happen. God is in control. And, in this new season of grandchildren, we're content to rest in God's sovereignty and enjoy the blessings we still have at home.

My 40s are flying by, and I have come to the conclusion that each new season has its own unique blessings. The year our first grandchild was born, I recall holding him in my arms and enjoying his intoxicating aroma. Nursing a child, touching soft skin, gazing into a content little face—oh, how I missed that!

At 2:00 a.m. I heard the first cry of the night. I waited until it got quiet again and knew my daughter was holding her little one in her arms and satisfying his needs. That's a good thing. I cuddled under my blanket and rested in the fact that a new generation is here, and that I get to be a part of it on a new and different level. And that's a good thing too.

Stacy Answers Some of the Survey Questions

1. How do you deal with the fear of increased miscarriage, infant loss, or birth defects? How can one handle that kind of pain, especially over and over again?

It's hard to know for sure, because we only faced one early miscarriage when I was in my twenties. I can't pretend to know the pain of repeated loss and disappointment that so many couples experience.

I do know that when we began to trust in God's sovereignty over the womb, we knew it had to go both ways. If we were going to trust Him to provide for us as He gave us children, we also needed to learn to trust Him with the children He chose to withhold or take home.

If God gave me a child who grew to be 90 years old, then praise the Lord! But, as a servant of the Lord, if He ordained for me to only hold my child in the womb for a few weeks or months, and never in my arms, then I wanted to praise Him for that opportunity too, as excruciating as the loss may be! *"Let it be to me according to your word."* (Luke 1:38)

2. How do you balance life with older kids and babies? Do you feel this is unfair to the older children? How do they feel about having more brothers and sisters? Is it being greedy to want more babies at the risk of not being able to meet the needs of the rest of the family?

God's ways are not man's ways, and our wisdom and logic always fall so short of His. Along with our children, we discovered the amazing truth in the mysterious dichotomy of gaining abundant life by dying to self and putting others first.

As they pitched in and served within the family as needs arose, our children not only learned the reciprocal blessing that comes from serving others, they also had the opportunity, particularly unique to homeschool families, to nurture close sibling relationships—relationships that may have been otherwise minimized or overlooked.

Each of us learned that it wasn't all about us—that God uses us in families to love and serve. If one is down, the others take up the slack. Our children were taught to thank God for the opportunity to serve one another and appreciate the learning experience. We discovered how God uses each family member and each circumstance to shape and mold us for His glory.

What families do.

It is not that any of us always did this perfectly. As God stretched us, we were all selfish at times. However, our five oldest children are now in their 20s, and all of them look back with fondness to those days when the younger ones were being born—when we had no choice but to work together like a well-oiled machine. And the younger ones look up to their older siblings with great affection and love and are now eager to help with their new little nieces and nephews!

Modern secular child rearing philosophies often promote narcissistic, self-indulgent behavior. A child who is never required to serve and give of himself to others will grow to be an adult who thinks the whole world revolves around him. Through God's providence, out of necessity, our children learned to help serve within the family by helping with younger siblings, the running of the household, assisting with our ministry, serving in our church community, and working in our family business. Though this was sometimes a challenge, it created in them a sense of family faithfulness and camaraderie that is sorely lacking in today's culture.

3. What about the ethical issues of repeated miscarriages? Shouldn't I avoid conception if I know that the chances of that child living are minimal? Am I enabling death when I should be promoting life?

If we truly believe that God is the author of life, then this won't even be a question. A healthy understanding of God's sovereignty is both a comfort and a relief. That being said, we should do all we can to be healthy and to seek medical assistance if our bodies are not working properly.

4. How do I deal with extended family members, friends, and even the medical community who disapprove of our continuing to want more babies as we get older?

James and I found that the best way to deal with critics was to stop fearing man and start fearing God—a healthy, active fear that communicates: "I'm going to glorify God in the way I know to be true and right. I'm going to be faithful to Him. And, while I want to be gracious and remember that many people are simply concerned, I'm not going to worry about what they think to the point that it manipulates me or distracts me from what God has called me to do."

5. How many mothers do you know who have had babies in their 40s? Share your thoughts regarding statistics and odds.

Over the years, I have had close relationships with many mamas in their 40s. Although many of us will readily admit that pregnancy and chasing little ones is more physically draining as we get older, in many ways the emotional side is easier. Older moms tend to have more confidence in what they are doing, which helps the mental fatigue of worrying if you're "doing it all right."

We *know* we're not doing it all right! But we also know that God is faithful, and that we don't *have* to do it all right for our children to grow in the nurture and admonition of the Lord. We just need to concentrate on being faithful to Him and learn to rely on Jesus to lead us with our little ones. It's the Lord that does the work in our children's hearts.

> *"He will tend his flock like a shepherd; he will gather the lambs in his arms; he will carry them in his bosom, and gently lead those that are with young."* (Isaiah 40:11)

Stacy McDonald *is the 46-year-old wife of Pastor James McDonald and the mother of ten children. She is a homeschooler, speaker, blogger, and author of the life changing books, Passionate Housewives, Desperate for God and Raising Maidens of Virtue (which has recently been revised and expanded). On her blog Your Sacred Calling and while traveling with her family she encourages women all over the globe on issues related to marriage, motherhood, homemaking, chastity, and Christian culture. At The Common Scents Mom, Stacy also encourages healthy eating, natural living, and the utilization of essential oils at home to promote health and healing in our own families.*

God Changed My Heart
By Molly Evert

I was a young bride. My husband and I married the summer before our senior year of college. If anyone would have suggested I drop out of college to start a family, I would have laughed at such an old fashioned notion—but no one did.

Several of my friends had married, but they were not starting families either. Every couple wanted several years to get established, to focus on their marriage, and to "accomplish things for the Lord" before being relegated to the role of parents. We laughed and joked each week during our couples Bible study as each woman's watch alarm sounded in turn, reminding her it was time to take the pill.

After graduation we left for the mission field. The Berlin Wall had fallen just a few years prior, and my sights were set on bringing the Gospel to a generation who had grown up under a communist, atheist regime. In my pride I believed that my obvious spiritual gifts would be squandered caring for children.

Some of the leaders in our mission agency pragmatically encouraged limiting family size to enable more ministry work. It was considered spiritual to sacrifice having a large family in order to accomplish more for God's kingdom. That was fine by me. It was a "sacrifice" I was glad to make. My husband and I embraced the message that we would be most effective for God's kingdom if we were unencumbered with children. Sadly, I don't think that message is unusual in ministry circles which often rely largely on female manpower. We had already encountered it both in student ministry and at church.

Ironically, an older woman I knew turned my concept of sacrifice on its head. As we talked over coffee, I waxed eloquent about the burden of children. Every mother I knew said that her children were a joy, and the sacrifices involved in caring for them seemed hardly noticeable. However, I was not so easily fooled; these same mothers appeared perpetually harried and exhausted to my young eyes.

My friend acknowledged that raising children does, indeed, involve sacrifice. She gently reminded me that Jesus said, *"Whoever wants to be my disciple must deny themselves and take up their cross daily and follow me. For whoever wants to save their life will lose it, but whoever loses their life for me will save it."* (Luke 9:23)

Finally! This was a vision I could get behind. I told my husband that I was willing to "take up my cross" and have a child. I laugh now at God's marvelous ways. I barely recognize the woman that I was back then. The Lord dealt with me gently through a series of transformational events.

Once we finally decided to have a child, four years into our marriage, it didn't take long to get pregnant. After just three months of trying I found myself holding a positive pregnancy test. I was surprised at the new emotions that raced through my heart. I felt *feminine*. I distinctly remember walking hand in hand with my husband through an open air European market. I was carrying a bouquet of flowers he had bought for me, and I thought to myself that it was, perhaps, the happiest moment of my life. I felt utterly content and womanly. For a moment, I tasted the idea that I was doing something I was created to do, and I savored the joy of new life.

But it wouldn't last. A few days later I went to the doctor for a routine visit, necessary to extend my missionary visa. The Hungarian nurse could not find a heartbeat on the ultrasound, though she pressed harder and harder with the machine on my stomach for what seemed like an hour. I had never had an ultrasound before and didn't know that it was probably much too early to see anything or that an ultrasound should not hurt or cause cramping. An hour or two later I started spotting, and that night heavy bleeding began.

Nothing, not even the book *What to Expect When You are Expecting,* could prepare me for the horrors of losing a baby in newly post-communist Eastern Europe. My husband and I were so naiive that we didn't know for sure whether I was losing the baby, though in retrospect we should have known. All the signs were there. We spent a sleepless night in prayer, begging the Lord for the life of the baby.

In the morning we made the hour-and-a-half drive from our rural community to the hospital. When my name was called, my husband was not allowed to come with me, so I lay on the table alone with God, praying for a miracle. My grasp of the Hungarian language was still developing, and I thought I heard the doctor say that the baby was "weak." My heart soared for a moment, believing the baby might survive. I had started this journey out of Christian duty and a desire to sacrifice for my Lord; now I found myself pleading with God to save my baby.

Of course, the baby was already gone. And my heart was forever changed. I would no longer seek to have a child out of a sense of Christian duty but for love.

Life was not esteemed very highly in post-communist Hungary, where in the 1990s the average woman had 1.2 abortions. I felt sick as the doctor told me not to cry over spilled milk. He said that I was young and could get pregnant again.

The communist medical system was set up to cow patients into submission, humiliating them. I was taken to a large room where three young doctors and a nurse were waiting. One of the doctors told me to strip naked and hang up my clothing on one side of the room and then walk to the opposite corner where my hospital gown was laid out. The nurse glanced at me, embarrassed, and looked away. I hesitated for a moment, and the doctor barked at me not to take all day. They pretended to consult their charts, but I felt their eyes burning through me as I took a walk of shame across the room.

A few days prior I had exulted in my femininity, but now I felt utterly barren. My body had failed me. I felt androgynous, unable to fulfill a creation ordinance. I was wheeled into a sterile operating room, scooped up, and dumped unceremoniously onto an operating table. Before I knew what was happening, my legs and arms were tied to the bed, and I was injected with something to make me sleep. "What is happening?" I cried out in terror just before drifting off. I was getting a D and C, but no one had informed me.

I woke up in a large maternity ward. Finally, I was allowed to see my husband for a few moments. We cried and prayed. Most importantly, we praised God, "*The Lord gave and the Lord has taken away. Blessed be the name of the Lord.*" (Job 1:21) A few minutes later David was ushered out, and as he made the long drive back to our home I fell asleep. Surrounded by women who were about to give birth, I felt utterly alone.

For years afterward I would be haunted by the thought that an incompetent nurse may have caused me to miscarry. Eventually I came to understand and accept that it didn't matter how it happened. Perhaps this suffering was a direct result of our missionary service, or perhaps it would have happened anyway. I found peace by resting in His sovereignty over everything and in trusting that our loving Father works all things together for our ultimate good and for His own glory.

Not long after the loss of the baby, we finished our initial stint on the mission field. We were faced with the decision of whether to return to the field after furlough. It was a time of soul searching, knowing that a return to the field would almost certainly mean another pregnancy in Hungary. After much prayer, we believed the Lord was calling us to another term, and I realized what taking up my cross to follow Christ might actually cost me.

I took three months to recover from the miscarriage, and we conceived again easily, after just three more months of trying. This pregnancy was fraught with difficulties which landed me in the doctor's office or hospital every single month, always with a fear of losing the baby again. Eventually I was put on medication and bed rest for three long months when my body threatened to go into pre-term labor.

It was 1996, and I had only just learned what the Internet was. We didn't have it at home, and there was no English television. Although my husband came home at lunch every day to make a meal for me, he spent most of the day working for the mission. Those were long, lonely months. I was determined to redeem the time and to not give way to fear but to trust in the Lord no matter what happened.

In order to derive the most spiritual benefit and to keep myself from going stir crazy, I organized a busy bed rest schedule for myself. I would spend an hour studying my Bible and praying, an hour reading a Christian book, an hour listening to a sermon on tape, and then have lunch with my husband. The afternoon was passed in similar fashion, with time allocated for reading about childbirth or caring for a newborn, time for napping, and time for correspondence. During that time I read *Stepping Heavenward* by Elizabeth Prentiss, and *Pilgrim's*

Progress by John Bunyan, two books which I have returned to repeatedly over the years; their influence on my life can hardly be overstated.

When my water broke two weeks early, I made that same hour-and-a-half drive to the hospital. I wanted to have a natural labor, but I had no preparation for childbirth and no clue how to manage my labor to that end.

Although it was not common, my husband was allowed to join me in the labor room. The nurse offered to give me a shot that would make everything better, and she said it wouldn't have any side effects. I didn't realize they were giving me a narcotic until it was too late. I had the strangest out-of-body experience and felt convinced that I was dying, and no one knew it except a big black dog that I saw standing by my bed during my eight-hour labor. Of course, no one saw the dog except me!

After a few hours of delirious labor, I heard the doctor say the word "C-section," and I began to cry out to him and to God, begging for just one more chance to deliver vaginally. Less than seven hours had passed since my water broke, but the doctor was in a hurry to get the job done. I saw him hold up a pair of scissors. Before I could ask, "What is that for?" I felt the searing pain of an episiotomy performed without anesthesia. That jolted me out of my stupor pretty quickly.

The doctor wheeled a table up to my bedside and climbed up on it. He made a fist, put his elbow into my rib cage, and pushed down on his clenched fist with his other hand as I gave a few pushes. Moments later, our son, John Christian (Jack), was born with a large bruise on his nose.

I put baby Jack immediately to the breast to nurse as I had read to do. He let out one cry, and the nurse snapped at me. "You are scaring him!" she said, grabbing him up and whisking him away. I fell asleep, still full of narcotics, and woke up hours later with my baby nowhere in sight. I found him in the NICU under bili lights. I was allowed to reach in and stroke his downy body, and I savored the wafting scent of warm baby lotion.

A nurse taught me how to feed him, but I was not allowed to hold him except when nursing. He was jaundiced, and because I had tested positive for Strep B, he needed antibiotics. Three days passed where I longed for my baby but was kept from him except at appointed nursing hours. My roommate taught me how to fill the empty hours by rolling my own maxi pads using cotton wool and gauze, and my wonderful young husband cheerfully joined me in storing up a good supply.

I struggled, waiting for my milk to come in. A hand-held pump was all that was available, and I worked it furiously until I was exhausted, trying to force the milk to come. I later learned that the nurses were supplementing my baby with milk from other mothers, women capable of producing an over-abundance of milk. Our son weighed just over 8 pounds and was 20 inches long, common statistics in the United States but apparently unusual in Hungary. On the maternity ward he was referred to as "the giant baby."

After three days my precious son was allowed to stay in my room, and I held him as much as I could, making up for lost time. The nurses came by occasionally to scold me for holding him more than I was allowed to, but I didn't care. He was mine, and I rejoiced over him.

But I did not feel capable in my new role. I wondered if he could tell what a novice I was. I was 26 years old and had never held a newborn baby. Losing our first baby (with the humiliation of that experience), the constant fear of losing our second baby, the months of lonely bed rest, a labor in which I felt I was acted upon like a spectator (rather than an active participant), criticism from the nurses about my breastfeeding techniques, the knowledge that other women had satisfied my child when I could not, and a lack of fellowship with any other young mothers all left me feeling inadequate as a woman and as a mother. It would take five more years and another baby before I would find my way and begin to feel confidence in my role as a mother.

I quickly found my footing where I felt most secure: in my job. As missionaries, my husband and I were in a unique position to job-share. He would work part-time while I cared for the baby, and then we would swap. Our mission leaders encouraged it, and it made sense to us. I still believed I was indispensable to what God was doing on a larger scale, and the job of caring for an infant seemed pretty straightforward. It was obvious that anyone could do it.

We followed our plan of job-sharing for almost a year. Neither of us were very happy with our situation, but it never dawned on us that we would be more satisfied by adopting traditional biblical roles. I often cried when I left my son to go to work, and I felt frustrated when I got home to find out my husband had accomplished little around the house. He took good care of the baby but didn't seem to notice the laundry piling up or the dust bunnies accumulating in the corner.

When my husband was offered a full-time position in the U.S.-based home office of our mission, we were ready for a change. My heart still rejected the idea that service at home was a valuable use of my time and efforts. As soon as we joined a church in the United States, I threw myself into women's ministry and quickly took on the leadership role in what would become our church's largest evangelistic community outreach.

After Jack's birth, a close relative told me I shouldn't try to get pregnant again anytime soon. I took those words to heart and went back on the birth control pill. Almost four more years passed before we decided to have another baby. It was still very easy to conceive, and three months after we started trying, I was pregnant again.

Knox Edward was born when I was 30 years old. I was determined to take a pro-active role in childbirth this time. My husband and I agreed to use a midwife and a doula to help me manage a natural labor. I was a little worried that having the doula there would take something away from the experience I hoped to have with my husband, but the doula actually enabled me to bond with my husband more.

During my first birth I felt like I barely saw my husband as he was too busy rubbing my back and applying counter-pressure for me to see much of his face. In this birth, the doula rubbed my back, got ice chips and heat packs, advocated for me with the nurse, and helped me take it one contraction at a time when the incredibly painful transition phase of my labor lasted for over two hours. My husband was freed up to hold my hand, stroke my face, and be a constant source of emotional support. He was always right there where I could see his face and talk to him, and I could hold his hand and feel his reassuring presence.

I wrote out a birthing plan and brought it with me to the hospital. One of my chief concerns was that I did not want an episiotomy and would prefer to tear naturally, if at all. Thankfully, I didn't need one. When I finally delivered Knox Edward after what is still, to this day, my most difficult labor, I felt like a marathon runner crossing the finish line. The exhilaration of delivery after a natural labor was indescribable.

Knox had a very large head, and my labor with him was difficult. For a couple months after Knox was born, I experienced excruciating pain whenever I had a bowel movement. The pain was so great that I had to pray for God to help me through it each day and often felt as if I would black out. I was so embarrassed that I didn't seek immediate help, but I finally told my doctor about it at my six-week checkup. I was referred to a specialist and found out that I had torn my sphincter muscle during childbirth, and it needed to be surgically repaired. I would have preferred general anesthesia so I could sleep through the procedure, but the doctor used an epidural instead. I was wide-awake while they operated.

That certainly ranks up there as one of the more embarrassing moments of my life!

The surgery was my first experience with an epidural. I got to find out all about what I had missed out on during my natural labor. The epidural made my legs tremble, and it required catheterization. When the catheter was taken out, it was painful, and although I felt like I desperately needed to urinate, I couldn't. I decided then and there that I never wanted to have an epidural again if it could be avoided.

After Knox was born I went back on the pill, and he likely would have been our last child had the Lord not graciously intervened. My husband and I each have just one sibling, and although we had never discussed it, two children seemed "right." We left full-time ministry shortly after Knox's birth but continued to devote many hours a week to serving the Lord through our church.

Knox was just over a year old when I found out I was pregnant again. I was shocked but thrilled. Up until that time, we had never heard anything about the pill being an abortifacient, and we had no idea that anyone would be against using it for any reason.

I can honestly say that the *moment* I learned I was pregnant, our first thought was "will being on the pill when I conceived harm the baby?" In that instant, our hearts told us what our minds had not grasped before, and we knew we would never again use chemical birth control. I had thought that I didn't want any more children and was trying to prevent a conception. Everything changed when I found out I was pregnant. Suddenly, I wanted nothing more than another precious baby!

During this "unplanned" pregnancy the Lord began a transformational work in both our hearts, giving us a vision for our young family, solidifying our commitment to home schooling, and changing our views regarding gender roles and marriage and a host of other issues. For the first time, I began to catch a vision for serving Christ through serving my family. I quit the church ministries I had been in charge of which so often took me away from my children, and I intentionally turned my heart toward home.

Colin Archer was almost born in the car. We lived one and a half hours away from the nearest hospital with a maternity ward, and I tried repeatedly throughout the day to be admitted, but the hospital refused. After being sent away we went to lunch at a nearby restaurant, and then we sat through a movie. I squeezed a stress ball with every contraction and tried to refrain from audible moaning. We went back to the hospital after several hours, but my labor had not progressed. A nurse said I was having false labor and sent me home.

At home, I took a hot bath and a Tylenol PM. I tried to sleep, but the pain was too intense. My husband insisted we needed to go back to the hospital, but I didn't want to. I was in too much pain to make that long drive again, and it was pointless since I was now convinced that I wasn't in labor. My pain seemed even more agonizing in light of the fact that I was **not** in labor; I couldn't imagine how bad the pain would be once I finally **was** in labor! Eventually my husband persuaded me to go back. I had a friend whose baby had died during a home birth a few months prior, and that was not a risk I felt comfortable taking. By the time I got checked in to the hospital I was fully dilated. Ten minutes later Colin was born; I had done the whole labor on my own. He was my biggest baby, weighing in at 9 pounds 7 ounces, and he was 21 inches long.

Colin was born a month after Knox's second birthday. My husband shared my newfound conviction about chemical birth control, but he wasn't yet ready to sign up for a large family. I now wanted to have as many children as the Lord would grant, but I needed to submit to my husband, who was not convinced that we should have any more children.

There was a time in our marriage when I would have spoken scornfully to my husband and tried to exercise leadership since I thought I was clearly right. The Scriptures seemed clear to me that children are a blessing and a reward, and I believed my desire for more children was biblical. But as convincing as those Scripture passages are, none of them spoke as definitively as this: *"Likewise, wives, be subject to your own husbands, so that even if some do not obey the word, they may be won without a word by the conduct of their wives, when they see your respectful and pure conduct."* (1 Peter 3:1-2)

My husband is a committed believer and a godly man. If a wife is to submit to an unbelieving husband, how much more should I submit to my believing husband! This passage goes on to say, *"For this is how the holy women who hoped in God used to adorn themselves, by submitting to their own husbands."* (1 Peter 3:5) Although I wanted another baby and believed with all my heart that my desire was from the Lord, I was convicted that I needed to put my hope in God and submit to my husband's decision. I did talk with him about it with passion and respect, but I made a commitment to him and to God that I would follow his leadership, even though it conflicted with my own desires and convictions.

This was challenging, but the Lord helped me to have a quiet spirit and to trust Him. If it were His will, He could change my husband's heart, just as He had changed mine. I prayed for my husband and gave thanks to God for blessing us so abundantly with three wonderful children—children I would never have conceived if the Lord had given me over to my own sinful, selfish desires.

I also purposed to change my attitude toward our home and children. Many times my husband found me discouraged and overwhelmed, and it is no wonder he thought it might not be the best thing for me to have another child. I was continually telling him and showing him that I was finding it difficult to manage the children we already *had*. I was like the foolish woman who tears down her house with her own hands. My husband had the responsibility of doing what was best for me and for the other children, and I had given him plenty of reason to believe that another child might be too much for me to handle. By God's grace I began to try (by reading good books and practicing what I learned) to become more capable, more confident, and more resilient to the stressors involved in raising a young family.

By the time my cycle started again, several months after Colin's birth, the Lord had changed my husband's heart. Although he wasn't willing to sign up for an unlimited number of children, he was willing to try and conceive again. Hallelujah! I just knew I would be holding another bundle of joy in a year's time, as conception had always been so easy for me.

But the Lord had other plans. We were finally embracing children and longing for another baby, yet I couldn't conceive. Three years passed before the birth of our fourth son, Calvin Rex. Several extra nurses came into my hospital room as I delivered him, and some remarked they had never gotten to watch a natural delivery before. I found that news incredible! When the nurse placed Calvin in my arms, I turned to my husband and beamed, "Let's have another one, right away!" By that time my husband's heart had changed, and he was willing to accept whatever blessings the Lord would send our way. As soon as I got my cycle back we began actively trying and praying for another baby.

By this time I was 35, and the days of easy conception were clearly behind me. I had no idea that my fertility would change with age, and I was disappointed to find that having another baby wouldn't be as simple as I had hoped.

Four more years went by. I was aware of when I should be ovulating, and some months I even took my temperature and charted my cycle but to no avail. Shortly after my 39th birthday I went in for a routine gynecological visit and got a wake-up call. I realized that I was almost 40, and my fairly passive approach to getting pregnant was not working. By this time we were no longer just willing to receive another baby, should the Lord bless—we were actively hoping and praying and trying to conceive. Out of desperation I made an appointment to see a fertility specialist. We weren't planning to do anything invasive to conceive, but I wanted answers. I feared there was something wrong with my hormones, and I wondered if there were any simple changes we could make which would enable us to conceive.

A few weeks before my scheduled appointment, I was lying awake at night, praying once again for another baby. I reminded the Lord that His Word says that children are a blessing, and I believed my longing to raise more children for Christ was consistent with His word and His revealed will. I even confessed to Him, for the first time in my life, that I had a secret longing for a daughter. Never before had I prayed about the sex of my babies, believing that we should receive with gratitude whatever the Lord deems right. And yet through the years of secondary infertility, I had felt a quiet desire growing in my heart to pass on what the Lord was teaching me about biblical womanhood to a daughter of my own.

It felt like a desperate prayer, one which would likely never be answered. I had only conceived once in seven years of constant trying, and a girl had not been born into my husband's family in 70 years!

The day came for my initial fertility work up. I could only be tested at a certain point in my menstrual cycle. It was a Friday, and I still had not started my period. The following Monday would be too late. It was December, and my insurance deductible was met, so the testing would be free. If I couldn't get the testing done that month, I wouldn't be able to do it at all due to the expense.

I was frustrated and angry with myself for waiting so long to take a proactive approach. I had finally decided to get some answers, and now my cycle wasn't cooperating. My husband suggested that maybe I was pregnant. I laughed. The thought was beyond ridiculous! But I took a pregnancy test anyway, and it was positive. Positive?! I was humbled, and I rejoiced in the faithfulness of my God.

I went to see my midwife right away. She was concerned that my progesterone was low and put me on progesterone supplements immediately. I continued to take Progestin for 14 weeks. Progestin made my usual morning sickness much worse than it had ever been. Every day seemed like a new mountain to climb, and each climb only brought me to the base of another mountain. I realized for the first time how weak my Christian character actually was in the face of physical suffering.

The Lord has used each of my pregnancies—as well as each of my children—to sanctify me. During this pregnancy, He showed me my sinfulness and weakness, and He enabled me to begin to *"rejoice in [my] sufferings, knowing that suffering produces endurance, and endurance produces character, and character produces hope."* (Romans 5:3-4) I didn't know how desperately I would need that endurance, character, and hope for the trials that lay ahead.

Although Keeper was born after my 40th birthday, I didn't have any additional symptoms or health concerns related to my age, only the usual heartburn, nausea and vomiting, fatigue, and varicose veins that troubled me in each one of my pregnancies.

Each of my boys were born at 38 weeks gestation, so at 37 weeks, when one of my older children needed to do a sleep study overnight at a children's hospital far from our home, I thought it would not be a problem. I was wrong. My water broke in the middle of the night, and I had to wake up my son, call my husband at home, and find a hospital where I could deliver the baby. I felt embarrassed being wheeled into an inner city hospital in the middle of the night by my 9 year old, and the staff were not very pleased to admit me when I had received no prenatal care at their facility and had no records with me.

The surly night nurse didn't want to cooperate with my desire for a natural labor, so I had to constantly advocate for myself. She wanted me to stay in bed, attached to a fetal monitor the entire time, and she threatened a vaginal monitor if I didn't comply. I went over her head and got permission to do intermittent monitoring from the doctor, but I still had to stay in the bed. Born at 37 weeks, Keeper was my smallest baby, but still weighed 8 pounds even. She is God's gracious answer to much prayer. Her name reflects the transformation God has brought about in me from my formerly feminist mindset to someone who takes joy in being a "keeper at home," which I pray she will one day be as well.

Although I had nursed all my babies successfully, I had a lot of trouble nursing Keeper. My milk wasn't coming in like it should have, and I had to start supplementing her from the very beginning since she was losing weight. It was a rigorous regimen. I spent about 45 minutes to an hour trying to get her to nurse, then I would offer the supplement, and then I pumped. About 30 minutes to an hour later, I would start the whole routine again. I tried to use a supplemental nursing system (SNS), which I taped to my breast to stimulate my milk supply and keep her from getting nipple confusion. Every time I gave her the supplement in a bottle she immediately became lazy at the breast. But the SNS was very difficult to use without an extra set of hands, and once my husband went back to work, I found it was too cumbersome. It also added even more time to an already exhausting and lengthy process, so I began to supplement her with a medicine dropper instead of a bottle.

This round-the-clock regimen of nursing, supplementing, and pumping lasted for an entire month. My local lactation consultants were wonderful, and they let me come in repeatedly to watch her nurse and check her weight. We tried a series of herbal remedies, but to no avail. Meanwhile, I was also continuing to bleed heavily. I called my doctor repeatedly and was always told that this was probably normal since I had given birth to so many babies.

I know my body and what is normal for me, and I knew that my recovery was not progressing normally. Two weeks after Keeper was born I was still in my pajamas lying in bed all day, unable to do anything other than nurse, supplement, pump, and catch the occasional 30 minutes of sleep here or there. I was 40 years old and had been trying for five years to have another baby. I knew she was likely my last baby, and I was desperate to be able to nurse her, just as I had nursed my other babies!

I realized afresh how little I knew about endurance. I had to call out to the Lord every time I needed to nurse or pump to give me the strength, the patience, and the moral fortitude to be faithful to keep going when it would have been so much easier to give up.

I might not have been as proactive about my slow recovery if nursing had gone smoothly, but the desperation of my nursing situation impelled me to find answers. Since my local doctor had not delivered Keeper, he assumed that everything was fine. He said my slow recovery was unusual but still within the realm of normal. I insisted it was not and continued calling daily until he agreed to do an ultrasound two weeks post-partum. The ultrasound showed that during the delivery the doctor had failed to deliver the entire placenta.

After performing a D and C my doctor told me he was amazed by how much placental tissue he found. My commitment to nursing and pumping 24/7 may have saved my life, as it kept my uterus constantly contracting when it could easily have hemorrhaged. I praise God for the marvelous way He created our bodies.

By the time the retained placenta was discovered and removed, it was almost too late to hope that my milk would come in, despite all my efforts. Nursing my baby meant so much to me! If she were to be our last baby, I wanted to enjoy the experience to the fullest. Although I have never had post-partum depression before, I was starting to struggle with depression over the potential loss of nursing my baby.

The lactation consultant said that I might try the prescription medication Reglan as a last resort. It came with strong warnings that depression is a common side effect. I was fearful that it would push me over the edge, but I knew if my milk didn't come in and I had to give up nursing, I might end up depressed anyway.

I took the first pill with fear and trembling, and waited—and nursed and supplemented and pumped and nursed again. After two more weeks of nursing and pumping around the clock, my milk finally came in. I was able to stop supplementing, and gradually I could stop pumping as well. What a joy it was to experience the fruit of so much hard labor! The Lord answered my prayers, and I never became depressed. In fact, the opposite was true; being able to nurse my baby and provide for her without supplements and pumping gave me great joy, and my spirits soared.

Before Keeper was weaned, however, I found, to my great surprise, that I was pregnant again! Since my progesterone was low during my pregnancy with Keeper my doctor put me on progesterone immediately. That meant that I had to wean Keeper cold turkey because progesterone supplements are not compatible with nursing. When the blood work came back a few days later, it showed that, indeed, my progesterone was low again, so it was a good call. I joyfully prepared for three more months of horrible nausea and stocked the pantry with crackers and soup.

The doctor tested my HCG level as well. I was on vacation when the midwife called to tell me that my HCG was hovering instead of doubling as it is supposed to. She told me that there may be a problem with the pregnancy, but I would need more blood work to be sure. Our vacation ended the day before Thanksgiving, and my doctor's office was closed for the four-day weekend. Ten days would pass from the time I found out that there may be a problem until I could be tested again. By that time I had started lightly spotting, but I still held out hope since my symptoms were nothing like my former miscarriage.

When we got the blood test results back, they showed that my HCG level had dropped a great deal, and there was no hope.

We had lost the baby. I braced myself for the heavy bleeding and cramping that was sure to come, but it never did. I continued to spot for about a week, and that was it. The doctor monitored my HCG level weekly until it returned to normal.

We cried and prayed with our children, affirming our belief in the Lord's loving providence and committing our family to Him. Although it was a painful and deeply disappointing loss, the Lord ministered comfort to our family and strengthened us.

That miscarriage was all the more disappointing as I believe it may have marked the beginning of the end of my childbearing years, and that is hard to accept. I learned recently that one of my fallopian tubes is blocked, and my ovarian reserve (the quality and number of my remaining eggs) is even lower than it should be for a woman my age. In short, the likelihood of conceiving again, apart from an amazing work of God, is slim.

Even before this surprising pregnancy, the Lord led us to start praying about adoption, something we had never considered before. The Lord used dear friends as well as some excellent resources to open our hearts to the plight of the orphan, and we began the adoption process on my 42nd birthday. We hope to bring home a toddler girl with a cleft lip and palate from China in 2013 sometime after my 43rd birthday. She will be our sixth living child, and there will be a 16-year gap between our oldest and youngest child. Although my fertile years may be coming to an end, I am grateful that the Lord has opened another avenue for us to continue being "fertile" and raising children for His glory.

My husband and I are finding great hope by realizing our fruitfulness can continue through our children. Our turn at center stage will one day be over. Our family revolves around our marriage and our calling right now, but soon our children will begin marrying and having children of their own. We will become their supporting cast as they live out the plans the Lord has for them.

That is as it should be. We are praying and endeavoring to raise children who will raise children who will raise children who will stand for Christ in their generation. By God's grace, we trust that our fruitfulness will continue in the coming generations through the multi-generational faithfulness of our family.

Isaiah 59:21 says, *"And as for me, this is my covenant with them," says the LORD: "My Spirit that is upon you, and my words that I have put in your mouth, shall not depart out of your mouth, or out of the mouth of your offspring, or out of the mouth of your children's offspring," says the LORD, "from this time forth and forevermore."* It is our greatest hope and most fervent prayer that our children—who have been given many spiritual advantages which we did not have—will grow up to exceed us in both love for Christ and godliness.

Molly Answers the Survey Questions

1. How do you deal with the fear of increased miscarriage, infant loss, or birth defects? How can one handle that kind of pain, especially over and over again?

As Christian parents, we trust our merciful and loving Father, believing we have every reason to hope that our unborn children are in Heaven with Christ. The Westminster Confession of Faith (chapter X, item III) states, "Elect infants, dying in infancy, are regenerated, and saved by Christ, through the Spirit, who works when, and where, and how He pleases." The Bible says that "*to live is Christ and to die is gain.*" (Philippians 1:21) Although I grieve, I also rejoice in the hope that my miscarried children are experiencing gain. Even through tears, I am grateful that the Lord used my womb to bring forth precious souls for Christ.

Even as we cry and mourn, we recognize that this world is not our home. We know that the momentary sufferings we experience here will soon give way to eternal joy. My husband and I try to look at our fears and pains with an eternal perspective, clinging to verses like 2 Corinthians 4:16-18 which says, "*So we do not lose heart. Though our outer self is wasting away, our inner self is being renewed day by day. For this light momentary affliction is preparing for us an eternal weight of glory beyond all comparison, as we look not to the things that are seen but to the things that are unseen. For the things that are seen are transient, but the things that are unseen are eternal.*"

As Christian mothers, we can march forth boldly into an unknown future, trusting our sovereign, omniscient, loving Father who works all things for our good.

2. How do you balance life with older kids and babies? Do you feel this is unfair to the older children? How do they feel about having more brothers and sisters? Is it being greedy to want more babies at the risk of not being able to meet the needs of the rest of the family?

The idea that having children is greedy implies that we are having children primarily for our own fulfillment rather than for God's glory. God says that children are a blessing and a reward, and I want as much of that reward as He will give me! But my motivation is not to store up children like a rich man hoards treasure but rather to raise them to love Christ and to put their hands to the plow for a lifetime of faithful Kingdom work.

Our children have been thrilled every time I have gotten pregnant. They were praying for us to adopt before my husband and I started praying about it. We are trying to teach our children to be pro-life, not just anti-abortion. Being thoroughly pro-life means embracing a culture of life, and being grateful for their younger siblings is a part of that.

It won't be long until our teens are parents themselves. These years in our home are meant to be a training time for them. That doesn't mean that our teens raise our younger children for us, or that they bear the primary responsibilities involved. What it means is that we allow them to learn from us as they walk alongside us. Our lives should proclaim to our children, "Follow me as I follow Christ."

Our children will be naturally selfish, just as we all are. Our culture indulges that sin and calls it a good thing, but as Christians we should fight against our selfish inclinations, and so should our Christian children. The Christian life is one of sacrifice and hardship, a life of taking up our cross daily. Our children should learn that from the beginning. We do them no favors if we teach them that Jesus is the cherry on top of a self-indulged life. Our

144

older children will have to make some sacrifices because of their younger siblings and vice versa. I don't see this as unfair. This is part and parcel of the Christian life: we sacrifice for one another out of our love for Christ.

Practically speaking, in our home, the younger children probably end up sacrificing just as much as the older ones do, if not more. Our two-year-old daughter is very flexible, as I don't have the luxury of regimenting her naptime as rigidly as I could for my oldest children. Many of her evenings are spent watching her brothers play football or basketball, and she sometimes gets put to bed late. None of our children get to sit around indulging themselves all the time. Our lives don't revolve around any of them. They all need to learn to give and take, to compromise, and to treat one another as they would want to be treated.

I don't believe that having more children puts my other children at risk of not having their needs met. I don't consider it my sole responsibility to meet everyone's needs alone. Yes, I do bear much of that load, but our whole family chips in to meet one another's needs, so it is do-able from an energy standpoint. Financially, there are many extras, which our culture defines as needs, yet they aren't truly necessary to a happy and fulfilling life. My children gain far more from the relationships they share with one another than they would from having their own rooms, for example.

3. What about the ethical issues of repeated miscarriages? Shouldn't I avoid conception if I know that the chances of that child living are minimal? Am I enabling death when I should be promoting life?

The Lord says "*See now that I, even I, am he, and there is no god beside me; I kill and I make alive; I wound and I heal; and there is none that can deliver out of my hand.*" (Deuteronomy 32:39)

Life and death are in the hands of the Lord. To conceive is to promote life, and we must leave the health of the child in God's hands. It is up to God to decide whether a person lives or dies, not up to us.

My babies who died in the womb have an eternal soul. I grieve for my miscarried children, yet I am grateful that God gave us those precious children who will live eternally.

This question also seems to indicate that science and statistics can predict how God will act and what God will do. The children of believers are precious to God, and we can entrust them to Him whether they live or die. I can't say it any better than Doug Phillips, who asks in his message A Hopeful Theology of Miscarriage, "What if miscarriage was God's means of showing mercy and love to a human soul, and what if He chose you to be the honored vehicle to usher that child into eternity?"

4. Do pregnancy, childbirth, and recovery get harder in your 40s? I already feel like I'm coming apart at the seams! How will I hold out until menopause if I keep having babies? Am I acting responsibly when it comes to taking care of my health?

God created women to bear children. A pregnant forty year old may need to be more careful about her diet and exercise than she was when she was younger, but if she is in normal health she should be capable of carrying a child without endangering her health. My pregnancy at age 40 went much more smoothly than my pregnancy at age 26. All pregnancies involve some pain and discomfort for the mother, no matter what her age, but these momentary trials pale in comparison to the inestimable worth of a precious child.

With that said, you should prayerfully and honestly consider whether the "threat" to your health is a general risk that would apply broadly to any woman your age. Or have you been told by a doctor that you have particular risks which would endanger your health if you were to become pregnant again? If a doctor or health professional has told you that having more children will seriously endanger you, then you and your husband may have good reason to be concerned about protecting your health, for your sake and for the sake of the family He has already given you. I would include in this category serious mental health issues, which may be exacerbated by pregnancy.

Much wisdom and prayer is needed in addressing each individual situation. What we must resist is the current cultural trend which puts forth the idea that childbearing is somehow bad for us. Often when people talk about taking care of their health, they may be thinking more about their figure or their creature comforts than about actual life-endangering problems. Our culture places so much emphasis on "taking care of me."

We must realize that as we age, our health and our beauty will degrade as a result of the Fall. Our culture is a death denying—and therefore an age denying—culture, where women are encouraged to take drastic, even unnatural steps to preserve their health and beauty. Our bodies serve a purpose, and bringing children into this world is part of that purpose for most women.

My body bears the marks of delivering 5 children, and it is not in the shape that it once was. But I glory in that! My body is only a temporary home for my spirit, and one day it will wear out, but the children God was pleased to bring into this world through my body will live eternally. I can think of no nobler use for my body than that. And even as I approach menopause, and my own body begins to bear testimony in its decline that this world is not my home, I rejoice in the knowledge that one day I will be given a glorified body without infirmity or blemish which I will be able to enjoy eternally.

5. How do I deal with extended family members, friends, and even the medical community who disapprove of our continuing to want more babies as we get older?

Having a large family in our culture is an opportunity to enter into Christ's humiliation. My husband and I have embraced the fact that the world already thinks we are foolish, so there is no shame in going all-out! I need to be willing to bear witness to the Gospel, and often my large family opens that door for me. People can be very nosy, and sometimes they ask rude, probing questions about my fertility or about our children. It can be embarrassing and awkward, but we try to meet these questions with humor and winsomeness. People say, "Are all those children yours? God bless you!" and I say, "He has blessed me!"

Some people will never understand our desire for more children. Many of these people don't realize their questions are inappropriate, and they ask out of good-natured ignorance. Sometimes we are too defensive.

Our first four children are all boys. When I was pregnant with our fifth, everyone stopped me to ask if we were trying for a girl. Often I felt annoyed by this insult to my four boys! But I don't think they meant it that way. Many people are just trying to make sense of what we are doing and to fit it into their culturally-influenced paradigm. Our behavior doesn't make sense to them as it is truly countercultural. People assume you are working toward some goal; they assume you want your girl, or you want an even number. The question, "Do you know what causes that?" implies that your pregnancy must have been an accident, as the speaker can't imagine anyone having so many kids on purpose.

My children have heard many of these unwelcome queries. I am particularly conscious when they are with me and try to be gracious, but brief, in answering. I always make a point to talk about the conversation later with my children. I want them to be fully aware of why we do what we do, and I don't want those comments to cause insecurity or embarrassment for them. I talk with my older children about being willing to live for Christ when the world, and even other Christians, think we are foolish.

We make a point to talk with our children regularly about welcoming children as blessings and embracing a culture of life. They will need to develop strong convictions and a thick skin if they are going to take their own stand for life one day.

Lord willing, we will soon be bringing a child with special medical needs home from China, and our family will be not only large but multi-racial. It is inevitable that we will draw attention whenever we go out in public. We are glad to draw this attention if it points people to Christ.

6. Will I have the energy I need to continue to raise children into my 50s if I have some in my 40s? Is it fair to the child to have older parents?

Would it be fairer for the child not to have been born? I am sure my youngest children would choose an older mother over never having been born. It's true, I am a very different mother for my two-year-old daughter than I was for my 16-year-old son when he was little. I probably have less energy now, but somehow I seem to accomplish a lot more! I definitely have far more experience, wisdom, and Christian maturity now. My youngest children have gotten the better deal by far.

7. How do you explain miscarriage to older children, especially if you have repeated losses?

I just lost a baby to miscarriage a few months ago. Our children knew that the baby's life was in danger, yet they prayed for many days with great faith and hope that our baby would live. And God's answer was, "No."

We have a family worship time most nights, and it was during one of those family times that we broke the news that we had lost the baby. We cried. I want my children to see my tears as they testify to the value of our precious baby. When a loved one dies, we cry.

We also prayed. As we walk together through seasons of grief, trusting our loving Lord, we model true faith for our children. "*Though he slay me, I will hope in Him.*" (Job 13:15) Even when our hearts are breaking, we love and trust our heavenly Father.

8. How does having babies in your 40s affect your relationship with your husband? Don't I owe him some of my best years?

My husband and I have grown closer through parenting, and it is a precious aspect of the relationship we share together. We are of one heart and one mind, and neither of us feels that our children detract from our relationship; rather our love for one another has deepened as our family circle has expanded. We see raising godly children for the Lord as our most important life's work, and it is an incredible joy to labor together toward that end.

My husband and I are intentional about spending time together. We have always been careful to keep our marriage relationship as the center of family life rather than putting our children and their activities in that position. Our older children are wonderful babysitters, so we actually get more alone time now than we did when they were all little. We try to meet for lunch, go out with another couple, or have a date night about once a week. We also take time to leisurely talk over coffee most evenings after our younger kids have gone to bed. For the past few years we have watched very little television, and it is amazing the number of hours this one change has redeemed. When a crying baby interrupts our special times together, we are experienced enough to keep it in perspective; we have been through these seasons together before, and we know that they pass by too quickly.

My husband has the opportunity to earn trips through his job, and last year he earned a wonderful cruise to the Mediterranean. He would have preferred for me to go with him (and I wanted that, too!) but it wasn't possible with our one-year-old daughter, who was still nursing at the time. Instead, he took some of our older children along as companions. That was a sacrifice, one that I will likely make again in the future as we hope to adopt another little girl soon. But when we put it on the scales and weigh a cruise to Italy vs. our daughter, it is obvious which side wins out.

Our precious daughter is of inestimable worth to us, and we would never trade her for anything! There may be some joys that we sacrifice in this life, including extended time alone together, but none of them will ever compare to all that we have gained, both in this life and in the life to come. And it is the life to come that we are living for.

9. Do you have any practical tips for high mileage mamas dealing with fatigue, pelvic separation, joint pain, varicose veins, etc.? In other words, what kinds of pregnancy issues did you have to deal with, and how did you deal with them?

Years of carrying and nursing large babies put a strain on my back and left shoulder, and I have lived with chronic pain in my shoulder for the past 13 years. A nightly backrub from my husband reminds me of what it is like to feel truly good for a few minutes. I have grown used to the dull ache and only get chiropractic care when the pain flares up to become constantly noticeable. I also sleep with a special chiropractic pillow at night, which has really helped. I recently started doing T-Tapp workouts, and this is helping stretch my back and neck.

I have also had problems with varicose veins, and last year one of my veins became so unsightly that I was afraid it may be dangerous. A vein specialist found problematic veins in both of my legs and recommended laser surgery.

Before my varicose vein surgery my legs often throbbed at night, keeping me awake. I had very simple outpatient laser surgery on my veins a few months ago, and my legs have felt wonderful ever since. The throbbing pain is gone, and I am sleeping much better. The new laser procedures are no more painful than a series of small stings, and my recovery was a breeze. I wore compression stockings for two weeks after the procedure and was able to go back to my normal routine the same day.

10. Are there real statistics (not skewed to the cultural norm) available regarding having babies in one's 40s? How many mothers do you know who have had babies in their 40s? Share your thoughts regarding statistics and odds.

I know five other mothers in real life (not counting my online friends) who had a baby in their 40s. Each of their children were born perfectly healthy.

After my recent miscarriage I spoke with a fertility specialist about conception statistics for a healthy woman in her forties. He explained that fertility rates drop rapidly after age 40. For a healthy 42-year-old woman with normal fertility for her age, there is only about a five percent chance of getting pregnant during any given month while actively trying. He used the word *chance*, but I know that God is sovereign over life, and I don't believe in chance. The doctor said that by the time a woman is my age many of her eggs are compromised, making it much harder to get pregnant or to sustain a pregnancy. He told me that my recent miscarriage was almost certainly related to a defect in the egg.

That was hard news to hear as I don't want my baby days to be over. I still feel very young and long for more children. But I rejoice in my God, who can work wonders whenever He chooses. I thank Him for giving me a baby girl two years ago, after my best years were supposedly behind me. I thank Him for all my precious children, including the little ones lost to miscarriage. I know that God controls the womb and I can only conceive at His pleasure; that was just as true when I was 25 as it is now at age 42. Statistics don't change that.

The CDC statistics say that a 42-year-old woman has a 1 in 65 chance of having a baby with Down syndrome. That number does seem to be skewed to cultural norms. Albert Mohler, head of Southern Seminary, recently reported that 90 percent of all children diagnosed with Down syndrome are now aborted. The fertility specialist told me that the actual statistic for a woman my age would be closer to 1 in 20 if abortion is taken out of the equation. Everyone seems to think that statistic is very high, comparing it to the much lower rate of Down syndrome among the general population. In reality, 80 percent of babies with Down syndrome are born to women under the age of 35, due to their higher fertility rates.

For the sake of argument, what if I do have a 1 in 20 chance of having a child with Down syndrome? I don't consider 1 in 20 to be a very high risk. If I thought that I had a 95 percent chance of winning a million dollars I would consider those odds to be pretty good, yet many people don't want to conceive during their 40s in spite of the fact that 95 percent of babies born to women in their forties are born without Down syndrome or any other syndrome. For me, that is an acceptable "risk," and even more so because I believe that God always works for my good and for His glory, and that any outcome would achieve both.

Our theology affects our view of risk. The Bible teaches us that God is sovereign over everything, and that I will have the children

He has foreordained for me to have since before the foundation of the world. There is no risk; there are only the perfect plans of my God. Many Christians have too low a view of God's sovereignty. They say they trust God, but then they don't want to do anything that seems risky. I want to live boldly for Christ and trust the outcomes to my loving, omnipotent, sovereign Heavenly Father.

To be truly pro-life is to say that all children are created in the image of God and are, therefore, to be embraced. It is tempting to say, "I can't take that chance because I couldn't handle that." God tells us *"My grace is sufficient for you, for my power is perfected in weakness."* (2 Corinthians 12:9) And Jesus said, *"Do not be anxious about tomorrow, for tomorrow will be anxious for itself."* (Matthew 6:34) God will give us the grace to handle whatever tomorrow brings—but He won't give that grace until tomorrow!

We are seeking to adopt a child with medical special needs, and although we are realistic about what that might involve, we trust that God will amply supply all the grace and strength we need when we need it.

11. Hind sight is 20/20. Do you have any regrets? Looking back, is there anything you would have done differently?

I do regret that we used birth control during our most fertile years. Although we were 20 when we got married, all but one of our children was born after I turned 30. I would love to have more children, but I have to trust God's sovereignty even over our ignorance and selfish sin. R. C. Sproul Jr. says in his book *Believing God* (p.94) that "Our calling is to repent and believe, not repent and regret. Repentance is a blessing. Remorse is not." I am grateful that God changed our hearts and in His kindness led us to repentance. We are seeking to raise our children to embrace a culture of life and to appreciate the blessings of a large family.

Molly Evert *is a 43-year-old mother of 5 (with one on the way via adoption), and the wife of 22 years to David. She is a contributing writer for the Visionary Womanhood blog and a writer and podcaster for Mentoring Moments for Christian Women. Her son's struggle with dyslexia led to the creation of a home business, My Audio School, which provides educational audio content for kids. She enjoys speaking to women's groups, and you can find her blogging at CounterCultural Mom and CounterCultural School.*

Not Our Plan, Yet Not Unplanned

By Ruth Einfeld

Growing up I loved to play house. I have distinct memories of my dollies all dressed up, hair brushed and beds created out of pillows and blankets. Each doll would have her own special name, names I hoped to use on my baby girls someday. I would have lots of babies—at least six or seven. In high school I read the book *The Family Nobody Wanted*, by Helen Doss, and loved the idea of a very large family. I also loved television shows about large families like *The Brady Bunch, The Partridge Family, The Waltons,* and *Eight Is Enough.* In college I met a family who lived on a large farm with over a dozen children. Their youngest child was the same age as their first grandchild. I spent a day with that family and loved every minute of it. My entire childhood and young adulthood was focused on the desire to marry and have many children. If asked, I would tell people that I wanted at least five children, and if I did not have a baby girl after the fourth baby arrived, I would adopt one.

In 1985 I was blessed to be able to marry Daryl, my best friend for over four years. In my desperation to be married, I had been engaged to another man the year before, but thankfully God stepped in and changed my course. The best husband for me had been right under my nose since childhood (our families went to the same church and we attended the same private school). Even before we ever had any idea that God wanted us to marry, we talked about things like marriage and children. We found that we both wanted to have five children – far above the average size of family. Little did we know what was to come.

During our engagement period, we talked further about having children. Since Daryl was going to be discharged from the Air Force in less than a year, we decided to postpone parenthood until we were more settled. We were encouraged by our pastor during premarital counseling to use birth control, specifically the pill, to postpone parenthood until we had time to settle into our marriage and were more prepared. So we followed the advice of my parents, my doctor, and our pastor, and I went on the pill before our wedding. We did not need it before then, but it was recommended to start early in case there were any problems with the dosage or reactions to it. The only problem I had before our wedding was gaining about 15 pounds due to the effects of the pill.

After our wedding we moved into an apartment near the Air Force base and started settling in. During those months I experienced PMS for the first time in my life. Mood swings caused me to go from hysterical happiness to deep depression in just a few hours. I remember telling my husband more than once during the low points of those mood swings that we had made a terrible mistake in getting married and that he was a terrible husband. After a few months of this, we began to see a pattern, and we were able to even predict it. That helped a lot, but it was still a nightmare.

A few months before Daryl was discharged from the Air Force, we went to California to get the training needed to be owners of a franchise we were purchasing in a partnership with his parents. While there, I realized I had not refilled my birth control prescription. We decided not to worry about it, not take it for a month, and start up again after my next cycle. It didn't exactly go as planned. That next cycle? It never came. The week before being discharged from the Air Force we got the results of the pregnancy test; we were expecting our first baby. We were surprised and shocked. So much for the five-year plan we had decided to follow! I was excited and intimidated.

My first pregnancy at 22 years old went by the textbook. I didn't have morning sickness, but I did have an aversion to meat cooking. I gained close to 60 pounds by the end of the pregnancy. I had dieted on and off since I was 11 years old (I even experienced anorexia twice). Being pregnant seemed to give me free rein on eating. We took our Lamaze class, toured the hospital's new labor and delivery wing, and packed our bags.

My labor started with my membranes rupturing the day after our baby was due. Once at the hospital and hooked to monitors, it became obvious that labor was not yet active, so I was given Pitocin. Around 5 p.m., the doctor checked my progress and found that I was 6 cm dilated. He decided it was safe to go home for dinner. An hour later I was at 9 cm. They tried to get in touch with my doctor to no avail. Finally a doctor on call showed up, and without asking, performed an episiotomy. With the next contraction our baby was born. Jeremy was 7 pounds 8 ounces and healthy. I had to sit on pillows for a week due to the pain from the episiotomy. I also struggled with nursing problems, at first due to poor latching, and then to diminishing milk supply when he was 4 months old. I had no idea that working, chemical birth control, and stress were things that can lower your milk supply.

After Jeremy was born, I went back on the pill. Only this time I had many problems. The regular dose that had worked before gave me terrible headaches; a lesser dose caused me to spot all month. We resorted to using the rhythm method, augmented with using a barrier form of birth control. We were planning to have more children, but we wanted them spaced according to what we thought best – just over two years apart.

Then one day I was listening to a broadcast from Focus on the Family (http://www.focusonthefamily.com/) and they were talking about the pill. They said it was an abortifacient. I had never heard of this—ever! Afterword, I checked with my doctor, and he said it was true. We never used the pill again.

As far as "planning" our next pregnancy, we decided that two years and two months apart would be perfect. So on the appointed month, we attempted to get pregnant. But to my surprise, my period still came. I was confused and sad. I remember calling my mother crying. She comforted me and told me to just wait, that in the right time we would conceive again.

She was right. The very next month I became pregnant. This pregnancy was much like the first, only I began to have some hip pain that prevented me from walking for exercise. On the evening before my due date, contractions began. I had an uncomplicated 10-hour labor. Jason, weighing 8 pounds 8 ounces, was born without an episiotomy and with little effort. I was careful during his infancy to protect my milk supply and was able to nurse him much longer.

The next couple of years were very difficult for us. Our cost of living went up, but our income stayed the same. We ended up moving into lower and lower living conditions. After much soul searching, we decided that it was time for Daryl to pursue another career and begin stepping out of our business. I committed to running the business and working full time so Daryl could go to school to become a machinist. We also decided to try to sell the business.

During this time, we planned to go back to using the barrier method after my first cycle, only that first cycle never came. Just after Daryl started school we found that I was pregnant. Once again, this was not in our plans. I had just committed to working full time for two years while Daryl went to school. I was to be supporting our family. We kept this pregnancy a secret as long as we could, so it wouldn't interfere with Daryl's education. Due to working many hours, I gained very little weight in the first two trimesters, making it even easier to hide the pregnancy. The pregnancy was uncomplicated and uneventful.

Unlike my first two babies, who came on time, this little one liked it in there! Two weeks past the due date, I was sent to the hospital for an induction. Once again, I was dealing with very difficult contractions right from the beginning. Around 7 p.m. I thought my water had broken, so we signaled for the nurse. She came in and lifted the sheet. She calmly said that my water had not broken, but that I was bleeding. She quickly got in touch with our doctor. He checked everything, and our baby sounded fine. They decided to increase the Pitocin to speed up delivery. I was soon having back-to-back contractions, 90 seconds long, with only 30 seconds in between. I had to be put on oxygen as her heart rate was doing down with the contractions now. It wasn't long before our first daughter, Jessica, was born, weighing 7 pounds 8 ounces. She was healthy and had no problems nursing. However, I experienced my first bout of mastitis while nursing her.

At 27 years of age, I was experiencing the most difficult year of my life to date. Working 30 hours a week and caring for three little ones was very taxing. The business wasn't selling. Daryl and I talked about the possibility of only having three children. Our future did not look good financially, and we were struggling to make ends meet. We had both desired a large family, defined then as five children, but reality seemed to tell us it wasn't a good idea.

Daryl and I desperately wanted to purchase a home for years. We were both nearing 30 years old now. We were tired of moving every year or so and were more than ready to be settled in a home of our own. When Jessica was 1, we jumped at an opportunity to participate in a program working with a group of families to build homes. This required a commitment of 35 hours per week. Just before breaking ground, our business sold, and I discovered that my cycle was late. I took a pregnancy test and it was positive. We were shocked. I didn't know how I could meet our commitment to building this home when our baby would be due the month after completion. Yet again, this was not how we had planned it. We didn't know how it was going to work out, but we knew that God had dropped this opportunity in our laps, so we forged ahead in faith. I worked most of the 35 hours each week. It was back breaking work for anyone, let alone a pregnant woman. I was so busy and tired, that if I slowed down I'd fall asleep.

When I went in for my 18-week check up, the doctor had trouble hearing the baby's heartbeat. He heard a beat or two, but it was faint. He asked if the baby was active; I had to stop and think. I did not distinctly remember this baby kicking at all. I had been too busy, right? He asked me to come back in two days. Meanwhile, I frantically tried to remember if this baby had made its presence known, and I just couldn't remember much movement at all. I became desperate trying to feel movement by lying on my stomach on our couch. But there was none.

I went to that next appointment, but there was no heartbeat. He sent me in for an ultrasound. The ultrasound was amazing—to see our tiny baby, all the fingers and toes. This was our first ever ultrasound. As Daryl and I marveled at this little baby we had not yet met, the technician was quiet. Then she excused herself. After she left, a man came in with a box of Kleenex. He told us that our baby was not living. He said that our baby was much smaller than expected for my gestation. He said he would contact our doctor, and our doctor would take it from here. Our doctor, who is a godly man, asked us to come directly to his office where he took time to talk, pray, and help us decide what to do next.

The next day we went to the hospital for induction. After four hours of horrible fever, shakes, headaches, and nausea from the medication used to induce labor when the health of the baby is no longer a concern, I thought my water had broken. Once again it wasn't water, but blood. The doctor broke my water, and out came Johanna Marie. She was tiny, but perfectly formed. I was told that she weighed just 3 ounces and was 7 inches long. Instead of being the size of an 18-week baby, she was the size of a baby at 14 weeks gestation. My uterus was the right size, but she had not been growing properly. We never knew for sure why Johanna died, but we firmly believe now that it was the well water from our previous apartment. The well was condemned for pesticides and fertilizer content not long after we moved. But I also know that our lives are in God's hands, and the promise of Psalm 139:16: *"Your eyes saw my unformed substance; in your book were written, every one of them, the days that were formed for me, when as yet there was none of them."* Johanna lived exactly the number of days that God ordained for her. I had been blessed to carry her. God has used our experience to comfort others who travel this same road.

During my grief, I poured over the Scriptures, especially the Psalms. God gave me this verse to comfort me, *"When the righteous cry for help, the Lord hears and delivers them out of all their troubles. The Lord is near to the brokenhearted and saves the crushed in spirit."* (Psalm 34:17-18)

Recovering from Johanna's birth physically was fairly easy. Putting away the pregnancy clothes, facing people, and the reality that I was no longer pregnant was very difficult. I poured myself into building our new home. During this time I dealt with guilt. I felt guilty that I had not been thrilled to be pregnant, that I had felt that the pregnancy was bad timing. I felt guilty that I had not noticed the lack of movement earlier, that maybe something could have been done. But God worked in me to overcome this guilt. It wasn't immediately, but over the years God has worked in me to create an understanding of His sovereignty and how He works all things together for my good. I have learned that in everything God is working for my good and His glory, as it says in Romans 8:28, *"all things God works for the good of those who love him, who have been called according to his purpose."* Johanna's life was His plan for her and His plan for me. More about about her birth story is found at http://11blessings.blogspot.com/2011/03/johanna-marie-february-22-1992.html

The next few months were a blur of working excessive hours to get the house finished. We moved in on schedule in the middle of July. It took weeks to recover from the lack of sleep and long hours of back-breaking labor. We were still using the barrier method of birth control, but I was tracking my cycles, and we only used it when I was fertile. But in order for that to work, you needed to remember to use it! I forgot—once. We soon found out that we were expecting again.

While we were still struggling financially, I was thrilled that we were going to be blessed with another baby. But then the fear came. I believe every woman who has experienced a pregnancy loss will experience fear in subsequent pregnancies, especially until passing the point of gestation where they lost their baby in the past. I was no exception. Even though this baby was very active, and I felt movement very early on, I experienced an inability to become fully bonded with this baby—just in case. It was a defense mechanism. There were so many nights that I spent hours unable to sleep, reliving the loss of Johanna. Having an ultrasound at 19 weeks and seeing that little heart beating and those little arms and legs moving was a great reassurance.

During this pregnancy, God used the book *A Full Quiver,* by Rick and Jan Hess, to open our eyes to the fact that we had been making choices without even thinking about God's choice. God changed our hearts, and we understood for the first time that God's Word can speak to us about everything in our lives.

For so long we had made decisions about birth control based on what others were telling us, what everyone else was doing, or what would be convenient or in our best interest as we saw it. But we began to realize that God is the giver (and taker) of life. When we tried to control conception, we were telling God that we didn't think that He knew what was best for us. We chose to release this to God. Thinking about letting go was scary – thoughts like "We'll have dozens of kids. What will others think?" went through our minds. But once we stepped out in faith, we found such peace. We no longer *had* to worry about whether or not it was the right time to add to our family. And even though we were currently expecting a baby, we became excited to see how God would work in our lives through our decision to trust Him.

After a very normal, uncomplicated 10-hour labor, Jonathan was welcomed into our arms. What a blessing to have a healthy baby after the loss of Johanna. As with the other pregnancies, I reached about the same weight full term. I was able to lose a little over half of my pregnancy weight after Jonathan. I didn't diet or exercise, but I was very busy with my little family!

The time had come for us to live out our decision to trust God with our "family planning." We found that we were expecting again when Jonathan was 14 months old. This would be my first pregnancy in my 30s. We began to looking into purchasing a new home on acreage, since we figured we would quickly outgrow our current home. My pregnancy was going well, but I still experienced times of fear, especially when I didn't feel this baby move. By the time I was 18 weeks I had only felt a few flutters. This was hard. When we had the ultrasound we found a very active little girl in there. Her placenta was attached across the front of my uterus, so even though she had been moving around, I was unable to feel her movements until she was much larger, and then only on my sides and near my ribs!

While we were working on purchasing land and placing a mobile home on it, several women that I thought were "normal" were asking me if I was going to have this baby at home. I really thought that was only for weird people and hippies! Well, I found I was very wrong. I began to research home birth and shared what I was learning with Daryl. We contacted a local midwife about the possibility of having this baby at home with her help. She agreed, so I kept seeing our doctor but also started having appointments with her in my sixth month.

We moved twice in my sixth and seventh month of pregnancy. My blood pressure crept up but went back down after settling in our new home. We moved in around the middle of January 1995. This baby was due at the end of February, so I didn't have a lot of time to get settled. I had a lot of difficulty with my hips due to walking and carrying boxes for the move. We were ready for this baby on her due date, but it would be three long weeks before she was born.

Our first home birth was beautiful. When it came time for the birth, my midwife suggested that I try the birthing chair. This worked really well – too well in fact. On the first pushing contraction my water broke and Rebekah was birthed all at once. The amniotic fluid was stained with old meconium, probably because the cord was wrapped around her neck, but she never showed signs of aspiration. She was very healthy and pinked up nicely. In spite of being over two weeks late, she was exactly the same size as my other babies. Rebekah was a new breed of baby for me. She talked early, but walked really late. She did not walk until she was 16 months old. We had weaned our other babies around the time they started walking. So I nursed her until she was nearly 18 months old. This meant that my next pregnancy was delayed quite a while.

During my next pregnancy, I participated in karate and learned about healthy eating and proper supplements through the midwifery correspondence course I was taking. This led to some major changes for us. We were eating healthier than ever. I was taking proper supplements and exercising regularly. Only gaining 15 pounds the entire pregnancy, I ended up 20 pounds lighter than all my previous pregnancies at full term. And true to form, being a girl of mine, Rachel was one week late.

My labor started in the early evening hours. My labor was weird. It would slow down when I was active and get stronger whenever I would lie down. Needless to say, this made it difficult to rest. My labor continued through the next day and into the evening, with little progress. I found later that the midwife had seriously considered transferring me, but due to the training I was taking, as well as my good health and exercise during the pregnancy, they decided to wait. By 1 a.m. I was nearly complete, but there was a part of my cervix that was stuck on the baby's forehead. Through several contractions, the midwife worked to release this "lip" of the cervix and finally succeeded. I was ready to push this baby out. After several attempts with no success, I was sure that this was the biggest baby in the world. Rachel was finally born with the cord around her neck twice, looking at the midwife as she emerged sunny side up. Thirty-one hours of labor led to one tired and worn out momma! During my midwifery training, I had read the book *Husband Coached Childbirth: The Bradley Method,* by Robert A Bradley, and had learned about the Bradley Method of labor management. I used this throughout my labor, and I know that it made it possible for me to remain home for this prolonged and difficult labor and delivery.

I experienced my only serious bout with post-partum depression after Rachel's delivery. I would cry for no reason, on and off all day and night. This went on for days. It was so bad that my husband was beginning to get concerned. I was still studying midwifery as well as nutrition. I came across a recipe for Adelle Davis's "Pep Up Drink" (http://adelledavis.org/press/adelle-davis-pep-up-recipe/) to help when experiencing severe health problems. I drank this several times daily. My depression was completely gone in less than three days. I believe that I was deficient in B vitamins, and that drink was full of them in an easy to digest form. After that my recovery went great.

My next two pregnancies and deliveries were nearly identical. Two boys, Reuben and Daniel, were born almost on their due dates. Both were unplanned water births, and with both I had a little trouble with postpartum hemorrhaging that was easily controlled with a shot of Pitocin.

When Daniel was just 7 months old, a dear niece of mine was killed in a car accident. This was my first experience losing someone close to me, and I was devastated. I did not understand the grieving process and tried to get on with my life after her funeral. But soon I began experiencing severe health issues. A naturopathic doctor ran testing and found that I was anemic, hypoglycemic, and suffering from adrenal insufficiency. She also asked me about what was going on in my life as well as my history of eating. She told me that I was suffering physically for two reasons. The first was that I was not processing my grief properly, and it was wreaking havoc on me physically. The second was the diet (high protein/ low carb) I had gone on before my last pregnancy. She put me on a new diet and gave me some herbal tinctures. She advised me to not avoid my grief but to experience it fully so that I could move on, in time. I followed her advice and began feeling better, but that kind of physical deterioration and emotional trauma does not mend quickly.

Just a month later I found out I was pregnant. I was concerned about being pregnant with my current health. I was excessively tired now. At seven weeks along, I started spotting. Very quickly it became obvious that I was losing this baby. On the third day the bleeding became so bad that I couldn't leave the bathroom. I took herbal tinctures for hemorrhaging, and they worked, allowing me to avoid going to the hospital. Recovering from this miscarriage was tough. I was grieving the loss of my niece, the resulting hardships in our family, and the loss of our baby, and now, once again, I was anemic and experiencing signs of adrenal failure. My midwife, mother, and others advised us to avoid becoming pregnant again soon; I needed to get healthy first. For a while we followed their advice and used "alternative" methods, but it didn't feel like we were doing the right thing. After much prayer and discussion, we decided that really nothing had changed, God was still sovereign, and we should not "worry" about getting pregnant too soon. I pleaded with God to close my womb while I worked to get healthy again. I asked for a six month break so others would see that our faith was not unfounded. I got more than I asked for – it was seven months before I got pregnant again, and by then I had recovered and returned to good health.

The next two pregnancies were very similar as well. I experienced high blood pressure in the last few weeks, putting me on bed rest. With both babies, I induced early labor (one to two weeks early) with castor oil when I became frustrated with bed rest. Both babies had problems with sucking, and both babies were smaller than my other babies; Dayton was just under 7 pounds 8 ounces, Elizabeth at 6 pounds 8 ounces. With Elizabeth I struggled with my milk supply and had to supplement.

After weaning Elizabeth, it took quite a few months before my cycles returned. When they did it was closer together than in the past – just 28 to 30 days apart whereas they had always been 35 to 37 days. I was also experiencing many signs of perimenopause. I went to a naturopathic doctor again because the night sweats and mood swings were becoming a nuisance, and the white-hot rage caused me to worry about my sanity. She put me on a form of black cohosh, and my symptoms went away.

After Elizabeth was born, I experienced my longest break between pregnancies—two full years. We were in the middle of building a new home in our backyard to replace our mobile home when we found we were expecting. After moving into the new home, when I was 24 weeks along, I experienced bright red bleeding. We decided to get an ultrasound to rule out placental bleeding or anything that would put the baby at risk. The ultrasound showed a perfectly healthy little girl. No sign of any bleeding that would cause a problem for the baby. It was probably just cervical bleeding like I had experienced in labor before.

During this pregnancy I experienced far more debilitating tiredness than ever before. My blood pressure also became a problem. I was put on bed rest at 35 weeks. Ten days before my due date I took castor oil, once again ready to be done with bed rest. When our midwife arrived, I was 4 cm dilated, so I relaxed in the tub. I had been experiencing some bloody show (more than usual for me), but I assumed it was from an exam that the midwife had performed earlier in the day. Just before midnight, I told the midwife that I thought my water had broken. Checking me she said no, it wasn't that; I was bleeding—badly. She got me out of the tub and moved to my bed. The bleeding continued, becoming alarming during contractions. We decided that we should call 911 to arrange transport to the hospital. When the paramedics and EMT arrived, she checked me again, and I was at 8 cm. Considering the rapidity of my previous births once I reached 8 cm, we decided to not transport but wait for the baby to be born and then re-evaluate.

On my first serious push, Esther was born. This was my shortest labor ever – just 4 hours and 20 minutes. She was very blue when she was laid on my chest. I looked at her as she was trying to take her first breath and thought that she looked a little Asian. I commented about her being our little China doll. I was talking to her and vigorously rubbing her to help her breathe, waiting for that first cry. She finally got a shallow breath and let out a tiny noise. Then I noticed she was getting cool, in spite of being skin to skin with me. I handed her to my midwife and then noticed that she was blue in the extremities and mottled gray over her chest and head. I knew enough to be very concerned at this point. About this time I began to feel the urge to expel the placenta, so my midwife told me to go ahead.

Once that was done, I began bleeding again. All the while she was trying to get Esther to open up her lungs and pink up, but nothing was working. When she tried using oxygen, Esther pinked up a little on her chest, but when it was taken away she would go gray again. She called in the paramedics and EMT and asked them to work on Esther so she could concentrate on stopping my bleeding. She gave me a shot of Pitocin, as well as another medication for hemorrhaging. The bleeding seemed to abate soon after that. I remember reaching out to Daryl's hand at one point, looking to him for comfort and support, but realized that he was facing his worst nightmare – his newborn daughter was not breathing on her own, and his wife was bleeding uncontrollably. The next 10 minutes were like an out-of-body experience. I was observing as things were happening. It was like my emotions were shut off, and I was just an onlooker; I think it was God's grace.

Just 15 minutes after she was born, Esther needed to be transported to the hospital. Daryl accompanied Esther along with our midwife. Her assistant remained behind to ensure that I also made it to the hospital. So Esther left my bedroom wrapped in a heating blanket, an oxygen mask on her little face, resting on the shoulder of the paramedic. A minute or so later, my midwife ran back into the room, and I asked her the question no one had dared to ask. "Does Esther have Down syndrome?" She replied that yes, she thought Esther did, and she ran out of the room to the waiting ambulance.

The next 30 minutes were surreal. Suddenly my bedroom was quiet and feeling empty – just me, my 18-year-old daughter Jessica, and the midwife's assistant. Jessica was in shock; she attended my last two births and enjoyed taking notes for me. She was not prepared for what happened; none of us were. Finally Daryl called, telling us Esther was at the special care nursery and better now that she was in an oxygen tent. He told me the doctor thought she had Down syndrome. Later Daryl shared with me that throughout the pregnancy he felt this baby would have Down syndrome. So God had, in a way, prepared Daryl for hearing this from the doctor.

When I arrived at the hospital, Daryl met us at the door. Weak from blood loss, I had to be wheeled to the special care nursery. There I found Esther resting under an oxygen tent, just five hours old. She had an IV and wires everywhere. Her color was good now. Exhausted, Daryl and Jessica returned home, and I remained there. After they left, feelings rushed in, and I began to cry. I thought of every person I had ever seen who had Down syndrome. I thought about how this would negatively affect our family forever. All I could think of were negative things. I realized I shouldn't be alone. I started calling my friends. Two dear friends immediately changed their plans to come spend the day with me. They kept me company while we watched the nurses care for Esther. (I couldn't hold her or even touch her because the nurses said she needed to rest.) They encouraged me to look for blessings, and we discovered how many things God had done to bring Esther safely into this world. The biggest was that I had started to bleed in labor, so the paramedic was already in our home when we needed him. We were able to transport Esther so much faster than if we had been forced to wait for their arrival.

Esther remained at the special care nursery for three weeks. They gave her a feeding tube because she would tire quickly when she took a bottle, but we continued feeding her with a bottle so she would not lose that ability. She just could not get off oxygen. We knew from testing that she had a heart defect, but her health seemed to be worse than the condition warranted. During this time, the outpouring of prayers and visits was such a balm. Even total strangers who had children with Down syndrome would call, encouraging me that this was indeed a blessing—that Esther would be a blessing to our family. They were right, but it took me a while to really, truly believe them. The Lord ministered to me in many ways while I was essentially cut off from friends and family. When Esther was 3 weeks old, she was transferred to Seattle Children's Hospital, spending two weeks there before being allowed home. After five difficult weeks at home, she became sick and was admitted again. After four more weeks of battling a virus, she was finally healthy enough to have the open heart surgery that she needed. She came home just four days after her surgery.

Esther was the best baby, rarely complaining about anything. I thought about not breastfeeding since I had such a hard time with Elizabeth, but after learning babies with Down syndrome do much better when nursing, I relented and started pumping when she was three days old. I never made enough milk to nurse exclusively, but every ounce was worth gold. She had a lot of trouble gaining weight, but that was mostly due to her heart defect. Once she recovered from the surgery, she began to pack on the weight.

Esther is indeed a blessing to our home; she loves to give and take hugs. She always greets everyone with enthusiasm when they come home. She loves to go away from home with us too. Watching her work hard to learn things that we take for granted is a joy. Her exuberance when she gets it right is contagious. When I hear of other mothers-to-be that may have a baby with Down syndrome, I pray for peace and grace for them, but in my heart I hope that they will experience the blessing of having a child with that extra special chromosome too!

My cycles returned quickly after Esther was born. She was just over 2 months old. I think this was because I was pumping and not directly nursing. Having gone through all we had, we still struggled with leaving our family planning in God's hands. For a time I kept track of my cycles, and if Daryl asked, I'd tell him if I might be fertile and leave it for him to decide. With time and prayer, we overcame our concern about getting pregnant again, at least most of the time. We found that it is one thing to believe something, but quite another to live it out. Many times we would find ourselves wanting to be in control, to track my cycles, to avoid pregnancy for one reason or another. But for us, it was more restful to leave it in His hands.

When they returned, my cycles were even shorter, lasting only 27 to 28 days, and now they were so heavy that leaving home or doing anything was nearly impossible. Following the heavy days, I would be exhausted and need to rest for a day or two. With the bed rest before Ether was born, and the long weeks in the hospital, I gained extra weight and was at my highest non-pregnant weight ever. I even weighed more than I had full term with my babies. Esther's first year I had to focus on caring for her, taking her to her various therapy appointments, and doing daily therapy with her to help her learn to hold her head up, roll over, sit up, and crawl.

Around the time she turned 1, I started an exercise and healthy eating program. This was very helpful in gaining back my strength and health. Losing weight in my 40s was tough. I was only able to lose 30 pounds through that program and then hit a plateau. Therefore, I was holding steady at the weight I used to get to when I was full term.

When Esther's second birthday came and went, and I still wasn't pregnant, we were beginning to think that my childbearing years were coming to a close. But God had other plans. Just a few months before Esther's third birthday, I had my worst menses ever. I didn't even dare walk around at home. I got dizzy from the blood loss and seriously considered going to the emergency room. It eventually lessened, my cycle ended, and life went on. I began to think it was time for my cycles to stop completely so when my next cycle didn't come on time, I was wondering if this was it. I was done. Then I started having strange episodes of dizziness. I got a pregnancy test to see if that was my problem before doing anything else. It was positive! We were shocked. I would be turning 48 during this pregnancy.

After our experience with Esther's birth, we knew that it was time for a hospital birth. We had formerly chosen to have our babies at home because we thought it was the safest place for a normal, healthy birth, but with my history, this was no longer the case. So we set out to select an ob-gyn early on, and it's a good thing we did. Around 8 weeks, I began to have trouble with spotting. I felt fragile, and the slightest thing could start the spotting. I had blood work done and everything looked fine, except that my progesterone was low (very common in women over 40). So I was put on a progesterone suppository until I was 12 weeks along. The feeling of fragility went away and so did the spotting. I had an ultrasound at 10 weeks, and everything looked good except for a spot that would indicate bleeding from poor implantation, but it was not really a concern yet. Everything looked healthy; no signs of polyps or cysts or fibroids. They scheduled me for another ultrasound at 12 weeks, "to see if the pregnancy was still viable." Oh, how I didn't like to hear those words. At 12 weeks everything was just fine.

Everything continued to be great until November. I was suffering from a very bad cold and was on antibiotics for bronchitis and a sinus infection. While sitting at the computer one morning, I passed out. Jessica called 911, and I was transported to the hospital. I had developed an ear infection and had lost consciousness due to dizziness. They gave me medications and sent me home with instructions to do nothing but rest and drink lots of fluids.

The cold never really went away. At my next ob-gyn appointment the following week, my blood pressure was high and my pulse was elevated. I told him that the elevated pulse had been going on for some time, but they thought it might be from the cold remedies I was taking. At my next appointment, when I wasn't taking those cold remedies anymore, I still had high blood pressure and an elevated pulse. I needed to see a specialist since these could be indicators that I might develop pre-eclampsia. I was a candidate for developing it since I was over 45 and pregnant, even if I'd never had it before. So, just before Christmas, Daryl took me to the University of Washington where they found I had developed high cardiac output (hence the elevated pulse). They put me on a low dose of a medication to control it and sent me home with strict instructions to do nothing to elevate my heart rate. It was okay for me to be in my recliner, but I was to do no housework whatsoever!

For the next two months I went to see the University of Washington specialist once a month but also continued to have regular visits with my ob-gyn. At 34 weeks they discussed having me come in twice a week, but I made a deal to come in once a week and have a non-stress test/ultrasound profile at every visit. At my next appointment with the specialist, they explained to me that with high cardiac output and hypertension, the life of the placenta is greatly diminished. They needed to keep a close eye on our baby to make sure that she was still growing correctly. At any sign that she was under stress or experiencing low amniotic fluid, they would need to induce labor right away. When I got home, we made plans for an early delivery and packed our bags. At my 36 week appointment the next week, sure enough, her fluids were low and so was her activity. They scheduled an induction for the following day.

Our first attempt at induction started with several different attempts to prepare my body for labor. It culminated with a cervix dilated to 4 cm, but I was not responding to Pitocin. After 36 hours I went home overnight and was admitted again the next day. They gave me Pitocin just after lunchtime. They explained to me that they had pints of blood on standby, and that I was required to have two IVs just in case I hemorrhaged as I had in the past. Throughout the day and evening they slowly increased the dosage of Pitocin, and by early evening I began to have some light, irregular contractions. We decided to allow them to break my water in hopes of getting my labor started. There was concern that with her head not well engaged and her cord near her head, as seen in an ultrasound the day before, that there might be trouble with her cord getting trapped or expelled with the gush of fluid, but all went well, and there was only a trickle of fluid when she broke my water.

As we watched the monitor, her heart rate went down during the contraction and stayed down. It slowly went back up after the contraction, but this was not good—not good at all. It did the same thing on the next contraction. I was told to lie down immediately, and the nurse checked me. She found what she thought was cord compression. She called the doctor, who confirmed it. She never removed her hand but held our baby's head off of my cervix to relieve the pressure being exerted on her cord. They called an urgent response code, and within minutes things were happening fast, and lots of people were running around. My doula prayed with me, and I told Daryl that I loved him—I knew I was headed for an emergency C-Section. I didn't have to be told. I was soon being wheeled down the hallway with my doctor perched on my bed.

Before I knew it, I was on the operating table being prepped for surgery. Those last few minutes were some of the worst in my life because I had not had an epidural, and they couldn't put me out until everything was ready. Eventually all was ready, and I was put under general anesthesia. The next thing I knew, I woke up under a very warm blanket with the sensation of having a hot knife on my lower abdomen (remember no epidural, so I was feeling everything until the morphine kicked in). I began asking questions before I could even open my eyes. I found out that Carese (meaning "the divine influence on the heart as manifested in the life") was born healthy and vigorously crying. She weighed just 4 pounds 14 ounces and was 18 ¾ inches long – our smallest baby by far.

They said she was a fighter, that I would be able to see her in a few minutes, and that she would not have to stay in the special care nursery. What a miracle! What a relief. Sure enough, just after talking with our pediatrician and being reassured that Carese was very healthy, but oh so tiny, Daryl walked in with her. She looked like a little doll. We praised God for His mercy in sparing her life and mine. We later found that my membranes had become "stuck" to my uterus, and that if I had delivered vaginally, I would have bled profusely, resulting in a hysterectomy or worse. I also found out that I did, in fact, still have my uterus, and everything looked healthy in there.

Carese and I spent 3 days in the hospital. The recovery was rough, and she had trouble latching due to being so tiny. But she was able to room-in with me the entire time and came home weighing less than 5 pounds. For some strange reason, they felt that I had enough experience to care for such a tiny infant. I chose to bottle feed her and pump right from the beginning. She was impatient waiting for my milk to come in, and she had no fat on her whatsoever. She started gaining weight from the first day. I like to say she came out hungry and has stayed that way.

We had a very difficult time moving from bottle to breast. She was stubborn, but so was I. I spent most of every day and night pumping, attempting to nurse, and then giving her a bottle, just to repeat it all in three hours. It took three different lactation consultants, but she eventually became very good at nursing. I had some problems with milk supply, but since going to full-time nursing, we've only had to supplement with one bottle each day. She is a precocious little girl, learning everything quickly. She's got a temper, but she also has the most amazing laugh, and her baby talk is the cutest thing in the world. I can't imagine our family without her.

My first cycle returned around the time that Carese turned 10 months old. I had to resume taking the black cohosh before that time due to mood swings. I have also had some mild night sweats return. I don't know if the Lord will bless us with another baby, but I am more than content with the blessings He has already sent our way. I am still nursing Carese, so my cycles are not regular yet. She has been walking for about two months, but I don't plan to wean anytime soon. So much for our weaning-when-they-walk routine. I figure she's probably the last baby I'll nurse, so I'm going to continue as long as we both enjoy it.

We are currently in the process of adopting a little girl who has Down syndrome from an Eastern European country. If we succeed in adopting her, we will have a baker's dozen! She is 2 and a half years old and is just learning how to sit. The Lord has taught us so much through Esther. He has opened our hearts to the plight of these rejected children. We want to be able provide the love of a family for a little one whom the world sees as defective and unworthy. You can follow our adoption journey on my new blog, A Seventh Sister, http://aseventhsister.blogspot.com/.

As I face uncertainty in the coming years as to the possibility of becoming pregnant again, or whether experiencing the final months of my fertility, I will hold onto the promise from my Lord for me found in Jeremiah 29:11, *"For I know the plans I have for you," declares the LORD, "plans to prosper you and not to harm you, plans to give you hope and a future."*

Ruth Answers the Survey Questions

1. How do you deal with the fear of increased miscarriage, infant loss, or birth defects? How can one handle that kind of pain, especially over and over again?

I have thought a lot about fear. After losing Johanna I experienced a lot of fear. Fear that tried to take over in every pregnancy after her loss. God has taught me that fear is not of Him. There are so many Bible passages that tell us not to fear but to trust God. Another form of fear is worry – something else that God tells us we are not to do. When facing fears, I try to remind myself to think of what is true, especially what is true about God and His love for me. I remind myself that God promises to give strength to the weak, comfort to those who mourn, and that we are held in His hand. I remind myself that He does all things well, and He never makes a mistake. He orchestrates all things in my life for my good and His glory.

I have not experienced repeated miscarriages (yet), and I can't say how I would handle that. I do know that fear thrives where there is lack of faith. God tells us in 1 John 4:18 that *"perfect love casts out fear."* Faith and trust are the remedy for fear and worry.

I have also learned that God will never give us more that we can handle in His strength. The very thing you fear most will not be sent your way without the grace that only God can give. When I have been in trying and difficult times, God's grace has enabled me to endure in ways that I could not have understood beforehand. So when I worry about the what-ifs, I am on my own. I experience the trials in my imagination—without the grace that God will provide if, and when, that trial comes to me from His loving hand. God does not promise that His grace is sufficient for the what-ifs—but He does promise in 2 Corinthians 2:9 that, *"My grace is sufficient for you, for my power is made perfect in weakness,"* and in Philippians 4:13, *"I can do everything through him who gives me strength."* He will give us the strength to do what He asks us to do and the grace needed for each day.

Philippians 4:6-7 pretty much sums this up – *"Do not be anxious about anything, but in everything by prayer and supplication with thanksgiving let your requests be made known to God. And the peace of God, which surpasses all understanding, will guard your hearts and your minds in Christ Jesus."*

2. How do you balance life with older kids and babies? Do you feel this is unfair to the older children? How do they feel about having more brothers and sisters? Is it being greedy to want more babies at the risk of not being able to meet the needs of the rest of the family?

Every day has its own challenges. The older children need me less physically, but at times they need my moral and spiritual support. They have learned to allow for interruptions. The needs of the little children can get in the way of our heart to heart talks. But God can use that in their lives to produce patience too! When I have my quiet time in the morning, I ask God to give me wisdom to know what is important to do that day, and that He will give me the strength and wisdom to do it. So far, all our children have always welcomed news of a new baby on the way. When we went longer than usual between having babies, they began to look forward to the next baby.

I really believe that God is in control, whether we believe that or not. God will act in our lives according to His will, and if we are not fighting against His will, we will be blessed, even through the tough times. I think it's a myth that having more children deprive the older children. I think it enriches their lives. They learn to be unselfish. They learn to care for babies and little children, and that prepares them for parenthood. They learn to meet the needs of others. They learn to turn to God when their parents are unavailable. God uses our lives as parents to mold our children as well.

When facing the probability that I, as a mother, will be on bed rest or even hospitalized, it's easy to feel that it will be a hardship for my older children as they care for the younger children. It will be. But God is in control, and He will use that experience to mature and develop Christ-like character in our children. We also look to our community to help during times of trial. It has been good for our children to experience this firsthand. It helps them to understand how hard it is on a family to have the mother or father unable to be present in the home. They now have compassion for other families who experience similar trials—and want to help out where they can.

It is so good to teach our children and remind ourselves that trials produce lasting benefits – James 1:2-4 says, *"Count it all joy, my brothers, when you meet trials of various kinds, for you know that the testing of your faith produces steadfastness. And let steadfastness have its full effect, that you may be perfect and complete, lacking in nothing."*

3. What about the ethical issues of repeated miscarriages? Shouldn't I avoid conception if I know that the chances of that child living are minimal? Am I enabling death when I should be promoting life?

The affliction of miscarriage is momentary, while pregnancy produces an eternal soul. *"For this light momentary affliction is preparing for us an eternal weight of glory beyond all comparison."* (2 Corinthians 4:17) I believe that God is the giver and taker of life. The era of easy access to contraception has given us the idea that we are in control of giving life. Yet how many couples want to get pregnant and can't? And how many do everything in their power to prevent conception and yet end up pregnant? Some forms of contraception actually allow fertilization but deny implantation, therefore causing death. With Carese, the probability of carrying her to term and that she would be completely healthy were slim (our chances of her having Down syndrome were 1 in 4), and yet here she is. If I had relied on my own common sense and not on Godly wisdom, we would have missed out on enjoying her every day as she grows and learns and blesses us all!

4. Do pregnancy, childbirth, and recovery get harder in your 40s? I already feel like I'm coming apart at the seams! How will I hold out until menopause if I keep having babies? Am I acting responsibly when it comes to taking care of my health?

Yes, pregnancy, childbirth, and recovery were harder in my 40s. I can't say that I long to become pregnant again. Both my last two pregnancies were very hard on me, and it took my much longer to feel that I was back to normal (whatever that is!). But it is all worth it. The rewards outshine the difficulties. I can't really compare with someone who has not experienced a pregnancy in their 40s, but from what I can tell, other women are experiencing physical limitations at this age too. Actually, I think pregnancy hormones keep you young! I get so many comments that people think I'm so much younger that I really am—even with all my gray hair.

I do take my health seriously. I try to eat right, exercise, and take herbal supplements and vitamins to maximize my health. If I wasn't facing the potential of another pregnancy, I might not be so serious about staying healthy.

5. How do I deal with extended family members, friends, and even the medical community who disapprove of our continuing to want more babies as we get older?

To avoid confrontation, I do not bring up the subject unless others do. With the medical community I try to lovingly tell them what I believe. I have found, however, that once we got past six children, we got less and less reaction from others. Maybe they thought we were so "out there" that we weren't worth the effort to convince. I will usually let them have their say, and then tell them that I believe God is in control, and He never makes mistakes. When they tell me I could die if I get pregnant again, I remind them that I could get hit by a truck too, but that doesn't stop me from leaving the house. I could die slipping in the shower, but I'm not going to quit taking a shower. He and He alone has numbered my days says Psalm 139:16, *"Your eyes saw my unformed substance; in your book were written, every one of them, the days that were formed for me, when as yet there was none of them."* I have no idea if today will be my last or if I will live to be 103 years old, like my grandmother, and have more days left to live than I have already lived!

6. Will I have the energy I need to continue to raise children into my 50s if I have some in my 40s? Is it fair to the child to have older parents?

Since I am still in my 40s, I can't really address this question. I have seen other women raise children (and in many cases their grandchildren) in their 50s and 60s, and while it may be difficult at times, with God's help and grace it is more than possible. I was born to a mother who was 36 and a father who was 43. I felt that I had older parents, especially compared to my classmates in school. But other than that, I saw no problem with their age. My husband just went snowboarding with our older boys, and I hope to go-kart with them again some day soon! My husband still plays volleyball regularly with our children, and I believe having younger children to raise in "our old age" will keep us young and on the move.

7. How do you explain miscarriage to older children, especially if you have repeated losses?

You tell them the truth. We did that even with our younger children. They can understand more than we give them credit for most of the time. They will learn from us in how we live through the trials that God sends our way. Do we fight God and become bitter, or are we looking for the lessons God is teaching us through the trials? Do we react to grief by becoming bitter and recoiling from God, or do we run to Him and find comfort in His Word?

8. How does having babies in your 40s affect your relationship with your husband? Don't I owe him some of my best years?

I owe him my devotion and support. I owe him my love and submission. I cannot control whether or not these are the best years of my life. I could avoid pregnancy but suffer from endometriosis, fibroids, or any number of physial ailments that I see other women my age suffering from that keep them from giving their husband "the best years. I try to keep my priorities correct even when I am physically challenged. God is first, husband second, children third, and then our home. When I am physically challenged my list ends there. Recently, during my last pregnancy and the recovery, I felt like I had been put on the shelf like the broken toys in *Toy Story*— out of sight and no longer good for anything. I rarely left home and was out of the loop with my friends and church family for months. During this time the Lord worked in my heart to learn lessons I could never have learned without being on the shelf. My husband and my children were my world.

9. Do you have any practical tips for high mileage mamas dealing with fatigue, pelvic separation, joint pain, varicose veins, etc.? In other words, what kinds of pregnancy issues did you have to deal with, and how did you deal with them?

I have learned that I need to take care of myself. Eating right, getting enough sleep (taking naps if necessary) and exercising are critical. I do a lot with essential oils and herbal remedies as well. I learned a lot about nutrition and I research a lot as well. Finding natural ways to deal with maladies usually has the best benefits in the long run. I started doing T-Tapp (http://t-tapp.com/) this past fall and I highly recommend it. It is good for your joints, muscles, and adrenal system. You can do these exercises during pregnancy with some modification too.

I personally have dealt with an undiagnosed sciatic nerve problem through nearly all of my pregnancies, only finding out in my last pregnancy what I was suffering from. A few appointments with a physical therapist corrected the problem for me. When pelvic separation starts to happen, I limit my activities so that I reduce all strain on that "joint"—trying to not do things that cause my legs to go in opposite directions, and walking carefully and with small steps. I learned this the hard way with Esther as I ended up walking only with a walker for the last week as it got really bad. With my last pregnancy, the moment I felt that developing, I became very careful not to aggravate it, and it went away.

10. Are there real statistics (not skewed to the cultural norm) available regarding having babies in one's 40s? How many mothers do you know who have had babies in their 40s? Share your thoughts regarding statistics and odds.

I know many moms who have had babies in their 40s. I also know of many who have experienced miscarriages. I think that overall it's not as difficult as what statistics tell us. Women who are not avoiding pregnancy and are aware of the possibility of becoming pregnant in their 40s usually take good care of their bodies. Those finding themselves pregnant when trying to avoid it might be less prepared. Also, today, prenatal care is so much better in many regards, but worse in others. Many medical techniques can lead to complications in pregnancy and birth, while many of the complications that come up in advance maternal age pregnancies are readily dealt with today with modern medicine. Educating ourselves and making knowledgeable decisions about our health care is of vital importance.

Ruth Einfeld *is 40 years old and has been married to her best friend, Daryl since 1985. They have been blessed with 12 biological children, and are currently working to adopt a little girl with Down Syndrome through international adoption. Their 11th child was born with Down Syndrome, so they have a heart for children with this disability. She runs her business, Snap-EZ Inc, from home. She also authors several blogs, including My Daughters and her adoption blog, A Seventh Sister.*

The Lord Directs Our Steps

By Terry Covey

My story of bearing and rearing children is one of growth, lessons, faith, and humility. Mine is not the usual one of a Christian mom-of-many who wants to have all the children God will give her so she can raise them for His glory. Mine is actually one of pride and selfishness. But the Holy God, the Creator of all things, chose to use that pride and selfishness for His good. He chose to use me and my frame and weakness to bring about His purpose. But isn't that always His way!

> *"...that all the peoples of the earth may know that the LORD is God; there is no one else."* (1 Kings 8:60)

One thing I find funny is that long ago when I was in high school, I told people I wasn't going to have any children. I was going to protect myself from the fear of the unknown, risk, and pain of pregnancy and birth. God does have a sense of humor! Read on and you'll see how those children I said I would never have—10 of them—came into being.

I began my journey of motherhood long before I became a Christian. I was 19 when we married, became pregnant six months later, and gave birth to a tiny baby girl who came three weeks

189

early. I was only 20 when she was born, but I was invincible! (You can read about my walk away from invincibility at http://www.visionarywomanhood.com/invincible-christ-alone/.) I read all the books and knew what I was doing. I would raise my children well (they would not be spoiled), giving them healthy food (none of that sugar) and good parenting according to all the books I read. I would breastfeed, discipline correctly, and gain their heart along the way. I had a plan!

Looking back, I see I didn't deviate from that plan until recently when, in His perfect timing, God showed me my true frame: one that is, and will continue to be, aging and changing with the seasons. I suddenly couldn't make a baby whenever I wanted; my children were growing up and leaving the nest, and I couldn't make them smarter, more capable, or have more character. I wasn't all-knowing, all-powerful, or all-capable anymore. God was humbling me.

My story is one of naivety and pride, yet amazingly, God loves me so much that He offers a way out even when I wonder why He would be so patient. I'm sure there are many unmet needs in my children that stem from my micro-managing style of motherhood, and amazingly those needs keep them on their knees before God. He continues to offer grace to cover our mistakes and meet our needs. He uses everything for His good and our growth in knowledge of Him.

"The heart of man plans his way, but the Lord establishes his steps." (Proverbs 16:9)

I was blessed with a body that handled both pregnancy and birth well, and I had perfectly healthy babies. They ranged in birth weight from 5 pounds 11 ounces to 7 pounds 15.5 ounces. Six of my babies came one and one-half to three weeks early. After my third child was born I was involved in coaching single moms at a crisis pregnancy center where I volunteered. This aided me in finding good doctors and midwives who allowed me to be fairly natural during my hospital births. Through my pursuit of the best birth experience possible, I had a variety of birth experiences.

Although my first five births were in the hospital, I always sought doctors who viewed birth as a natural process, limited medical intervention, would allow my husband in the room with me, and let us take pictures. Back then some still didn't allow dads in the room, and others didn't allow pictures for fear the flash would ignite the oxygen. My sister had her hands strapped down during labor, even in 1980! After my first doctor gave me an episiotomy during the birth of my five-and-a-half pound baby, I found a doctor who would avoid that unnecessary procedure for my second. For my third, I discovered midwives, CNM's (Certified Nurse Midwife), who were willing to be present for the entire labor and would offer a more natural experience. This led to my discovery of what I consider the most natural birth experience possible: home birth.

For my fifth baby I wanted to have a home birth, but my CNM talked me out of it. Actually, she scared me out of it. But my fifth birth involved a long, grueling labor, spent in the hospital for almost 20 hours, simply because of a hospital policy. So before my next pregnancy, I studied, researched, and talked with doctors and midwives to be sure home birth was safe (taking into consideration high risk pregnancies, of course). This sealed our decision to switch to home births in the future. We went on to have five of our babies at home, providing wonderful memories of birth the way, I believe, God intended it to be! Natural, family centered, and home based, if at all possible.

I continued my education in birth by apprenticing and assisting local midwives for six years. My midwifery experience helped me to see birth as a normal body process, not an anomaly. I continue helping others have natural birth experiences by assisting my oldest daughter, who is a licensed midwife.

"May you be strengthened with all power, according to his glorious might, for all endurance and patience with joy, giving thanks to the Father, who has qualified you to share in the inheritance of the saints in light." (Colossians 1:11-12)

Along with my book knowledge of birth and being a good momma, I read studies that "proved" the best age gap between children. The "experts" said that children thrive when they have three years of individual attention and teaching. So I purposed to offer each child plenty of time and energy before the next baby came along. But by the time my baby reached 15 months, I was aching to hold another babe in my arms, so I quickly adjusted that three-year equation down to two. Two worked well for me. We were on a roll.

My husband's job required him to work long days, seven days a week, every 18 months. This work lasted several months at a time, so we decided it would be best if our babies didn't arrive during one of those times. I wanted my husband around to welcome his child and help during the adjustment periods. We used barrier birth control methods to keep our babies from coming too closely.

That planning worked well for us. God allowed our first four babies to arrive about two years apart, and we never did have a baby during one of those crazy work schedules. Why God chose to allow for my need to be in control, I'll never know, but I believe He just wanted our 10 children to be born. You see, my selfishness and impatience would never have tolerated having them close together. I'm sure I would have chosen to stop having more babies. God always knows best!

"And we know that for those who love God all things work together for good, for those who are called according to His purpose." (Romans 8:28)

Exactly two years after my first, baby number two came along. She came two weeks early with only a few hours of labor. I was overjoyed. My purpose in life had been set, and I was in heaven! Unfortunately, I did not realize the selfish streak that ran through me, along with the anger problem I had. I remember cutting out shapes in construction paper and writing reminders on them to post around my home. They said, "Smile, don't yell," and "Give hugs, not hurts." Those days seem so very far away, yet my notes all over the house were reminders to "take my thoughts captive" even before I knew what it meant! God offers us His ways even before we acknowledge Him.

> *"We destroy arguments and every lofty opinion raised against the knowledge of God, and take every thought captive to obey Christ..."* (2 Corinthians 10:5)

The battle over God's plan for our family began about this time (it was 1984, and I was only 24). My agnostic brother discovered that baby number three was coming. He asked, "Don't you feel socially responsible to not bring more children into the world?" I was offended. I was raising them to be socially responsible and productive members of society! His cutting words could have squelched me, could have easily convinced me of my "guilt" before the world. Remember, I wasn't a Christian. Looking back, I know God used my strength of character (or strong will!) to do His will. I'm grateful that He never stops working on us.

> *"Remember the former things of old; for I am God, and there is no other; I am God, and there is none like Me, declaring the end from the beginning and from ancient times things not yet done, saying, 'My counsel shall stand, and I will accomplish all My purpose."* (Isaiah 46:9-10)

My view of social consciousness involved being responsible to raise our little people well: seeing that our family worked as a team, knowing the value of hard work, and loving each other. I made it my goal to prevent the resentment that an older child might feel when a younger sibling enters their world. You know those children's books written about the spoiled child who welcomes home his new sibling only to feel threatened and unloved? I read those books, but I didn't buy the lie! Looking back, I believe God blessed me with common sense, even before my conversion, to overcome many of the traditions and habits that the world was throwing at me.

> *"He will tend his flock like a shepherd; He will gather the lambs in his arms; He will carry them in his bosom, and gently lead those that are with young."* (Isaiah 40:11)

I devoted myself to preparing each child for the next baby. We would read and look at the beautiful pictures in Lennart Nilsson's A Child Is Born, tracking our baby's growth each week. We let them hear the baby's heart beat within me. We brought them to my doctor or midwife appointments so they could anticipate this new life as much as we did. For our entire family, our children's births were like parties, and we share fond memories of them. When our third was born, we started a tradition of bringing ice cream to the hospital to celebrate after the birth. This continued for every future birth. When we had hospital births, the nurses enjoyed our huge crew in the birthing room. Once a nurse put on a "Quiet—No Visitors" sign on our door, and when each new nurse would enter our room, they would do a double take and then laugh! We had nine people in that room! What fun memories!

> *"…I have set before you life and death, blessing and curse. Therefore choose life, that you and your offspring may live, loving the Lord your God, obeying*

*his voice and holding fast to him, for he is your life
and length of days..."* (Deuteronomy 30:19-20)

A new battle was beginning to brew in our marriage, and it
relates to the one begun in the garden of Eden—the one that pits
me against my husband for power. Before baby number three came
along, my husband and I began the cycle of discussing having
another baby. This cycle began around the time my second baby
reached 15 months old and continued for over a decade. I would
yearn for a newborn in my arms. But when I was ready for my
third, my husband was not on the same page. We had no biblical
understanding. We only went to church for holidays, based on my
upbringing in the Catholic Church, and we knew nothing about
living for or trusting God, in our daily life or for instruction in our
roles as husband and wife.

I truly wanted more babies, but my husband had been raised
in a family with only one brother, so all he knew was life in a small
family. He adamantly argued with me, using the reasoning that
children take so much time when they're older, and he didn't think
he wanted the work. But as you can tell, I won, and fortunately,
because of my guy's gentle nature, each child was warmly welcomed
by both of us. I now understand the implications of arguing with
my husband, but what a blessing that God uses our sin to challenge
us and bring us to our knees before Him. He knows what the
future holds for us and what to allow or disallow.

> *"To the woman he said, 'I will surely multiply your
> pain in childbearing; in pain you shall bring forth
> children. Your desire shall be for your husband, and
> he shall rule over you.'"* (Genesis 3:16)

Baby number three arrived when I was 25, again, an early and
easy delivery. We had just moved to a new state. I even brought him
home to a hotel for 10 days until our house was move-in ready!
I explicitly remember commenting about our new community,

"Everyone we meet is a Christian!" God used our first three years there laying a plan for our salvation by placing new friends, and even the contractor who built our home, in our path. And yes, they were all Christians. Our fourth child was born when I was 27. Soon after, in 1989, we became Christians. I was also beginning to understand that God wanted us to trust Him with the timing of number five.

However, I was not quite ready to trust—not quite ready to give up my micromanaging. "What about those babies who wouldn't get enough time with their busy momma?!" So I fretted and worried about having another baby. "How would I have enough time for all of them? What if I couldn't be patient and give them what they needed?" But I prayed and gave my timing to God, and He delivered. Literally! When I discovered I was pregnant, I was talking to my husband on the phone while holding the pregnancy test with a clear, blue line on it. I slumped to the floor, sorely depleted in my own strength. I was trying in my heart to trust God, but I was "undone" as they say in the old movies!

I continued to wonder how I would make this transition and still be the kind of mom I always wanted to be. Where would I get the strength? I know the answer now, but not then. I was used to deciding when I was ready for another baby, and this time I wasn't prepared for my sense of inadequacy. It's not as if she came too soon after our last child; it's just that I wasn't ready. I had yet to learn it isn't in our own strength we obey. Rather than offer my life to the Lord the way I so much wanted to, I fought and convinced myself that I couldn't do this. I hate to admit it, but I even wished I would fall off my horse and lose the baby! I was in such a battle with God over my will and releasing my life to Him. That battle would last for many more years.

> *"For the mind that is set on the flesh is hostile to*
> *God, for it does not submit to God's law; indeed, it*

cannot. Those who are in the flesh cannot please God.
You, however, are not in the flesh but in the Spirit,
if in fact the Spirit of God dwells in you... But if
Christ is in you, although the body is dead because
of sin, the Spirit is life because of righteousness."
(Romans 8:7-10)

When I became pregnant with this transition child, I decided I would conquer my need to have babies. I wanted to avoid my sense of vulnerability to God's control for the timing of my babies. So I convinced my husband to get a vasectomy before this next baby was born. That way, when I saw her and fell in love, the decision would already be taken care of. I definitely had a control issue!

Our plan was for my husband to have the vasectomy around my sixth month of pregnancy, giving us plenty of time to recover and not risk another pregnancy. And we wouldn't look back! But, when my husband called to set up the appointment, he was informed that the doctor required both husband and wife to be present at the first visit. Oh, my! I didn't want to deal with the reality of having to say "no" to more babies. I just wanted it to be done and behind me. Crazy, I know, but this was my reality. Yet God would have His way. He knew just what I needed, what we both needed, what He needed of us!

So on the day of our appointment, I awoke in a tizzy. I couldn't see straight. I couldn't think. I was tingly all over. I just couldn't do this! I couldn't make this permanent decision to stop having babies. I wrestled with God all morning – remember, I was now a Christian, albeit a new one. So I called my husband at work, telling him of my odd sensations. I really felt crazy, as if someone else was controlling me. My husband listened and considered my words, deciding that it must be a sign, and we could not go through with this. We both knew that God was taking charge. The appointment was cancelled.

We are so grateful for God's intervention. Permanent birth control leaves God out of the picture. It avoids the possibility of revelation from Him for new direction in our lives. We lose the opportunity to pray and examine our motives, our life purpose, our finances, and our health as we "plan our way," and give God His rightful place to "direct our path."

"You, however, are not in the flesh but in the Spirit, if in fact the Spirit of God dwells in you." (Romans 8:9) *"And he who searches hearts knows what is the mind of the Spirit, because the Spirit intercedes for the saints according to the will of God."* (Romans 8:27)

God took care of all my worries when our baby was born. All I had to do was look into her sweet oval eyes and see her perfectly shaped red lips, and I fell instantly in love. I've always said that God knew what He was doing when He created babies! To think that people throw away such a perfect and grand gift! I instantly became the loving mother I had always been, and my worries were over. I adjusted, got organized, and elicited the help of my growing brood. We were a team and it was quite fun!

One thing I need to share here is the effect my attitude had on this baby, my daughter. I know without a doubt, that throughout her life, her confidence in my love has been much lower than my other children. Some will say that a baby can't sense the feelings of the mother while in the womb, but I would disagree. This daughter was well into her teens before she trusted God enough to give her life over to Him. She struggled with insecurity, lying, and trying to be "good" enough and loved like her siblings. I believe she inherently knew she wasn't wanted while she was growing within me, and that insecurity played out in her childhood years. I pray for her pain to be overcome by my actions and God's love and restoration.

" . . *Return to the Lord your God, for he is gracious and merciful, slow to anger, and abounding in steadfast love; and he relents over disaster." "I will restore to you the years that the swarming locust has* eaten…" (Joel 2:13, 25) *"Do nothing from rivalry or conceit, but in humility count others more significant than yourselves."* (Philippians 2:3)

One thing I distinctly remember all through my mommy years was praying for my babies. I'm sure it came from my Catholic background, praying when I was young, and knowing there was a God somewhere. Each night as I tucked them in bed, I would pray, "God watch over them, God be with them always." Exactly those words! I know now, beyond a shadow of a doubt, that He honored that prayer even though I was not a Christian at the time.

> *"Likewise the Spirit helps us in our weakness. For we do not know what to pray for as we ought, but the Spirit himself intercedes for us with groanings too deep for words."* (Romans 8:26)

Around this time, we heard biblical teaching that woke us to the idea of allowing God to decide the number of our children. We were advantaged to have many friends with large families, which I'm sure helped us to be confident in our lifestyle. Although not quite ready to have babies a year apart, we were ready to give the number to God. We decided that natural family planning was the best course of action for us. We decided to use self-control rather than birth control during those important times of the month as we felt it left God in control to alter our plans as He saw fit. When I was 33, baby number six was delivered, and my husband was sold—no more arguing. He was as much in love with all these children as I was!

From my first baby on, I was always confident in breastfeeding. Being rather independent from what the world deemed normal, I breastfed all my babies for 19-20 months. I usually stopped when I was halfway through my next pregnancy and my milk was diminishing. One luxury I didn't have (and it seems to be more common with women today) was the expected six-month space with no ovulation that usually occurs due to lactating. My periods began within two months of birth, even though I demand fed all of my babies. This lack of natural spacing was another reason we chose to be cautious about getting pregnant.

Our next three babies, arriving when I was between the ages of 35 to 39, were a comfortable fit for our family lifestyle. We simply expected that "momma" would be having a baby every few years. Now, instead of worrying if we could handle another baby, we honestly didn't know how we'd handle it when the babies stopped coming! Everyone loved their newest siblings, and we were fairly organized and capable as a team. Note the fairly adjective! I have a friend who said, "God knew there was too much of me to go around, so He keeps giving me more children!" This is so true of my life. God tamed me a bit at a time through each child He added to our brood. I learned organization when I'm not the least bit organized! And I have learned to be a servant when I started out selfish and stingy. He uses all things to bring us to His ways.

> *"But all things should be done decently and in order."* (1 Corinthians 14:40) *"...but rather let him labor, doing honest work with his own hands, so that he may have something to share with anyone in need."* (Ephesians 4:28)

One thing about having a large family that I never got comfortable with was the scene we'd make when we'd go in a restaurant or out shopping. All eyes would be on us. Remember, there were no Duggars to pave the way for large family normalcy. I can't count how many times I saw people pointing and counting, literally aloud! And we received the usual questions: "Are these all yours? How do you do it?" My favorite reply was, "One at a time!" And to the comment, "You must be a saint!" I'd reply, "No, actually I'm selfish and had them because I love babies!" And then there is the all-time favorite comment for large families: "Don't you know what causes that?" Silly! Of course we do. That's why we have 10!

I was beginning to wonder when my baby-making days would be over. I was 40 and knew those days were numbered. But I was caught completely off guard when my 10th pregnancy ended in miscarriage. I worked for a midwife as an apprentice/assistant for four years, so I owned a Doppler and could listen to our baby's heart tones. At nine weeks along, I couldn't find a heart beat. I was stunned! How could this be? I hadn't lost any babies, and my worst fear was happening. At 10 weeks, I miscarried. It was quite difficult and left me tired and saddened. I stared at that empty crib in my room and pined for my lost child. Now I could understand when other women shared about their losses. I know God allowed my suffering so I could help others.

> *"Blessed be the God and Father of our Lord Jesus Christ, the Father of mercies and God of all comfort, who comforts us in all our affliction, so that we may be able to comfort those who are in any affliction, with the comfort with which we ourselves are comforted by God."* (2 Corinthians 1:3-4)

The Lord saw fit to let us become pregnant only two months later, and at the age of 41 ½, I gave birth to a healthy baby boy, our youngest child, who is now 11. Each time I get to play with him, or he comes to snuggle with me in bed in the morning, I thank God for giving him to me. I especially see him as a blessing, knowing he came in the middle of four years of miscarriages and pre-menopause!

Looking back at my births, one thing I see that varied as I got older was my body's way of dealing with labor. In particular, my final labor lasted 30 hours, starting and stopping all along the way. I would have a few hours of good contractions, then they would slack off or stop for hours. I'd have another few hours of contractions, then more rest time. It was as if my body needed to regroup and build the necessary hormones for labor. The human body is amazing. God created us to do the hard work of delivering babies, even in our older age. It just takes a bit more patience!

One thing I highly recommend for older moms is more rest, better nutrition, and supplements to recover from birth and boost their milk supply. It's especially important to understand our changing needs due to age, higher activity level in a growing family, and lagging hormones. As we protect our health, we'll have more energy and be more productive to serve God and our family.

> "*So Sarah laughed to herself, saying, 'After I am worn out, and my lord is old, shall I have pleasure?' The Lord said to Abraham, 'Why did Sarah laugh and say, 'Shall I indeed bear a child, now that I am old?' Is anything too hard for the Lord?*" (Genesis 18:12-14)

Two years after my 10th child was born, I had two more miscarriages, at 7 and 10 weeks. It is quite trying when we see a phase of our life ebbing. I liken it to a man retiring; our sense of usability is altered, and we must re-invent our identity. It was especially hard to realize I would not be creating new life. My children loved having babies delivered to them, and now I couldn't provide them with this gift and joy. It was what I lived for and loved doing. My sadness was overwhelming and complete. It can be such a hard transition for a woman, but one in which we can only trust that God will provide for our need and reveal what lies on the other side.

My years of miscarriages lasted four years and came with signs of impending menopause—hot flashes, erratic cycles, foggy thinking, and moodiness that came and went with no apparent reason. Unpleasant is how I would describe this season. Those years have turned into 10 now, but in the last few years, since my periods have stopped, it's gotten better. I still have hot flashes, which I seriously would like to end. But the moodiness and the PMS of the past is, well, in the past. And I am glad for that. I am more balanced and only occasionally get grumpy for no apparent reason. Hmmm. I better ask my family if that's true!

I have been on progesterone cream for the last 10 years, age 42-52. I went to an ob-gyn/midwifery conference a few years ago, where it was recommended to stay on the cream for the rest of my life. I'm not sure if I'll follow that advice, but I do feel it has helped me maintain balance during these trying years. When I miss a day on the cream, it is obvious in my mood, my irritability, and my nerves. Now, instead of dealing with cramps, PMS, or the uncomfortable symptoms of pregnancy, I deal with the joint pain of old age. God never promised us it would be easy!

> *"For everything there is a season, and a time for every matter under heaven."* (Ecclesiastes 3:1)

> *"For we were so utterly burdened beyond our strength that we despaired of life itself. . . But that was to make us rely not on ourselves but on God who raises the dead."* (2 Corinthians 1:8-9)

In looking back over my pregnancy charts, I realized I didn't struggle with my weight until my last few babies. I was pretty much 120-125 pounds at the start of my first seven pregnancies. I honestly didn't know that! My memory of those years was one of being overweight and having to fight it, but my records show that it was only the four to six months after birth that I was overweight. I did begin to put on more weight during each successive pregnancy. With my first babies I gained about 25 pounds, and my largest gain was 50 pounds with my eighth child. After my last baby, at 42 years of age, I was 15 pounds heavier than when I was first married.

Now, being 52 years old and in menopause, I am finding that each year gets harder and harder to maintain my weight. I now weigh 150 pounds and am struggling to keep the pounds from rising. My activity level is much lower without little ones around, and I sit much more than I used to. My joints ache often, but my research is revealing that it may be caused by lack of exercise. I'm realizing my need to care for myself in ways I never did before. I have to be much more careful with what I eat, or my weight goes up. If I don't exercise, my weight goes up and my bum gets wider! Becoming overweight has become my biggest frustration. I can feel the stress on my joints and heart and lungs. It's amazing how even 25 pounds can weigh us down both physically and emotionally. I highly recommend preparing for this season in life by getting into a routine of exercise and eating healthy. This year I have a plan to change my diet and find ways to exercise and become more active.

> *"Or do you not know that your body is a temple of the Holy Spirit within you, whom you have from God? You are not your own, for you were bought with a price. So glorify God in your body."* (1 Corinthians 6:19-20)

My next season of life, grandmothering, entered while I had a houseful of activity and children. It has been nothing but an adventure! Becoming "Grand-momma" has had a learning curve of it's own. It didn't come naturally for me, simply because I wanted to give my grandchildren the same love and attention I gave my own children. But how does one do that when these children are not your own? How do you help while not taking away responsibility from their parents? How do we treat these little ones as we would treat our own children but at the same time know our boundaries? These were new questions I hadn't thought of before.

This season offers new territory, new choices, and new mistakes to be made. You can read more of my mothering/grandparenting journey at momsmanylessons.com. Now that I have six grandchildren and am four years into grandparenting, I'm seeing that it does get easier. I can see the full circle of life that God created; children become adults, and adults become parents, and parents become grandparents. Each season adds to our experience and maturity; each offers us new sanctification as we seek to become more like Christ.

> *"Grandchildren are the crown of the aged, and the glory of children is their fathers."* (Proverbs 17:6)

I have had the privilege of giving birth to babies in three decades: the 80s, 90s, and one in 2002! I never intended or thought I would one day make that claim, but it truly is an amazing gift and responsibility. I have seen changes in how babies and birth are viewed in our culture. I have seen women give up their rights to know about their bodies and about what is best for their babies. But given how our society thinks about children and the unborn, that is not surprising. I encourage women to defend their right to care and provide the best for their children. One way to do that is to be proud of our children, never forgetting that they are blessings from God. We must be confident in our role as co-creator with God and take that privilege seriously.

> *She opens her mouth with wisdom, and the teaching of kindness is on her tongue. She looks well to the ways of her household and does not eat the bread of idleness. Her children rise up and call her blessed; her husband also, and he praises her.* (Proverbs 31:26-28)

This experience of reliving my baby-making years makes me marvel at what God has done! I am humbled that He would allow me to mother so many of His children. I am astonished by my body's ability to do all the work necessary to create a little human. I am amazed how God made a woman's body capable of sustaining life and adjusting to those seemingly tortuous months of growth, only to be capable of contracting back down to a pre-

pregnant state! Simply awesome! Add to that our ability to provide sustenance to our babies – milk that offers them all they need for half a year, and more! I am simply in awe that God would allow me, and provide me with the grace, to do this job of motherhood. And I praise Him for that!

> *For you formed my inward parts; you knitted me together in my mother's womb. I praise you, for I am fearfully and wonderfully made. Wonderful are your works; my soul knows it very well. My frame was not hidden from you, when I was being made in secret, intricately woven in the depths of the earth. Your eyes saw my unformed substance; in your book were written, every one of them, the days that were formed for me, when as yet there was none of them.* (Psalm 139:13-16)

Looking back on my years of fertility and mothering, can I say that I have done this well, this role of motherhood and bearing children? I would have to say, "Yes!" And how can I say that? Where does my confidence lie? Oh, it can only come from seeing life as one that my Father has set before me! It comes from knowing that He gives me the strength to do this job. He orchestrates and conducts it for His glory. And now that I am well over halfway finished (in a normal life span), I can see that He is constantly at work. He has given me this life and my abilities, and even my pride and selfishness are not beyond His control. More importantly, He has used it all for His glory, not my own! At the end of this life, I will proclaim that I ran well because of Him, by His strength, and for His glory. Amen, and amen!

Terry Answers the Survey Questions

1. How do you deal with the fear of increased miscarriage, infant loss, or birth defects? How can one handle that kind of pain, especially over and over again?

I am past the child bearing years, so the fear of miscarriage is also past. But I certainly had to deal with it from my early 40s until my complete cessation of periods. At first I was shocked to be in the stage where my hormones were inadequate; I had been so fertile all my life. I was now dealing with the reality that this pregnancy might be my last. For so many years, I almost looked forward to that time when I didn't need to worry about getting pregnant again. But now, looking at my empty cradle was a new sense of loss with which I was not familiar.

Miscarriages are unpleasant and a bit scary. One of my miscarriages was worse than the others, resulting in excessive bleeding. The next two were not severe, but I still had the depression that comes from hormonal adjustment and loss. The pain of laboring and knowing there would be no more pregnancy and baby at the end was discouraging. Yet, I knew that God was in control, and if He desired another child in our home, I was certainly ready!

2. How do you balance life with older kids and babies? Do you feel this is unfair to the older children? How do they feel about having more brothers and sisters? Is it being greedy to want more babies at the risk of not being able to meet the needs of the rest of the family?

I'd have to say that I was quite greedy wanting more children for my own purpose, but I stand amazed at how God used even my self-indulgence to build a family for His purpose. As far as the risk of not meeting our other children's needs, if you asked my children, you would not hear of risk or negligence. As a matter of fact, they would probably laugh. We have adult children who are now having children of their own, and they love having younger siblings. And our youngest children play with their nieces and nephews on a regular basis. We all would have it no other way!

There is a sacrifice that comes with being older in a large family, and yet, that sacrifice pays huge dividends in love, experience, and responsibility all along the way! Our older ones never regretted having so many younger siblings. They got the perks of hugs, joy, and togetherness that is incomparable in our world.

There is a balance in the family design that offers exactly what we each need at the various seasons of our lives. The older children gain responsibilities when each new child comes along, making them ready and capable for their adult years. And the younger ones, who don't get as much attention as their older siblings received, gain their adult skills in a different way. They learn to adapt to the adult world and gain experience serving and being responsible in caring for their nieces and nephews. Then, the first grandbabies born have young aunts and uncles who play and teach them as if they were their siblings. Added to that, each adult sibling gets a multitude of counselors and friends as they venture into adulthood, parenthood, and marriage! It really is like one huge, caring family! I truly believe that our culture has lost the real value of family as God intended it.

A huge benefit of large families comes in the variety of personalities and talents among the children in a large family. No socialization or diversity awareness problems here! Always someone to learn a new skill from—talents in our family include: woodworking, computer, photography, sewing, Civil War reenacting, gardening, music, remote control airplanes, coffee roasting, midwifery, and more! There's always someone to learn from, defer to, and be flexible for—lots of opportunity to learn unconditional love.

Believe it or not, our family often finds our life rather boring with only eight of us in the home! All our children are trained for the most part, and they know how to behave, sit still, and talk calmly (well, for the most part!). We miss all the excitement and activity of a full house. It seems that as soon as we figured out how to live with the chaos and work of lots of children, they began leaving, and now our home is quiet. Large families only have a few years when all the children are in the home at the same time. It is the most busy and exhausting time in their life, and then it's over. I'm so glad I enjoyed it while I could!

3. What about the ethical issues of repeated miscarriages? Shouldn't I avoid conception if I know that the chances of that child living are minimal? Am I enabling death when I should be promoting life?

This question really makes me consider life and death and choices. God is our Creator, and He gave us intelligence. We are to use that intelligence for making plans like it says in Proverbs 16:9, trusting God to direct us through those plans. We use intelligence to consider the cost when starting a project as in Luke 14:28. God also gave us our intelligence to use and care for our bodies, and yet the ultimate question is, how much do we trust Him? How much control are we saying we need in this life? Each family needs to determine that from prayer, counsel, and discussion.

God knows what we each need. He will decide which babies live and which die. I believe 'ethical' relates to causing death or injury. If we avoid pregnancy because of the possibility of miscarriage, how much trust are we placing in God? If we avoid pregnancy because our last miscarriages were high risk, can we consider it wisdom? Only a husband and wife can answer those tough questions.

It's important for women to know the risk of miscarriage increases as we age. It's a simple fact of decreasing hormones. Some women have miscarriages in their 20s, and others not until their 40s. Some women have major pre-menopausal symptoms like hot flashes and sporadic cycles, others just stop having periods and it's over! It's just the way of a woman—God's grand design.

4. Do pregnancy, childbirth, and recovery get harder in your 40s? I already feel like I'm coming apart at the seams! How will I hold out until menopause if I keep having babies? Am I acting responsibly when it comes to taking care of my health?

As far as the basic idea of childbearing getting harder in my 40s, I'd have to say no. Of course, I was older and got more tired, but I felt that pregnancy kept me younger, more alert and energized. Studies show that pregnancy hormones keep us young and are good for skin, mental health, and alertness. Motherhood is exhausting, but as my brood increased, I had children who could hold down the fort while I was nauseous or tired. And they loved helping out; it made them feel a part of this new sibling's life, even before it was born.

One thing we can do to help our aging bodies is to avoid being super mom. In other words, if we're doing it all, we're doing too much! I've seen so many frazzled, tired moms doing all the hard work of maintaining their entire home and family, singlehandedly. Our bodies wear down and need more rest as we age. Plus, we do our children no favors when we don't delegate the various duties in a home. There is a two-fold benefit: it gives us the rest we need, and it offers them the practice necessary to prepare for the adult world. I was raised by a mom who did most of the housework, so when I married I felt inadequate for the many duties of adulthood. I compare my early years of marriage to what my son-in-law shared one day, years ago. He called on my daughter's birthday to thank me for raising his wife the way I did. He was grateful that she was completely capable of running the house, cooking, caring for him, plus keeping their budget in check by being frugal. I was humbled because I knew I couldn't take all the credit. She hadn't learned all this from me, but out of the experience of sharing the workload as she grew up in our home. And I got the benefit of being well rested for my next baby!

Overall, our responsibility is simply to be more aware of our body's needs as we age. I'll always remember something my Granny said on her deathbed, "I don't feel 83; I still feel 17 in my mind." That is so true! I see myself in the mirror and really can't believe I'm as old as I am. I mentally feel like I did when I was in my 30s and in my prime. We can easily forget our body has new needs, so it's so important to care for it.

5. How do I deal with extended family members, friends, and even the medical community who disapprove of our continuing to want more babies as we get older?

Most often I simply ignore the negative comments or just smile at them. Why? Because they are ignorant. And I don't say that rudely, just as a statement of fact. The definition of ignorant is: lacking knowledge, information, or awareness about something in particular. Those who disapprove usually have only a knowledge of current trends and limited experience. They honestly have not seen women having babies in their later years or having numerous babies in their lifetime. Our own mothers most probably had the "large" family of four children, if that many. Many didn't breastfeed, and they often left home to work while their children attended public school. They don't know any differently. When I told my mother-in-law we were expecting again, she would always say, "That's a lot of work!" She had two children, five years apart. That's all she knew. We had to prove it worked by example, through our pilgrimage into large family life, and home schooling. We simply had to trust. But we did prove it. Now they see the difference. Now they know.

211

Because it isn't taught as the norm in medical schools, the medical community doesn't relate well to women bearing children into their 40s. They view pregnancy and birth similar to a state of illness, as something to correct. Some doctors don't have the opportunity to observe a normal birth, one that allows the body to progress through labor and birth naturally. This affects how they view the mother's ability to birth, especially an older mother, which then affects how they treat her as a patient.

I've dealt with the medical community for over 32 years, coaching unwed mothers, working with my own doctors/midwives as I strove to have natural births, assisting midwives, and dealing with doctors and nurses during hospital transports. Numerous times I've seen health practitioners' attitudes and treatment completely change as they observe the confidence of a birthing mom as she trusts her body to do what God intended. If a woman understands the medical community's view of normal birth, she can learn to communicate with practitioners more easily, with the hope that she can have a better birth experience.

6. Will I have the energy I need to continue to raise children into my 50s if I have some in my 40s? Is it fair to the child to have older parents?

Well, I guess this is my question! I am 52, have six grandchildren, and six children still in the home. Albeit, two who are at home are young adults, but they still have needs for conversation and advice. The age range in our home at present is 11 to 23. We continue to be a busy family but nothing like when we had babies and toddlers in the home. We have weeks when our grandchildren are visiting, and yes, I do get tired. Tired of the noise, or the bustle, or the distractions, and it makes me wonder how I did it all those years! As much as I miss those hugs and "pick me up, mommy's" and pitter-patter of little feet, I can't imagine having to be on-call all the time. My energy level is definitely lower, but I have quite enough for those currently in my home. I am seeing God provide just what I need. He gives young moms with more physical energy the job of caring for and nurturing little children, and He gives older moms the job of caring for their older children along with the occasional care of grandchildren. His timing is absolutely perfect.

I know one advantage of being an older mom: I can offer wise counsel based on experience. While my older children had a mom with more energy and confidence, they also had to deal with my zealous nature that often acted out of lack of experience and the pride of youth. My younger children have a mom with a more mellow nature, but with that, I have less energy and excitement to try new things. They also have a mom with a deeper faith, based on decades of lessons and growth. Again, God knows just how to bless the life and responsibilities in a family.

As I enter into my older years, I'm finding the need to be a prayer warrior. I balance the differing needs of my multi-aged children by spending lots of time on my knees. Life slows down in the physical sense, but speeds up in the emotional sense. The varying stages of life are now much broader with adult children: courtships, careers being forged, and launching out to live on their own. We need to be there for support, encouragement, and advice! It can be tiring. So don't think for a minute that when the babies stop coming you'll have much time to sit and relax; not if you're a mom of many, at least. But your prayer life will increase dramatically.

I highly recommend reviewing your family's goals with your husband often, especially during the changing seasons of life. There are new interruptions, like technology, along with new expectations, like dealing with in-laws and a young adult's freedom. And none of them are without challenges, so put on your seatbelt (or your knee pads!) and get ready for the ride! It's not just about you and your immediate family any more – there are new families to adapt to and new needs to meet. It's easy to get sidetracked helping the older ones launch while letting the younger ones fend for themselves. Review your goals often to be sure you're on the right track. Remember that letting go is often painful and confusing as to where your role begins and ends, so go into it with prayer and open eyes. Ask God to give you joy, as it's easy to let this out-of-control feeling get you down. Trust me, it gets better! Actually, just trust God.

> *"Therefore, my beloved, as you have always obeyed, so now, not only as in my presence but much more in my absence, work out your own salvation with fear and trembling, for it is God who works in you, both to will and to work for his good pleasure.*
> (Philippians 2:12-13)

Is it fair to be an older mom for my younger children? I am quite sure that they would rather have life with an older, wiser, more tired momma than to never have been born! My younger ones love our life. They love their momma. They get my best years when it comes to wisdom and patience and time. Oh, I have no doubt that it's quite fair. Yes, my son will have very old parents (God willing) as he enters into his parenting years; yet, he has many older siblings, some 22 years older, who are and will be like second parents. They love their little brother and will be there for him through thick and thin. They will not hesitate to offer counsel and support as he ages when we can't or are gone. We would rather have that option than to have never loved and lived with our younger ones. Oh my, no!

7. How do you explain miscarriage to older children, especially if you have repeated losses?

My children have always understood and been a part of our pregnancies, births, and losses. They have also watched kittens, goats, and chicks be born, so it is not a mystery to them. As we share in the beauty and wonder of creation at all levels, it is not a shock when death occurs. It is the cycle of life.

Miscarriage helped everyone to learn to deal with disappointment and death. Our children learn best from true-life experience, not from living in the box of ease and sterility.

8. How does having babies in your 40s affect your relationship with your husband? Don't I owe him some of my best years?

We have certainly struggled in our relationship over the years, but the majority of those struggles came from misunderstanding the roles God gave to men and woman. We both loved it when I was having babies; we loved caring for and nurturing our little people. I think that because having babies was all we had known for 30 years, it wasn't a hindrance to us. We believe the only true pathway to a loving relationship is constant and completely open communication between husband and wife.

As I look back on my 40s, I was pretty hard to live with, come to think of it! Having to be competent in handling all the children and the running of our home for twenty years made me too strong. Now that we are past those stressful years of constant motion in our home, I can see how hard it was on our relationship. We were pushed apart by constant busyness. And I compensated for our marriage deficits through my relationships with my children. This pushed my husband and I further apart. But that's a risk in any marriage, not just in our 40s. We, as women, need to realize that our children will leave. It's hard to picture that when the house is full, but it's true. And we are left face to face our husbands when our children leave. We must ask ourselves the question, what will be left in our relationship with our man? That can be a fearful thing if we haven't kept our marriage healthy. Take time now to stay close to your husband.

I am a very different woman now that I'm past my childbearing years. The transition hasn't been easy. We have both had to adjust to my change of roles. It was a sort of retirement for me. A change of perspective. Now I have more time to give my husband, but we both wouldn't trade those years of having 10 children in our home for anything! I have wisdom to offer him. I have been tamed by my Father. I am not so in control. I listen better. I am more patient. It's a good time in our life!

9. Do you have any practical tips for high mileage mamas dealing with fatigue, pelvic separation, joint pain, varicose veins, etc.? In other words, what kinds of pregnancy issues did you have to deal with, and how did you deal with them?

I am very blessed to have had few problems in pregnancy. I always had Braxton Hicks contractions beginning at two months and continuing throughout pregnancy. I dealt with fatigue and nausea for the first three months. That was never fun, and I did feel guilty having my children cover for me during those times. I had pubic bone weakness and had to limit my activities, but I viewed that as part of life. I think my children learned to love and appreciate me more in those years. One great tip for pubic symphysis dysfunction (severe pain that interrupts normal activity) is to walk backwards. It sounds silly, but it works. It keeps the joint from separating.

I took prenatal vitamins and tried to eat healthy but never took it to extremes. With the discovery of home birth, I learned about herbs and began drinking red raspberry tea through my pregnancies and beyond. It's been used throughout history and is said to be good for balancing hormones. My main source of exercise was found in caring for my growing number of little ones and taking lots of walks. We've always been a walking family. It's what we did most days—walk up and down our street, or around our property. Anything to get out as a family, talking and spending time together.

The basic recommendations I'd offer to busy moms: rest, drink lots of fluid, take vitamin supplements, exercise as able. Care for your body—it's doing a lot of work making babies! Give yourself a break and don't think you'll earn a merit badge for being super-mom. You'll wear out. You want to be available for your family in your latter years.

> *"You shall teach them diligently to your children, and shall talk of them when you sit in your house, and when you walk by the way, and when you lie down, and when you rise."* (Deuteronomy 6:7)

10. Are there real statistics (not skewed to the cultural norm) available regarding having babies in one's 40s? How many mothers do you know who have had babies in their 40s? Share your thoughts regarding statistics and odds.

I actually know many moms who've had babies in their 40s. For the most part, the moms I knew or assisted in their deliveries were healthy, normal and happy, and had great births! I don't think any of them would have changed a thing after living with and loving their children.

I do know of two families who had Down syndrome babies in their 40s, but I also know of two who had them in their 20s. We are at higher risk for birth defects as we age, but we each have to determine our level of faith in that area. One mom shared with me about her sense of guilt when her baby was born with Down syndrome. She felt as if she shouldn't have wanted another baby so much. She has worked through those feelings and loves her child completely. It is by prayerful consideration and trust in God's sovereignty that a husband and wife make decisions about what risks they are comfortable with. Motives of the heart are more important to God than outward actions.

I the Lord search the heart and test the mind, to give every man according to his ways, according to the fruit of his deeds. (Jeremiah 17:10)

11. Hind sight is 20/20. Do you have any regrets? Looking back, is there anything you would have done differently?

I have absolutely no regrets! I'm guessing many people wouldn't believe that we aren't a have-as-many-babies-as-God-allows family when they find out we have 10 arrows! And I'm sure many people are surprised to find out we spaced our children. But it worked for us. I think God knew what we needed in our two-year space between babies. I was raised in a short-tempered family and was quite spoiled going into my parenting years. Looking back, I honestly believe that I would have not been a good mom if the pressures were greater than they were. God gives us just what we can handle. And because God uses all things for our good, I see that He grew me right where I was, in His timing, using my personality. He certainly knows just what we each need to serve Him and give Him glory.

I wish I had trusted God more, but He uses our life as a classroom in which to learn that trust. As I completely trust God, then there is nothing I would change, because He uses it all for His glory anyway. If He had desired any difference in our family size or lifestyle, He would have changed our minds back then or let me get pregnant even when I didn't choose it! I find this absolutely amazing! He gave us the perfect family size complete with all the beautiful family relationships and wonderful memories along the way! Yes, I can truly trust. As I write this, I am cuddling my five month old grandson while I watch my 11 and 15 year old sons play Nerf wars with their toddler nephew. Would I change a thing? Not a chance!

But Jesus looked at them and said, "With man this is impossible, but with God all things are possible." (Matthew 19:26)

And he made from one man every nation of mankind to live on all the face of the earth, having determined allotted periods and the boundaries of their dwelling place. (Acts 17:26)

Clap your hands, all peoples! Shout to God with loud songs of joy! For the Lord, the Most High, is to be feared, a great king over all the earth. He subdued peoples under us, and nations under our feet. He chose our heritage for us, the pride of Jacob whom he loves. (Psalm 47:1-4)

Terry Covey *is 52 years old, Bruce's wife for 33 years, mom to ten (ages 32 to 11), "Grand-momma" to six, and home educator for 22 years. Her website, A Mom's Many Lessons, was designed to mentor and encourage women to fulfill their calling as wives and mothers. She apprenticed with home-birth midwives and now assists her daughter, a licensed midwife. She and her husband support Family Life's ministry and encourage couples to fight for their marriage.*

God's Faithfulness in Life and Death

By Heather Olsson

Although I had a desire to be married, I can't say that I was altogether prepared to be a wife and mother. I had an idealistic view of what it takes to manage a household. During my teen years I had quite the babysitting business, and I felt prepared for the challenge. However, there is a significant difference between a four-hour job and the day-in-and-day-out challenges of serving as a wife, parenting, washing dishes, running laundry, sweeping, and other household tasks.

I was 19 when I met Eric. He came into the bookstore where I was working, wearing his Navy uniform, and swept me off my feet. A little over a year later we eloped, exchanging vows in a small cinder block building nestled right next to the towering Circus Circus Casino in downtown Reno. Cupid's Chapel of Love offered everything, including witnesses, for a small fee. The polyester-suited, gold-toothed "minister" was an added bonus.

221

Ten months later as we were preparing for a six-month deployment, I found I was pregnant. Morning sickness struck me like a load of bricks. This was unlike any kind of stomach virus I had encountered before. I was miserable physically and emotionally. Eric headed out to sea when I was two months along. The next time I would see him would be when I was full with child and almost ready to deliver.

My eating habits were poor, and my sleeping habits were worse. I'm not sure that I took any kind of prenatal supplements, and if I even had a hint of a headache I would run to the medicine cabinet for my handy-dandy Tylenol. My introduction to natural remedies and healthy eating habits came years later.

Two days before the due date I lost my mucous plug. Of course, this didn't mean I was in labor, but for some reason I felt I was going to have a baby that day. It was a 40-minute drive to the military hospital, so we headed down there just in case. Of course, they were obliging and examined me, but I was barely at 2 cm, so they sent me out to walk. We walked to a local mall, and I could tell something was happening, but the pain felt like menstrual cramps. We decided to head home. It wasn't more than a half hour after entering our door that I realized that I was in full labor. We headed back down to the hospital and ended up stuck in traffic due to a car accident just ahead of us. We made it to the hospital in time, but laboring in the car was not ideal.

I will never forget the night our beautiful daughter Rebecca was born. I was ill prepared for the pain I encountered. During a few difficult contractions I realized Lamaze wasn't working for me. Rather than focus on something external, I began to focus on what my body was doing. That was hard to do while hooked up to monitors and lying in a bed. My gut said I needed to be up and walking, but the hospital regulations wouldn't allow for such out-of-the-box thinking. Rebecca was born at a military hospital where the mother had little voice on how she wanted to birth her baby.

The whole experience was sterile and methodical. This was before labor, delivery, and recovery rooms, so I was whisked away to the operating room where everyone wore masks and gowns, and I just obeyed. I was mentally unaware of what was going on because of the Stadol dripping into my system through an IV. Eric told me that our baby girl was a healthy 7 pounds 12 ounces, and I'm sure I got a glimpse of her before she was carried away to the nursery. I do not fondly recall this delivery, and the hours after the delivery were no better.

Since Becca was born around midnight, I went without food until the first morning shift. I was in awe at what I had just experienced but also incredibly lonely since hospital rules wouldn't allow Eric to stay through the night. I shed tears in those dark, early morning hours as I experienced the first of many overwhelming moments. Becca had her first diaper explosion around 2 a.m., and I remember thinking, "What am I doing here? I'm hungry and I have no idea how to take care of this little creature." The nurses were kind and lent helping hands, but even they could not help me with the overpowering emotions.

Life as a new mommy was not easy. My idealistic daydreams came crashing down as I tried to figure out what to do with my crying little one. We soon realized Becca was not gaining weight. After a month of weekly visits to the clinic, the doctor told me it was time to switch to formula. His conclusion was that my poor diet was the culprit for a lack of healthy breast milk. In my naivety, I believed the doctor was always right, so I started the endless cycle of doctor visits for everything from vaccinations to multiple ear infections to eventually putting in ear tubes.

Twenty months later we said hello to our sweet son Nathan. Eric was no longer in the military fulltime, and my homemaking skills improved after Becca's arrival, so I was eating healthy and taking better care of myself than I did throughout my first pregnancy.

With this pregnancy I had very little morning sickness. I only felt awful when I went too long without eating, so I always carried around a bag of crackers to fill the emptiness before the nausea. I had a nasty bout of stomach flu when I was seven months along. With the outside temperature reaching above 105 degrees and no air conditioning in our tiny farmhouse, misery was my companion as I dealt with the heat, vomit, and a big belly.

As for my friends, most were using a midwife. This was a new term to me, but I liked the idea of having a female assist in the delivery. My midwife was a new breed in the doctoring arts. She could not deliver at home according to California state law, and to have hospital privileges, she had to work under the umbrella of a doctor. My midwife, Barbara, was a part of a very small practice and was well loved and respected by the nurses of the hospital where I would deliver. On my first visit with Barbara, I was shocked by her warm care and attention toward my growing belly and me. It became clear, while in the hospital laboring, that if I wanted something to eat, I could because Barbara said so. If I wanted to walk around, rock in a rocking chair, or take a shower, I was able to do so because Barbara had garnered the respect of the nurses.

One morning I woke up leaking quite a bit of blood. It was a week before my due date, but even so, the blood scared me. My nervousness was enough for my midwife to send me to the hospital. She later explained to me that sometimes the pressure of the baby sitting on the cervix can burst a blood vessel. Nathan, a healthy 9 pounds 1 ounce, was delivered four hours later in a new labor and delivery wing of our local hospital, built to be quiet and beautiful. They made the rooms look like home, and this time I was able to labor, deliver, and recover all in the same room. The luxury of warm blankets piled on top of me while nursing my sweet boy was an amazing improvement over my first experience. I even had a hot meal delivered to my room right after the birth.

Although I enjoyed being a mom, I was not as content with our marriage. I began to work out at a local gym and enjoyed sweating off all that baby weight. However, the atmosphere of the gym and the friendships I began to develop did little to encourage me to be a homemaker. Many of my friends were having affairs. By the grace of God I never walked that road, but I became rather discontent with my situation. My friends thought my husband was overbearing and controlling, which gave me ammunition to complain about my situation. When my complaining didn't change things, I became bitter.

At one point I was so upset about our lack of communication that I took the kids and went to my parents' home. This shocked Eric, but it didn't bring about the change I thought it would. I stayed one night, and my parents insisted I go home after hearing wise counsel from an elder in their church. Back home, Eric, with his ring off, told me I could leave, but he had made a vow and would not walk out the door. I stayed. We ended up in counseling at the church, and we changed areas of our lives that were inhibiting our marriage. Not only was I no longer going to the gym five days a week, but I also attended a small women's group and began to be mentored by older, godly women.

These women encouraged me to see what the Word of God said about my role as a wife. They were instrumental in helping me see the importance of submitting to and respecting my husband. Through this teaching the Lord started reforming my heart. As I was changing, so was my marriage to Eric. The Lord graciously began to build a solid marriage, growing our love deeper; yet we had much to learn when it came to fully understanding the sovereignty of God in the role of conception. Eric wanted one more child, but I wasn't keen on having an odd number of children, and the thought of having four didn't work with my idea of family.

Eventually I gave in to Eric's wishes to add one more child to our family. I had been on the pill for about two years and had been told it might take a while to get pregnant, but within a month I was expecting baby number three. This pregnancy was uneventful. Thankfully, midwife Barbara was not as anxious as I was to hold little Mallory. Our darling daughter waited two long weeks after her due date to make her entrance. After witnessing my delivery of Nathan, Barbara asked if I would try to have this child without medication. She convinced me that I was missing out on wonderful physical and emotional feelings by dulling my senses with medication. With her confidence supporting me, I decided to take her advice, and my third born became the first birthing experience with no intervention.

I enjoyed every moment of my hospital stay, but a few weeks after arriving home my joyful disposition took a turn. I cried at the drop of a hat, and the littlest things annoyed me. I couldn't shake the cloud hanging over me, and I started to feel like I was losing my mind amidst the crazy emotions. My home life seemed to be better than ever, but little did I understand the power of hormones. I was experiencing postpartum depression. If it weren't for news reports of a famous actress abandoning her family due to PPD, I would never have known what I was dealing with. I began to pray that the Lord would relieve me of this powerful blanket of despair. He did, but not in the way that I would have chosen.

At five months, Mallory began to cry and want to nurse constantly. I realized my milk was drying up no matter how much I nursed. When talking to a friend about this, she suggested that I might be pregnant. Pregnant? My mind just could not fathom having another child while dealing with emotional upheavals and the many to-do items on my daily list. How was I going to break the news to my parents? We didn't live the life of luxury but instead lived on a tight budget. I was sure that there would be some concern from friends and family. All our friends had one or two children, three at the most. I was hesitant to even visit my primary doctor because I worried how he would react. He chuckled and asked me if I knew how these things happen.

The year I was pregnant with baby four was a banner year of busyness. Becca was now in kindergarten at the local public school. I not only worked in her class but babysat for another family one day a week so the mother could work in the class as well. I began singing in our church, leading a mom's Bible study, and teaching piano lessons. I also helped take care of my niece most days as my sister-in-law, who was a single mom, tried to make ends meet. Postpartum depression was slowly drifting away with the surge of pregnancy hormones, but now I was being swallowed up by the details of daily life. There were many days I wanted to walk away from my home, yet I had just started learning about how to be a supportive wife. The pressure was sometimes overwhelming, but my life was about to get crazier.

Although it was a rocky start to my fourth pregnancy, all did go well. I would sometimes hold Mallory and cry because I thought this pregnancy was taking my time away from her. I had no idea how I was going to manage taking care of two little ones so close together. Eric and I still did not have an adequate understanding of Who presides over the womb and that He is able to strengthen us for the challenges set before us. We needed a change in our understanding. Sadly, the needed change only came after we'd followed in the footsteps of those friends who were making sure they didn't have any "accidents."

Something had to give in my hectic life. I was a bit nervous that the cloud of despair would hover over me yet again after I gave birth to number four. I started cutting back on my commitments and started looking forward to the time when I would have two children attending school in the fall.

Our fourth bundle of joy was due on May 4. That day passed, along with many more, before I held our baby in my arms. Paige was born May 24 and became my 28th birthday present. By May

23 I had it in my mind that she was going to be born on my birthday; so I employed a pregnant mother's best friend, gravity, to help bring her into the world by walking. I walked almost ten miles that day. A dear friend brought over ice cream to celebrate my birthday and then walked with me some more. I had some contractions during the day but nothing substantial or bothersome. By 6 p.m. I asked Eric to take me to the hospital to get checked. I informed the gal checking us in that I honestly thought they would be sending me home, but I wanted to know if I had made any progress.

Everyone was in a buzz after I was checked. I thought I was at 1 or 2 cm but I was at 6 cm. Eric told the nurses that my last three deliveries went quite fast when I reached 5 cm. It had been my modus operandi to take awhile getting to 5 cm, but once I was there I held my baby within an hour. The nurses were unimpressed with Eric's opinion but called Barbara to the hospital anyway. This time I took a shower and walked around a bit but still didn't feel like I was very far along. During this time, Eric ran home to get the video camera. It took him all of 10 minutes to run home and get back. If it had taken any longer he would have missed the baby. As soon as he walked in the door I asked if I could lie down. As they helped me up on the bed, my midwife quickly began breaking down the bed and asked for help in getting everything ready. Paige's head was right there, and out she slid. I don't even remember pushing. It still amazes me how short that labor and delivery was. I was elated. Eric cried tears of joy as he did at the birth of each of our children. It was the only time I ever saw him cry. The video camera never even caught a moment of this crazy (or quick) birth.

I had been so worried about how I could manage four children with two only 14 months apart, and yet it wasn't long after bringing Paige home that I realized it wasn't hard—as long as I was willing to die to my own desires. My day went smoothly if I didn't have grand plans outside of taking care of our home. In all my worrying I had forgotten that I had a 5 and a 6-year-old who were incredibly helpful and cheap entertainment for the younger two.

We decided that Paige would be our last child. I drove Eric down to the local urologist for a vasectomy. This doctor was well known for his ability to make sure that you didn't have any "accidents." I cried most of that day. At the age of 28 I left my childbearing years behind. We were looking for the perfect family situation. I wanted to be that mom who had a clean house and cookies baking in the oven when her children came home from school. But worst of all we caved to peer pressure from our Christian friends who said you should only have as many children as you can afford. We never asked whose standard we were following.

Life never slowed down for us. We bought our first home, and Eric's dad was diagnosed with Lou Gehrig's disease. Eric and I were still holding strong even through all of these challenges. The greatest challenge of all was to shortly rear its ugly head. A few weeks after Eric had his vasectomy his breathing became labored. I remember sitting in a very crowded ER waiting room for hours only to be given the simple answer— an asthma attack. Eric was sent home with some prescriptions and advice on how to live as if breathing through a straw.

Researching the correlation between asthma and a vasectomy yielded information I wasn't necessarily looking for. There were multiple sites on the Internet talking about the morality of cutting off the ability to bear children. I began to read articles discussing the Biblical mandate to be fruitful and multiply. I had my suspicions and questioned our decision before Eric went in for the surgery but did not follow through with the research. This quest for answers was only the beginning of yet another reformation within our family.

Six years passed between the first surgery and the reversal. Six long years of grieving as I was reminded monthly of our inability to bear children. I would beg Eric to please go for the reversal surgery. My constant nagging did nothing but prove that King Solomon was right when he wrote *"It is better to live in a corner of the housetop than in a house shared with a quarrelsome wife."* (Proverbs 21:9). One of the hardest lessons I have ever learned was learned during this time: say what you need to say once; then keep your mouth shut and pray.

Eric surprised me during a Valentine's dinner by telling me he had already made arrangements to fly out to Texas for the reversal. I believe I was more excited about answered prayer than I was about the surgery. The statistics showed the rate of success diminished every year between the two surgeries. I knew that the chances were very low, but every month, like clockwork, I wondered if this could be the moment I had been hoping for. I even dreamed of how I would break the news to my husband and how we would tell the kids. Each month I would become a crying mess as I asked God, "If children are such a blessing, then why aren't you blessing us with more?" I was so fragile that I choked back tears when someone told me they were pregnant.

Eric and I did not feel as if our family was complete. Since God was not giving us any more children through biological means, then maybe we were supposed to consider other avenues. Eric was convinced that we should adopt. It was quite costly to adopt, so I wasn't holding out hope that would be feasible for us. I had many friends who had adopted through the state system, and their stories scared me away from California's foster/adopt program. It was during dinner with our pastor and his wife when we found out about Acres of Hope in Liberia, West Africa. That night I came home from dinner and promptly looked up the orphanage online. I fell in love with the pictures of sweet children with bright, big smiles. I wasn't sure how we would be able to afford adopting, but looking at the adoption process of Liberia gave us hope because the fees were much lower than other countries.

It took almost a year from beginning the adoption process to bringing our children home. My pregnancies had been complication free, but the adoptions were filled with multiple complications. From adoptions being completely stopped due to accusations of child trafficking, to our 6-month-old contracting Malaria and needing to be put in foster care, we were on the longest emotional rollercoaster we had ever encountered. After much protesting, the government reopened adoptions, and we were back on track. We thought the drama was over, but it was quite the challenge to adopt our 4-year-old boy and 7-month-old daughter.

When Eric arrived in Liberia, he was given full custody of our children. He had to quickly adapt to our new son's English dialect and deal with the symptoms of malaria that both children were struggling with. He was only expected to be gone for one week but ended up in Liberia for three weeks as he patiently waited for our daughter's passport to be signed. We had many advocates trying to help get the needed papers so they could leave the country, but day after day they seemed to be only getting doors slammed in their faces. At one point, Eric called to prepare me for the possibility that our baby girl might not be able to come home with him. She might have to be escorted home a few months later. I began to sob, and I remember thinking this was harder than any of my four birthing experiences.

Week three was upon us, and Eric had to come home with or without our little baby because of a commitment coming up with the military. It was on the last day he could manage to stay in country that one of the Acres of Hope staff was able to convince the government official to sign that passport. Eric drove as fast as he could to the airstrip with luggage, children, and newly signed passport in hand.

Because of the gracious gift of friends, I was able to meet Eric and the kids in New York and fly back to San Francisco with them. What a sight. That day I knew utter joy and relief as I held my 12 pound bundle of brownness and hugged my precocious, smiley little son. That was the longest and hardest "pregnancy." We had decided months before to rename our African children. As had been our tradition, we gave our new son a Biblical name. Foley became Joseph. It is my daily prayer that our Joseph will be a strong man who may bless his people in Liberia with the Bread of Life just as Joseph, son of Jacob, gave his people bread during a famine. Priscilla became Gabrielle, which means strength of God.

Adoption is not for the faint of heart. That first night together as a family was as crazy as my first night as a new mom. I couldn't help but chuckle at the thought that my first night with Becca was forever remembered because of a poopy diaper just as my first night with Gabbie would be. Gabrielle's first bowel movement in America put diaper changing into the category of an extreme sport.

We spent two days together before sending Eric off to Hawaii for his two-week Naval drill. Four days later I headed to the airport with our six kiddos to board the next flight to the Islands. With the stomach flu and hives floating around the family, we tried to enjoy the seven days in paradise.

After coming home from Hawaii, Eric found the route for his job was being cut drastically. He took advantage of this announcement and started developing his pool business. He had always wanted to own a business where he could be outside with the children. Each day he would take a different child with him to help him scrub pools. I was one content momma. For the first time in eight years I had a baby in my arms. Actually, Gabrielle went from babyhood to chubby toddler in a matter of months. She went from having only four teeth to 15 teeth in one month's time! Joe and Gabbie kept me busy.

We enjoyed every new little detail of life that Joe and Gabbie discovered. I remember when Joe saw ice for the first time. He was giggling and entranced by the frozen water in front of him. He would give the biggest, most charming smile when he held a straw for the first time and a grimace when he bit into his first Oreo. Seeing the world through this rambunctious kid was enlightening.

While one part of our life was filled with wonder and excitement, another part was filled with worry. Eric's breathing was becoming more difficult. His inhalers and medications were not keeping his airway open. Nights were filled with the terror of waking up to heavy gasping of air. Pounding him on the back gave some relief.

Right after Thanksgiving Eric had a severe attack. He had already been to the ER multiple times, so I assumed that this visit was just like the others, to give him help by administering oxygen and more powerful drugs. Becca, our oldest, heroically drove her dad to the hospital and called 911 to make sure they were ready. I stayed behind to make sure the kids were settled for the night before having Nate, our son, drive me to the hospital, completely unaware of what Becca was going through. When I arrived, I was pulled aside and asked all kinds of questions. They were very concerned, yet when I went back to see him he was sitting there smiling at me. One concerned nurse decided she had seen him too often and wanted to do more tests, so she ordered him a room. It was not easy to sleep knowing there was something terribly wrong with my husband.

The next day, while doing a CT scan, Eric went into an attack, sending the nurses scrambling. They were not prepared for this, and neither was I. As they raced around to perform intubation (a breathing tube down the throat), the doctor told me that he believed Eric's body was in a fight or flight mode. Maybe after years of dealing with asthma his body no longer wanted to fight but just wanted to flee. This sure didn't sound like the man I had married. I needed answers to why this was happening.

Eric was in the hospital six days in a sedated state to give his body time to heal. I was able to ask questions of many different doctors but couldn't get good answers. I was blessed to have a church community that surrounded me with kindness and hospitality by bringing us meals and sitting with Eric so I could go home to shower and nap. He was released from the hospital in a very weakened state, but we were thankful to have him home. We still didn't understand how severe this physical ailment was. I remember thinking he would more than likely get his strength back but knew we would always have to deal with this ailment called asthma.

He needed weeks of rest, but we were self-employed, and he kept pushing himself. Even so, he seemed different. He didn't have the get-up-and-go that he was famous for. Of course, some of that is to be expected after such an ordeal, but there was something that had changed. Eric was known for not forgetting, yet he was regularly forgetting small details.

We enjoyed the Christmas holiday and celebrated Eric's 41st birthday, but soon his health began to deteriorate again. It seemed that every time he finished up a round of antibiotics, his symptoms would come back with a vengeance. Waking several times during the night to the sound of him struggling for breath was now part of our daily routine.

The day I hoped and prayed would never come happened January 25, 2008. After Eric kissed me good-bye, he said, "I love you" and drove off with Paige by his side. A few hours later I received a phone call from a woman who said she was with Paige, and Eric had collapsed. This woman had seen Eric struggle and called 911 for Paige who couldn't get through to the dispatcher on Eric's cell phone. The next hour was such a blur of calls ranging from the fire chief to the detective who had taken Paige to the hospital. Eric was in a town about a half hour south of us, so I had no idea where the hospital was, but Nate just started driving anyway. Running into the ER, I saw Paige and the detective. I still thought that I would go back and see Eric sitting up with a breathing mask on, but instead the detective introduced me to the chaplain. This confused me, but I thought maybe it was protocol for this particular ER.

The chaplain was new and didn't realize that taking a wife back to see her husband in an emergency situation was against the rules. I walked into that room utterly shocked to see a man sitting on top of my husband compressing his chest. I ran over to kiss the hand of my husband's lifeless arm dangling off the bed. The doctor was obviously angry with the chaplain and asked her to please take me out of the room. Before she did though, the doctor pulled me aside and told me that I would have some hard decisions to make. I just looked at him in the most quizzical fashion. What did he mean? It all seemed surreal.

The chaplain ushered me out of the ER and told me to wait in an adjoining hallway. I have never felt so alone with so many people bustling about. I wanted to throw up or scream or crawl into a hole. Four days later I had the gargantuan task of declaring my husband legally dead. With my pastor/friend and dad by my side, we told the kids their dad was gone. He was now in the presence of his Creator.

I walked out of that hospital praying the Lord would use me and that I would walk this path of suffering with grace. My motto became "I don't understand, but I trust." Twenty years of growing together and loving is a pretty wonderful gift. An added bonus was six beautiful children. For the first time I was content with the family God had blessed me with. I am ashamed to say it took the loss of my best friend to shake me out of my state of discontent.

I had been given multiple reasons to trust God Almighty who promised to take care of my children and me. Looking back, I now realize how incredibly difficult that first year was. There is so much of that year that I can't remember. I do remember praying, hoping, and believing that God would have me marry again soon.

About nine months after Eric passed away, we were at our church's first family camp. A friend and I talked about the single men in our church community. None seemed to fit the bill, and even if one did, would he really want to take on a 40-something widowed mother of six? She asked if I had thought about Phil, a young single guy that had taken a liking to Joseph while at camp. I had noticed him but pushed any hopes of his interest in me out of my mind because I was almost seven years older than he was. Five months later Phil began joining my table every Sunday at our church's weekly luncheon. We started having long conversations and finding out we had a lot in common. Secretly, I was hoping that this funny, handsome guy would take notice of me. Our friendship grew into a courtship. After four months of courtship we set the date for our wedding.

Beautiful memories flood my mind as I think of our wedding day. Phil swept me away to Hawaii for our honeymoon, and then it was back to reality. We weren't starting from scratch but working with a full house! At some point I realized that the dream I had of having the perfect little family was based on a faulty perception of what a family should look like. I finally began to see that God is the one who forms a family in the fashion that He sees fit. I had taken pride in being married for so long and having a rather tidy family with Eric. God was (and still is) molding a new family that will hopefully bring honor and glory to His name. We have half-siblings, adopted siblings, and a step-dad. It is a beautiful mess that causes me to reflect on His goodness and faithfulness.

As soon as Phil asked me to marry him, I began to think about the possibility of having more children. I could feel those old anxious feelings begin to emerge as I wondered if I could even conceive. One of the hardest moments in our courtship was asking Phil if he was okay with the possibility of us not being able to have any more children. I was 42 when we were married, and it had been 16 years since my body had carried a child.

Month by month passed, and I started to feel that disappointment that was all too familiar. I cannot fully explain how excited I was when, six months after we were married, I found I was pregnant. I knew there was a big chance of miscarriage, but I had gotten pregnant. That meant it could actually happen.

I was quite sick, yet I was the happiest pregnant woman you've ever met. Although I was incredibly happy, I was also worried by all of the online information I was reading about women having babies in their 40s. I was definitely not going to go the traditional route of using an ob-gyn in a hospital, and the midwife working with an ob-gyn seemed to now be a glorified nurse. I surely didn't want to be questioned constantly about all the tests they give older women, so a home birth seemed to be the only option. Eric had never been keen on the idea of birthing one of our babies in our own home, but Phil was willing to let me if it was what I wanted.

My first phone call to a midwife ended up being two hours long. I didn't call any other midwife. Dawn was a kindred spirit. She was like a sister to me. With tears I write this because my dear, sweet friend, who helped deliver my last child, recently went to be with the Lord. There were many of "Dawn's babies" at her memorial.

My pregnancy was free of complications, but there was a big difference in my energy levels. My body tired quite easily, and I had a nice bout of indigestion that didn't seem to ease throughout my pregnancy. But the pain in my hip that continued to bug me prior to pregnancy was now gone thanks to an abundance of Relaxin, a hormone to help flexibility. I did experience the worst case of influenza I have ever encountered. For days I couldn't even make it to the bathroom without help. I decided not to take any over-the-counter drugs to protect our baby; however, concerned that the flu might turn into pneumonia, we were extra cautious.

One thing I was nervous about was my inability to understand and read my body. I didn't know with my other four if I was truly in labor. They were fast births, and I was worried that my midwife, who lived an hour away, wouldn't make it to the birth. Those last few weeks of pregnancy were filled with all kinds of anxiety. My son was getting married only 10 days after our baby's due date, and with my track record of late babies, I had to work through the emotions of maybe not being able to attend his wedding. My midwife also began to prepare me for the possibility of complications. We had our entire list of phone numbers set up for worst case scenarios: call the fire department if we needed oxygen; call the ambulance if there was umbilical cord prolapse; call the hospital to alert them of our arrival if we needed help. Everything was laid out and ready to go. Probably the most important thing we did was pray. We prayed that God would work out all the details.

Ten days before my due date, I cooked a few meals for friends, went to my chiropractic appointment, and then headed home. I thought I felt something going on, but it was rather early. I probably stood too long while I was cooking.

By the evening I realized I was having constant aching and cramping, so I called my midwife. She suggested that I rest in the tub with a glass of wine; I wasn't too concerned. In fact, I was happy my body was doing something. Around 10 p.m. I started to think I might have a baby in the next day or two, because the aching didn't go away. Dawn decided to come reassure me. When she arrived I was walking up and down our long hallway and stopping with every contraction to mentally work at relaxing my body. At midnight we all laid down to rest, but soon after, contractions started hurting and coming closer together. Phil ran tub water again, and as I relaxed in the warm water my labor slowed.

I asked Dawn to allow me to do as much of the birthing as I could on my own. I really wanted to feel the different steps of labor, yet I did not feel capable of birthing my baby on my own. Although Dawn and her assistant, Jacquie, had to remind me to breath deeply, I really took possession of this birthing experience. I felt the moment my body opened up, and I was able to push. I pushed a few times and felt the baby's head crown— that burning ring of fire. With control I slowly breathed while Dawn made sure I didn't tear, and our little baby slid out without any need of a push. We were all quite taken back by this quick entrance. Baby would have been placed up on my chest except that she was wrapped in her cord. It was around her neck and around both her arms. She was such a slippery little thing while Dawn was trying to unwrap what looked like a backpack. After she was unwound, I enjoyed her sweet body against my chest. Warm towels were continuously laid on us as we waited to cut the cord and deliver the placenta.

I informed Dawn that with my last birth, the midwife ended up extracting the placenta from the womb because it did not deliver itself. Before this birth, we discussed the length of time that the placenta can take to deliver. Of course, in the hospital, waiting 45 minutes to deliver a placenta is just too long. Time is money. However, at home we had time; so I nursed and rubbed my belly waiting for the placenta to finally emerge. After administering herbs under my tongue, delivery of the placenta happened. I was then helped into our warm comfortable bed where I gratefully held our baby in my arms. It was just past 2 a.m. when we ushered in Joe and Gabbie to meet their sibling. Mallory and Paige were able to witness the birth of their young sister.

Cora was a healthy 9 pounds 1 ounce. One of the funniest moments was when Dawn asked Phil to read the scale. Every woman in that room did not believe his answer. He must have read it wrong because she sure did not look like a 9-pound baby.

My recovery was much harder than when I was in my 20s. I remember just getting out of bed and getting on with life— not this time. I became dizzy regularly because my normally low blood pressure had climbed to 130 over 80. This came down over the span of two weeks, but at first it was quite alarming. Nursing wasn't hard, and in fact, I enjoyed it. For the first time I saw it as a privilege rather than a duty. I knew there was a possibility that

Cora would be my last so I wanted to enjoy every moment of her next to me. I also realized that time quickly marches on. My older children were a testimony to that!

There were some bumps in the infancy road; for instance, Cora had a pretty bad case of colic, and within a few days of her being born we had to help her have a bowel movement. Again, those bowel movements forever etch my first memories of parenthood. I felt like such a novice!

Six months after Cora was born, I began to sporadically have periods again. According to what I have read online, I more than likely was not ovulating. The month of Cora's first birthday I had my first 28-day cycle, and the next month I found I was pregnant again. This time I was healthier and eating a diet of organic foods, so I felt I could nurse and be pregnant at the same time. I didn't lose my milk, but I had a lot of people question my decision to continue nursing Cora. All the same, we were thrilled and thankful for God's gift of another child.

Again, I was a happy momma to be dealing with morning sickness. However, this time we had a month long excursion from California to Colorado and back during the first trimester of my pregnancy. Thousands of miles having to sit rather than lay in my comfortable bed didn't sound too appealing. The day arrived for us to hit the road, and I was feeling good. I was 10 weeks along and thought maybe the Lord had answered my prayers of relieving my weary stomach. A few weeks later I started to spot. I was 12 weeks along now, so off to bed I went in hopes of keeping this baby in the womb. When we arrived back home we made an appointment with a local ob-gyn. The ultrasound confirmed that our little baby had died around 10 weeks.

I felt every labor pain. I cried through every contraction. This was indeed the hardest delivery that I had ever worked through. After a few hours I delivered a beautiful, perfectly formed baby. We may never know why this little "gift" was ours for only three months, but we know the One who ordained our child's life, and we praise Him for such a blessing.

Through this loss I became fully aware of the silence in the church regarding miscarriage. We rejoice over the announcement of a pregnancy, we pray for those who are pregnant, and we rejoice over the birth of a newborn. We even mourn over the loss of a stillborn child birthed at full term. But what about the thousands of souls whose lives end earlier than full term? We need to remember those babies that God gives us for such a short amount of time. I am truly thankful for this experience and the wonderful lessons it has taught me.

It took me eight weeks to stop bleeding after the miscarriage. I finally decided I needed to find out why I was still bleeding when, quite by surprise, I passed another large mass. The bleeding stopped within a couple of days, and my hormones seemed to calm down.

Recently I had blood tests done which showed that my hormones are quite low due to adrenal fatigue. I am working closely with our doctor to recover my adrenals in hopes of regulating my hormones. According to medical textbooks, fertility dramatically drops at the age of 45. Even though I am 46 now, I prefer not to put my trust in science but rather in the God of creation. Mentally I am preparing myself for the next phase of life, yet still praying the Lord might bless us with another child.

Dr. Seuss once wrote, "Don't cry because it's over. Smile because it happened." There is a smile on my face as I realize how good God has been to me. An amazing story, a loving husband, eight children and two grandchildren, with hopes of many more to come. It all adds up to a blessed life.

Heather Answers the Survey Questions

1. How do you deal with the fear of increased miscarriage, infant loss, or birth defects? How can one handle that kind of pain, especially over and over again?

Whenever I am fearful or anxious, I recite and obey the words of Philippians 4:3-7. *"Rejoice in the Lord always; again I will say, rejoice. Let your reasonableness be known to everyone. The Lord is at hand; do not be anxious about anything, but in everything by prayer and supplication with thanksgiving let your requests be made known to God. And the peace of God, which surpasses all understanding, will guard your hearts and your minds in Christ Jesus."* I have known this peace when I submit to His will and His word. I also remind myself that Paul again admonishes us to take every thought captive to obey Christ (2 Corinthians 10:5). I have dealt with the fears of birth defects in particular because I sometimes worry about medical debt. These are the moments when I must remember God's promise to always take care of our needs. Jesus said to those following him, *"Look at the birds of the air: they neither sow nor reap nor gather into barns, and yet your heavenly Father feeds them. Are you not of more value than they? And which of you by being anxious can add a single hour to his span of life?"* (Matthew 6:26-27)

For a Christian, there is only one way to deal with the pain of loss: trust in God's perfect will. When we allow ourselves to be spun around and led about by worries and fears, we show a lack of trust in our heavenly Father, who instructs us to look to Him for our daily needs and says He will sanctify us through trials. Leaning on His Word is of utmost importance while trusting Him with fertility.

2. How do you balance life with older kids and babies? Do you feel this is unfair to the older children? How do they feel about having more brothers and sisters? Is it being greedy to want more babies at the risk of not being able to meet the needs of the rest of the family?

Balancing life between older kids and babies is just plain complicated. My two oldest children live thousands of miles away with their growing families, and I rely on technology to help me keep up with them. Sometimes this has meant being on the phone with one of them while nursing my little one.

One of the hardest issues I have had to deal with is not being readily available for my older children as they began having children of their own. We were able to visit with my son and daughter-in-law after their first child was born, but it was hectic, and I was hardly helpful as I was taking care of my own 1-year-old. But there were sweet moments on that trip such as when I was nursing Cora while sitting next to my daughter-in-law who was nursing my grandson.

Siblings are one of the means that God uses to sanctify our children. Older children learn to be self-governing, concerned for others, helpful, and patient when they have younger siblings. It might be good to remind our older children that they were placed within our home by the graciousness of God just as our younger children are.

In regard to our children's feelings about having more brothers and sisters, they have been excited every time we tell them that we are expecting. They have all been taught that children are a gift from God. Gifts are good!

If you feel it might be greedy to want more babies at the risk of not being able to meet your family's needs then maybe you need to re-evaluate your priorities. You might have scheduled too many activities for your children, leaving you to be a glorified taxicab driver with little time to connect. You might have high expectations of how your house should look. Maybe a lack of organization is keeping you from getting your daily tasks done. Whatever the issue, we all need to constantly reform our focus and remind ourselves what our goal is in raising a family. We should align ourselves with the answer to the first question in the Westminster catechism, which says, "Man's chief end is to glorify God and to enjoy Him forever." We cannot rightfully say we are glorifying God if we are perpetually at our wit's end.

Cutting back has been a long struggle for me. I love to organize events, and yet my children suffer if I stress out over these obligations. We are very careful to not overextend our lives with busyness. Our children might be involved in a tumbling class or a school co-op, but I make sure that none of these fill up our calendar. I try to condense my errands to a few days each week, which allows me to stay home the majority of the time.

An area that I need to constantly work on is my desire to have my home look like it was the stage for the latest Pottery Barn photo shoot. It is such a distraction from loving and connecting with my children because I get uptight when things are in disarray. The focus should not be on how beautiful I keep my house but on taking care of the family God has given me.

3. What about the ethical issues of repeated miscarriages? Shouldn't I avoid conception if I know that the chances of that child living are minimal? Am I enabling death when I should be promoting life?

Each child conceived is a living, eternal soul whose days were ordained by God. Whether your child lives for 60 days within the womb, lives for a few hours outside the womb, or is blessed with 100 years on this planet, his days were determined. Job 14:5 states, "*Since his days are determined, and the number of his months*

is with you, and you have appointed his limits that he cannot pass."
The Psalmist says, *"Your eyes saw my unformed substance; in your book were written, every one of them, the days that were formed for me, when as yet there was none of them."* (Psalm 139:16)

You will not have any more children than what the Lord has ordained. A friend once told me that your quiver is full with the last child you have. Right now our quiver is full, unless God gives us another baby. With each conception you are promoting life and learning to live by faith in the One True, Living God.

4. Do pregnancy, childbirth, and recovery get harder in your 40s? I already feel like I'm coming apart at the seams! How will I hold out until menopause if I keep having babies? Am I acting responsibly when it comes to taking care of my health?

In my circumstance, pregnancy was not harder than when I was in my 20s. I tired quickly, but I was older and wiser in my 40s; I would listen to my body and take a nap or go to bed early. Age did help me as I cared much more about nutrition and health than I did when I was younger. This benefited both my baby and myself.

There were mental hurdles that I had to overcome when it came to birthing Cora versus birthing my other four. When I was in my 20s, I just went for it and talked my way through the process. My mind seemed much more cluttered with doubts and questions when giving birth to Cora. Mentally I had to work hard at relaxing my muscles.

Recovery was probably the most difficult for me. My body was tired. It is tired! I just assumed that I would be able to push myself as I did when I was in my 20s, but it was a few months before my body began to feel back to normal. For the first time in my life my blood pressure was 130 over 80 and had worked its way up to 150 over 90 when I was given my RhoGAM shot. Looking up information on the Internet about high blood pressure after birth did nothing to calm my fears and lower it, but within a few weeks I was back to my normally low readings. My bleeding seemed to be normal as well, although my hormones took much longer to get back to normal. I didn't seem to deal with postpartum depression as I had with my other pregnancies, but I attribute that to healthier eating habits and nursing.

My midwife friend reminded me that God created our bodies to have babies until menopause. It does get harder to conceive during perimenopause years, which gives you the ability to rest between pregnancies. I encourage you to take care of your health by exercising and eating good, whole foods. Also make sure that you are resting regularly. Have a daily quiet time where everyone is reading or sleeping so that you can rejuvenate your body.

5. How do I deal with extended family members, friends, and even the medical community who disapprove of our continuing to want more babies as we get older?

I am so intimidated by the medical community! There, I said it. It has been an ongoing struggle to find doctors who would provide care that does not include pressure to immunize or take prescription drugs. I am not against mainstream medicine altogether but find it is mostly only helpful in medical emergencies. I have to face the fact that I am an anomaly according to the medical profession, and much of that community does not care for people interested in other means of healing. If I truly believe that God has called me to bear children until I am unable to do so, then I must trust Him and not allow others' thoughts to affect my disposition. I'm speaking to myself right now because what people think has been way too important to me over the years and has caused a lot of stress in my life. I am learning to let go.

6. Will I have the energy I need to continue to raise children into my 50s if I have some in my 40s? Is it fair to the child to have older parents?

Children are such wonderful gifts. I have found that raising kids has made me feel younger, and many people believe I am younger than my age. In fact, many people are astonished that I have children in their 20s and grandbabies as well. Over the past couple of years I have pushed myself into adrenal fatigue, and because I want to enjoy my children as they grow, I am determined to change my habits by slowing down, eating a whole foods type diet, staying away from foods that my body can not tolerate, and getting lots of rest. It is important that we help our energy levels by filling our "tank" with all things good.

I also have to know my limits. I can no longer carry my chunky little 2-year-old up the stairs when she is fully capable of climbing them herself. I am active in different ways with my little ones than I was with my older one. In some ways I think that my older children were the ones who missed out on a more relaxed mother. As I have aged I have mellowed and not worried about some of the little things that made me crazy when I was a young mother. Although my older children enjoyed camping with their mother when she was still able to sleep on the ground in a tent, my younger children will enjoy other adventures tailored to my energy levels.

7. How do you explain miscarriage to older children, especially if you have repeated losses?

We are very honest with our children. As much as I would like to keep my children from the pain of death, it is a part of our journey here on earth. God uses the loss of a loved one, even a baby that you have only begun to be excited about, as a way to sanctify us. We talk about God's sovereign plan for each of our lives and how we do not know the days God has ordained for us. We talk about how the days of the little one that we are laying in the ground were precious and how that child has forever changed our lives even though they are no longer with us.

I am very happy to introduce myself as a mother of eight even though one of my children is gone. I think this is important for the children as well. We do not sweep the miscarriage under the rug or tiptoe around the subject but address it head on.

8. How does having babies in your 40s affect your relationship with your husband? Don't I owe him some of my best years?

Having Cora has been a wonderful addition to our marriage. There were a few moments where I was wishing that Phil would sweep me off my feet and carry me to some exotic island, but they were few and far between. I especially felt this way when we took Cora with us on a weekend retreat a couple of times. Romance was not easy with a demanding infant around.

Since I am no longer nursing, we were able to get away for a couple of days and had such a wonderful time together. It was a great reminder that few are the days when our children are so dependent. We do acknowledge that refreshment is important for every couple, so Phil is very good about making sure that we go out on a regular basis, even if it means just grabbing a coffee or going grocery shopping together.

The question of owing some of my best years to my husband is hard for me to answer. My husband and I are partners. We work together in nurturing and growing our family. He is getting the best of me as we walk this path together.

9. Do you have any practical tips for "high mileage mamas" dealing with fatigue, pelvic separation, joint pain, varicose veins, etc.? In other words, what kinds of pregnancy issues did you have to deal with, and how did you deal with them?

I have had very little experience with pregnancy ailments. But I have been a friend to many women who have dealt with these issues. I think if I were to have problems, I would need to learn to ask others for help. Make sure you are in a good church community that can help assist you in your time of need, and then be available to do the same for other pregnant mothers. I also think praying through the physical pain is important. Pain can sometimes leave us short-tempered. Longsuffering, a fruit of the Spirit, is not learned through easy living but rather hard circumstances.

10. Are there real statistics (not skewed to the cultural norm) available regarding having babies in one's 40s? How many mothers do you know who have had babies in their 40s? Share your thoughts regarding statistics and odds.

I do not know of any hard statistics. In fact, when I was pregnant I worried myself needlessly by looking up information on having babies in my 40s. There are pages and pages on the Internet full of maybes and what-ifs. But really, should we be relying on statistics anyway? God has designed our bodies to carry babies until we step into the phase of menopause. Each child is precious in His sight.

When I announced I was pregnant, I had quite a few women in our church approach me with not only congratulations but also stories of their pregnancies in their 40s. All of these women were now in their 50s, with teenage children. What a blessing it was to hear their tales and be accepted into a very elite club!

Heather Olsson *is married to Dr. Phil Olsson and is the mother of eight children. At the age of 46 she enjoys cooking, teaching piano, knitting, schooling her children, reading good books, thinking deep thoughts, and playing Words with Friends with her husband. She and her family are members of Central Valley Presbyterian Church in Central California. They commute from Oakdale, the cowboy capital of the world.*

Embracing His Plan

By Sue Liesmaki

God is amazing. Twenty-five years ago, if the Lord had given me a glimpse of who I would be today, I would have laughed— long and loud. In so many ways I am a very different person today. What changed me? GOD.

He sought me and He bought me with His redeeming blood, as 2 Corinthians 5:17 says, *"Therefore, if anyone is in Christ, he is a new creation. The old has passed away; behold, the new has come."* Praise the Lord! I am a new creation in Christ, a new person!

Twenty-five years ago I was in college pursuing several degrees (not because I was so smart; I just kept changing what I wanted to study). I wanted to be some big important person living in a prominent city and making a lot of money, totally self-sufficient. I had big plans! (Do you smell a feminist here?) This is when I met my husband; what he saw in me I will never understand, but we became friends, started dating, and a year later we were married. Within the year we became pregnant and had our first daughter. What a joy! This pregnancy was fairly easy; I felt great and enjoyed being pregnant. I loved watching my belly grow and thinking about the little person within me. One thing I was not prepared for was gaining almost 60 pounds.

251

My due date came and went. Seven days after my due date, during the night, my water broke; I was excited and scared! My husband and I kept track of contractions, and in the morning we went to the doctor. After examining me, the doctor concluded that I was leaking amniotic fluid. After laboring for several hours, the doctor discovered that I must have had a twist in the amniotic sac (allowing the leak the night before), so she decided to break my water to get the labor progressing. I labored for 24 hours, actively pushing for the final three hours.

During labor I received an epidural, which scared me to death. I thought I might become paralyzed. My patient husband helped me through getting the epidural, and it did help me to progress, but it wore off before delivery! That was in the old days. I am so glad epidurals have come so far along. The Lord blessed us with our first little lady, Stephani. She was perfect. We were in awe at this little life placed in our hands, beginning our journey of parenthood.

After two days in the hospital, we took our precious bundle home. We had one night with her alone before my mom came to help. We were so nervous! I remember sitting in our little living room, looking at our sweet girl and thinking, "I don't even know how to lay her down so she doesn't die from SIDS!" Well, she survived that night and many more. The Lord has been so gracious to gently lead us. As I gazed at her, my heart melted. I could hardly believe I could love this person so much. I treasured this child and wanted to be the absolute best mom I could be to her. I still feel that way even now as Stephani is 24 years old.

Another precious little lady was born to us two-and-a-half years later. We conceived easily and had another wonderful pregnancy (something I certainly took for granted, and now I realize how arrogant we were—as if we would always be able to "decide" to have another baby). Again, our baby wanted to stay inside my cozy womb 16 days past her due date. I went to the doctor weekly for the last month, just hoping to be dilated at all, but I never was. I cried at the last visit when she once again told me to go home and wait. As it turned out, my doctor was going to be on vacation the following week and told me if I didn't have the baby by the time she got back, we would schedule an induction for the day she returned.

I tried everything anyone told me about how to jump start labor. Everything that is, except a cartwheel. I stopped there as I wasn't sure that was anatomically possible! Longing to meet our new baby, I went in for a scheduled induction. Little did I know that scheduled inductions would be my normal routine. My doctor scheduled me to come in the night before the induction to receive prostaglandin gel which was supposed to start the process, and the following morning I went in with my husband to be induced. I was not dilated enough to break my water, so she started me on Pitocin. After progressing a bit, my doctor broke the water and labor progressed. This time around, not a 24-hour labor, but six hours. Yippee! Our sweet little Abbie was born. She was so worth the wait. What a miracle to be able to look into the face of our little girl, this precious gift from God. She is now 22, the age I was when I delivered her.

Our next pregnancy was very much like the first two. We loved having children and thought we would like another baby. We tried, conceived, and had a wonderful pregnancy. This time around I had heartburn and was told it was due to the baby having a lot of hair. I wasn't so sure; nevertheless, this little darling was born with a full head of hair. To this day she has the thickest hair in the family. Oops, I just gave it away, our third baby was another girl! We didn't find out the sex of our first three children prior to delivery, so each was a surprise as they entered the world.

At our fourth baby's 20-week ultrasound, we were told there was a possible marker for Down syndrome. We had a level two ultrasound, and they said the baby was probably "normal," but they could not be 100 percent sure. We wanted to prepare our hearts if she was to be born with Down syndrome as it would be an adjustment. We were excited to welcome another little one into the world. Labor and delivery were almost identical to our second pregnancy. This time around I was over due by seven days, so I went in for prostaglandin the night before. The doctor started me on Pitocin and broke my water the next morning, and I went into labor. I was surprised because people told me that each labor would be shorter and shorter. After five hours of labor, I was discouraged that I didn't yet have a baby in my arms. A few hours later, she entered the world after 11 hours. The extra labor didn't matter once we held her in our arms. She is our precious Nicole (now 20 years old). Nicole does not have Down syndrome. It grieves and unnerves me to think of all of the precious babies—those with Down syndrome and those without —that are aborted for fear of a disability. Every baby is perfectly made by God. I know many children with Down syndrome whom I love and whose families know that they are "perfect." God doesn't make mistakes!

Wouldn't you think that after three wonderful pregnancies and three wonderful labor and deliveries we would have wanted to keep going? We had three sweet daughters, no problems conceiving, and no problems in delivery or post-partum. However, we (my husband & I) thought three was just right. We were happy, life was good, and so we decided to stop having children.

Life was good. We became Christians when baby number two was a year old, we were learning the Bible and trying our best to raise these little ladies in the fear and admonition of the Lord. My husband had a good job, and I was able to be a stay-at-home mom and home school our little brood. However, almost no one in our life had more than two or three children at this time, and we had never heard of allowing God to plan your family size. We just made our plans and thought that's what we were supposed to do!

A few years later, we were at a Fourth of July parade and met some friends of my parents. One of the women began telling us about her children. She said that she and her husband had three daughters, had a big gap, and then had their fourth daughter, several years later. I thought, "Oh, how cool. When the older three move out, they will have fun with a little girl at home to do things with and kind of spoil as if she were an only child." Well, I think the Lord used that family to strike a chord with me. Steadily, He worked in my heart in a way that allowed my mind to be open to another baby. We decided to try to have another child. Again—we easily conceived and had another great pregnancy and delivery. This time, we decided to find out our baby's gender at our 20-week ultrasound. We were having another sweet baby girl! It was fun to know the gender ahead of time. The girls talked to my belly and enjoyed getting to know their sister while she was still in my womb. We welcomed Megan into the world after 11 hours of labor. I was awed at the fact that this was the same little person who was growing within me. The little movements she made were the same ones I felt inside. From day one she had us all smiling, and she continues to do this at age 14. At the time of her birth people in our life thought we were crazy for having four children—especially after a five year gap! We were so pleased; our precious family was just the right size—or so we thought.

In the following couple of years we moved and started meeting people who had larger families as well as several who had miscarriages yet still continued to get pregnant. I was perplexed. One mom in particular talked quite openly about letting the Lord have her womb and allowing Him to give her and her husband the children that He desired. I later listened as she told me of yet another miscarriage. How devastating! I wondered if "letting God have control of the womb" was even good for your body. The questions continued coming to my mind, and I wasn't sure how to deal with them.

At this time I had another new friend who started chatting with me regarding adoption and having more children. She said she was praying that God would open our hearts to having another baby or adopting a child. I flippantly responded, "You go ahead and pray. We'll see what the Lord says about all of that!" I look back sadly at how arrogant I was, thinking I had it all figured out. Was I letting God be the Lord of my life?

Fast-forward eight years. The Lord was doing great work in the hearts and minds of my husband, our children, and myself. The girls were growing into lovely young women who loved the Lord. We had moved out to the country, had many people in our lives now who allowed the Lord to give them the children He desired, and our minds were soaking up Biblical promises and truths. At this time we repented of trying to control our womb and asked the Lord to forgive us. Psalm 127:3 says, "*Behold, children are a heritage from the Lord, the fruit of the womb a reward.*" We told the Lord we would lovingly accept any and all children He would give us. We had deep regrets that we didn't have 12 children at this time. I do know that the Lord had a good plan for us, and if He had wanted us to have 12 children, we would have 12 children. However, it is hard knowing that we were closed to having more children at previous times in our lives.

We tried to conceive again but found we couldn't! Oh, how sad we were. Every month I grieved that I was not pregnant. I didn't want to make an idol of it, but we really wanted to honor the Lord with our womb and have another baby. I was 35 or 36 at the time, and the doctors were saying that I was already at an advanced maternal age and that I should be happy that I had four children already. I was thrilled that I had four children, but that wasn't the point. I hadn't been obedient to the Lord, and I wanted to honor Him. After a couple of years of trying and not being successful, we finally had a positive pregnancy test! The news was a real shocker to many of our friends and family. After all, it had been eight years since our last pregnancy. At the 20-week ultrasound we were blown away to find out that this little baby was a boy. He was healthy, which was a blessing considering that my advanced maternal age was even more advanced—I was now 38. Again, I enjoyed a great pregnancy. Even though I was much older, I didn't feel much different than I had during my other pregnancies. I was overdue again and had another scheduled induction with Pitocin, the same routine as before.

We had the joy and privilege of having our daughters in the delivery room with us (ages 18, 15, 13, and 8), making that experience far from routine. They stayed at home when we went to the hospital, knowing that it usually takes hours for me to progress. We had a wonderful nurse who knew we wanted to have our daughters present for the birth. We asked if she would let us know when it would be a good time to have them come to the hospital. Our house was 20 minutes away, and we knew they needed time to drive over without rushing. In the early afternoon we were chatting with the girls on the phone, telling them that I had received an epidural and was progressing slowly; therefore, they wouldn't need to come for a while. Although disappointed, they continued to do their schoolwork, pray, and wait until they could come. Once we hung up, the nurse said, "Well, as long as I am here, I might as well check you to see how much longer it will be before the girls should come. It will probably be a couple more hours, but let's see." She checked me and said, "Quick, call the girls and tell them to come now!" She followed up by saying, "Oops, we are not ready for you yet!" and pushed the crown of my son's head back in! I couldn't believe she did that. Epidurals are awesome; I didn't feel a thing!

My husband called the girls back, and they left immediately. We had planned on our two oldest daughters (18 and 15) being present in the room when I delivered. The two younger girls were going to wait in the waiting room until the baby was born. Since

I had an epidural, it didn't look like I was in any pain, so my husband told our third daughter that she might want to be in the room also. (She is very sweet and sensitive. She would not have wanted to see me in pain.) My husband was on the phone with them while they were driving and told them that if daughter number four wanted to, she could be in the room also. The girls and the doctor arrived at the same time. The two older girls helped the nurses, and everyone was there to see their precious brother enter the world. Tears were flowing as we laid eyes on our little man—Jack. We had an incredible time; it was such a blessing from the Lord. What a gift for our daughters to see a new life enter this world and to be a part of their little brother's birth. I will never forget all of the love shared and the awe for what the Lord does each time a baby is born.

At this time in life our fourth daughter did not know how babies came out of mommies. She thought you went to the hospital, and God helped them come out. She came in to a full labor and delivery situation, and this led to a great talk afterwards!

Remember the friend I mentioned who had been praying for us to have another baby and/or adopt? Thanks to her prayers, the prayers of many others, and God's mercy, here we were with our new son. Her prayers didn't end there though. When we were unable to conceive (before Jack was born), we had decided to pursue becoming foster parents. We thought maybe God would allow us to foster and then adopt a child since we were not becoming pregnant. We became licensed foster parents the same month we found out we were pregnant. We fostered several children, loved them up, and told them about Jesus, but we always had to send them back. It was hard, but we knew it was what the Lord had for us to do.

When Jack was about 14 months old, we received a call from our county licensing worker asking us to consider a unique mother-daughter placement. It was for a 15-year-old girl and her

10-month-old baby. Our social worker felt we would be a good foster home because 1) the mother still needed to be parented, and we were parenting our teenage daughters, and 2) she had a baby and needed to learn how to parent, and we had a baby we were parenting. We prayed about it and met the mom, baby, and extended family. For many reasons, we felt this was an open door from the Lord and agreed to the placement even though up until this point we had never been open to taking teenagers.

Our life changed drastically. Our little bubble was burst in many ways. It was probably the hardest year-and-a-half of our lives up to that point. However, God used the difficulties to grow us and draw us closer to Him. We had to learn to trust Him. To make a long story short, after living with us for several months, trying to parent a growing toddler while attending high school, the mom made a very courageous decision and asked us to adopt her daughter. Feeling that this was God's plan for the mom, the baby, and our family, we adopted our precious Emma right before she turned 2. She is now 5 years old and is our sixth baby. We still have a relationship with the mom and her extended family.

Almost right after Jack was born, I wanted to be pregnant again. I felt so good, and I loved having a baby again. We tried again and conceived! Our pregnancy ended in a miscarriage that time. I was devastated to say the least. We had such stress in our lives due to all that was going on with this foster placement. I had to work at not being bitter about losing this baby. We tried again, conceived, and had another miscarriage. What was the Lord doing? I trusted Him, knowing that He knew what was best, but this was so hard. We were pretty sure that both miscarriages were twins. I had always wanted twins, and now we had two twin pregnancies but no babies! My heart was broken. We continued to give our womb to the Lord. With every period, I grieved. I wanted another baby.

As time went on, I learned that I no longer wanted what I wanted but rather what God wanted for our family. He knows what is coming in the future, and only HE knows what we can handle. It became easier to trust Him once I gave up trying to control everything. The older I get and the more life I live, the more I only want what He knows is good for me. I want ME to get out of the way. That doesn't mean I am at that point every day, but the times in between are getting shorter and shorter. I am thankful that He will never leave me or forsake me.

During this time the Lord was also working on me regarding my health. Self-discipline has never been a strong suit for me, so this was a huge challenge. I did a lot of reading and decided it was time to make a change. The Lord was my constant help as I cut out sugar, dairy, wheat and coffee. I lost 25 pounds and felt great! I added several supplements to my diet, two of which were cod liver oil and magnesium. I continued to take my prenatal vitamins, always hoping to be pregnant and have all of the good stuff in me before I conceived.

After losing the weight I almost immediately became pregnant. I was shocked. My husband had me take three tests before he believed me. This time around I went to my ob-gyn immediately and asked if there was anything I could do to help keep this pregnancy. She said that she didn't see any reason why I lost the last two, but that if I wanted, I could go on progesterone. Because progesterone is a hormone normally produced during pregnancy, my doctor said it wouldn't hurt to take it. So I did for the first 13 weeks. This was new for me, and it made me so tired. I had to take it twice a day: once before bed (that was easy because I just fell asleep afterwards) and once in the late morning, (that dose was a rough one). I would take it and then lie down exhausted, feeling like I needed to sleep and sleep. It was difficult wanting to be able to serve my husband and six children, but needing to depend on our daughters more. They were fabulous and pitched in like troopers. We were still homeschooling, had two preschoolers, and needed to coordinate schedules, activities, and life for our family of eight. After 13 weeks, I slowly weaned myself off of the progesterone, still scared that I would lose this precious life.

We continued to entrust this baby to the Lord, and at 20 weeks we went in for an ultrasound to find out that the Lord had graciously given us another son. What a blessing! I was then, according to the medical community, at an extremely advanced maternal age—43. My doctor mentioned that they didn't have many statistics on such old mommies. After the 13 weeks, my hair started falling out. After a few tests, my doctor attributed it to going off of the progesterone. But the baby was doing great! The second trimester flew by, and I felt fabulous. We got to the third trimester, and I started getting bigger and bigger. I was carrying a lot of extra amniotic fluid that made me so uncomfortable, just riding in the car was quite a chore. I stayed home a lot.

We got closer to the due date, and, as usual, I showed few signs of being ready to deliver. Because of my age, my doctor was afraid to let me go past my due date even though I was late with all my previous babies. She allowed me to go past my due date if I agreed to go in for an ultrasound or a non-stress test every week. If they saw anything abnormal, I would immediately be induced. I agreed, and each ultrasound showed a happy active baby. It was a joy to see him in my womb every week. I still didn't go into labor on my own and was induced one week after my due date. According to my last ultrasound, they found that not only did I have a lot of amniotic fluid, but that the baby was huge—at least 9 pounds! Well, they were wrong—he was born 7 pounds 10 ounces. He did have long legs and a bit of a big head, and we found out that their weight estimate was based on those measurements.

On the day of the scheduled induction my husband and I went to the hospital and brought our second daughter with us. She was in the process of becoming a birth doula. She is fascinated with

God's design of the human body, health, and natural health care. I had my precious daughter serving as my doula for her brother's birth!

My progression was similar to all the others: Pitocin, water breaking, labor, wait, labor, epidural, labor, wait, labor, wait, and then a delivery with the four oldest daughters present. What a joy and blessing to welcome our son Caleb into the world with a room full of people who love him! This precious little guy is a delight to our entire family. He is 18 months old at the time of this writing and keeps us all hopping! He walked at 9 months and has been running since. What a blessing to have babies in our older years. It is a privilege to share him with his big sisters and his big brother.

All of our babies took to nursing like troopers, and so, with the seventh baby, I didn't even think about the fact that though I knew how to nurse, each baby had to learn on their own. We found out that Caleb had a non-nutritive suck; he was sucking, but not getting enough milk to sustain him. I am so thankful for my lactation consultant at our local hospital. She'd been working as a nurse for over 30 years and knew mamas, babies, and nursing really well. She figured out what was going on in the first five minutes and set us up with a pump, bottles, and a plan. We returned home to try to nurse, pump, feed with a bottle, clean up, and basically start all over again. This ended up being an incredibly long, labor-intensive journey; however, I knew the long-term effects would be worthwhile for my baby and myself. I carried on. Thankfully, he got the hang of the bottle and began receiving the nourishment he needed.

The next day however, he started turning blue. We took him to the ER only to find out that he had contracted the RSV virus. This sweet son of ours was only three weeks old! He was so sick and we were so scared. He could not breathe on his own and was so tiny, vulnerable, and helpless. After the visit to the ER, we had an ambulance ride to Children's Hospital, where we spent a week watching, waiting, and praying. While there, the Lord used doctors and nurses to keep our little man alive. The Lord carried us through that very rough week. It was a time of deep soul searching and learning to trust the Lord more fully. This sickness drew us all closer to the Lord in new ways.

The Lord was gracious in allowing us to find out about Caleb's non-nutritive suck before we ended up in the hospital. Once at the hospital, Caleb was so weak he would not have been able to get any milk from me, and the bottle kept him well nourished. At the hospital I kept up the routine of nursing, pumping, feeding, and was so thankful that he did not have to learn to take a bottle at the same time he was battling RSV.

We left the hospital after seven days. Still concerned for his health and recovery, I continued to nurse, pump, and feed until Caleb was seven weeks old. My lactation consultant said that often when an infant reaches six weeks, their suck develops further, and babies who had problems up until this point are able to nurse completely on their own. Sure enough, right around six weeks I found myself having such a surplus of milk (due to pumping and nursing) that our freezer was filling up with little bags of frozen liquid gold. By seven weeks he was being nourished 100 percent from the breast. Oh, the joy and pleasure of persistence! All along I had wanted to nurse him as long as I could—this was such a victory. As I write, he is still nursing. It brings him and me such comfort. God designed a good thing in nursing.

I do not know if the Lord will allow us to have more children. We are trusting in God's good plan for us. Only He knows what we can handle and what we cannot. I would love to have another baby if the Lord would allow that; however, if my childbearing years are over, I am okay with that too. I want to honor the Lord with my whole life. I don't want to make an idol out of conceiving or having a certain number of children. I want to be obedient whether that means having 12 children or seven.

I am thankful that the Lord has promised never to leave me or forsake me. He is a patient, gentle Savior. We have big age gaps in our family, and sometimes it feels strange, but most of the time I have a deep peace knowing that the Lord has planned for our family to look just like it does. Do I wish those gaps were filled in with other children? Yes, but I also know that my Savior does not make mistakes, and He knows what is best for me and for all of our children. He loved me through those incredibly arrogant years, ugly as they were. I have not arrived but feel utterly thankful and undeserving of His love and guidance all along the way. John Piper says, "God is most glorified in us when we are most satisfied in Him." I don't want this quote only to make me think; I want to live it! I desire to glorify God, and I want to be satisfied in GOD alone.

Sue Answers the Survey Questions

1. How do you deal with fear of increased miscarriage, infant loss, or birth defects? How can one handle that kind of pain, especially over and over again?

After our first miscarriage I battled some fear during subsequent pregnancies. Each time we conceived I learned more and more how to relinquish control and put my trust in the Lord for each child's future.

> *"When I am afraid, I put my trust in you. In God, whose word I praise, in God I trust; I shall not be afraid. What can flesh do to me?"* (Psalm 56:3)

> *"You keep him in perfect peace whose mind is stayed on you, because he trusts in you."* (Isaiah 26:3)

During my most recent pregnancies I learned to praise the Lord for the lives growing within me, whether that was for a few weeks or full term. I felt such excitement each time the Lord allowed us to conceive in our 40s. I wanted to treasure every moment of having life within me. I had experienced having that life taken away and decided to celebrate each day I was pregnant.

Looking back, I realize that much of the pain with my first miscarriage was my disappointment in not being able to follow through with my plan. I was thankful the Lord allowed us to get pregnant again so quickly after our son was born, and then, when I miscarried for the first time, I was grieved that we would not get to raise the twins that had begun growing within me. I was sad that my other children would never know those siblings this side of heaven. Yet, the Lord is gracious. He gently showed me that He has a good plan for my life, even in miscarriage. It has been a blessing to have babies spaced further apart than I would have chosen. We have terrific older siblings who love spending time with, and caring for, their little siblings. I know the Lord doesn't make mistakes. He is the One who causes babies to grow inside the womb, and He takes them when He knows it is best. It has been a hard and good lesson to learn. Our children here on earth and the children we have in Heaven are all gifts from the Lord, whether I have seen them yet or not. I praise Him for each one.

2. How do you balance life with older kids and babies? Do you feel this is unfair to the older children? How do they feel about having more brothers and sisters? Is it being greedy to want more babies at the risk of not being able to meet the needs of the rest of the family?

This is a loaded question! Life is very full right now. We have three adult daughters, one teenager, two kindergarteners, and a baby living at home. Daily life is a unique balancing act. Every member of our family enriches our home, and we work together to keep family life running smoothly. I do not feel that a large family and little ones are unfair to our older children as I have seen what a huge blessing it has been for them to grow up with siblings of all ages. It has taught our children to be less selfish, to be patient, and to be an integral part in the work of the Lord within our family.

I cling to the verse in Isaiah 58:12 where God says, *"And your ancient ruins shall be rebuilt; you shall raise up the foundations of many generations; you shall be called the repairer of the breach, the restorer of streets to dwell in."* I did not grow up knowing the Lord personally or trusting in His promises. As I look to my children's futures, I am praying that the Lord will increasingly build, strengthen, and establish our children in His ways. I am asking Him to continually guide them on the path lighted by His Word and draw them ever closer to Himself. My husband and I learned many truths and promises from God's Word later in life, including the blessing of having many children. I am thankful that the Lord continues to reveal His truth to us, giving us hope that our posterity will, by God's grace, continue to embrace the renewing, sanctifying work of the Lord.

3. What about the ethical issues of repeated miscarriages? Shouldn't I avoid conception if I know that the chances of that child living are minimal? Am I enabling death when I should be promoting life?

The Lord is the Author and Giver of life. Only He knows who will live and for how long. I don't want to put my trust in myself, my foreknowledge, or my timing, but in His all knowing hands.

Romans 8:28 says, *"And we know that for those who love God all things work together for good, for those who are called according to his purpose."*

4. Do pregnancy, childbirth and recovery get harder in your 40s? I already feel like I'm coming apart at the seams! How will I hold out until menopause if I keep having babies? Am I acting responsibly when it comes to taking care of my health?

In my younger days I let a lot of decisions concerning my health fall by the wayside. I had youthful energy and health, but it wasn't a result of healthy choices and might not have lasted into my 40s. I have found that by taking charge of my health in a more proactive manner the past several years, I actually feel better, have more energy, and in many ways don't feel a lot different than I did in my 20s. With my last baby I felt so great that I only stayed one night in the hospital after the delivery. That was certainly a positive change. I have also experienced many health benefits that have accompanied pregnancy and nursing. Personally, I feel that pregnancy has improved my health.

5. How do I deal with extended family members, friends, and even the medical community who disapprove of our continuing to want more babies as we get older?

Smile, love them, and trust God with the outcome. Extended family members, friends, and the medical community are not always cheerleaders when it comes to having more children. Our heart's desire is to welcome all of the children God wants to give us whether others encourage us or not. Because He is the Author and Giver of life, we trust that if He sees fit to give us another baby in our 40s then He knows it is good. Our hope is that walking in obedience while loving those unfamiliar with our convictions will bring glory to the Lord. We will lovingly accept every child that the Lord chooses to bless us with.

6. Will I have the energy I need to continue to raise children into my 50s if I have some in my 40s? Is it fair to the child to have older parents?

I guess I would say it is no less fair than it is to have a baby when you are young. When we were young we had very little money; my husband had to work very hard to establish himself in his career. We hit lots of bumps in the road figuring out marriage; we were not very wise, and we didn't have enough life experience to know what was really important. For us, raising children in our late 30s and 40s has been more peaceful and fruitful in some aspects. We have learned that certain things aren't such a big deal, and we've learned how to let the little things stay little things. As we get older, walking with Christ, we want to continue to grow in understanding what is truly important, and Lord willing, we will focus on those things.

As far as the energy, I am trying to eat healthy and be active so that I can be the mom my little kiddos need for a long time! My older daughters remind me when I am weak and want to eat junk food that not only do our little ones need me, but my future grandchildren will want me to play with them too. No to the Doritos; yes to the Greek yogurt. I want to love, train up, and serve not only my children but also my grandchildren!

7. How do you explain miscarriage to older children, especially if you have repeated losses?

We want all of our children to understand that God is in control, and He knows what we can handle and when. Talking about the great possibility of meeting our babies in Heaven has helped us all to find comfort in the loss, knowing that we have children/ brothers/sisters waiting with Jesus for us in Heaven.

8. How does having babies in your 40s affect your relationship with your husband? Don't I owe him some of my best years?

Having babies keeps us smiling! We are in this together, and it has been a joy to parent many children of all ages at the same time. We don't regret any of our pregnancies and only wish we had more. There is a real, genuine happiness in the midst of crazy-big family life that we love and that we wouldn't exchange for a decade of alone time.

9. Are there real statistics (not skewed to the cultural norm) available regarding having babies in one's 40s? How many mothers do you know who have had babies in their 40s? Share your thoughts regarding statistics and odds.

I personally know eight women who have had babies in their 40s.

10. Hind sight is 20/20. Do you have any regrets? Looking back, is there anything you would have done differently?

Yes, I have regrets. I regret not allowing the Lord to control our womb. Back when I was Fertile Myrtle and thought I knew it all, we likely could have had several more children. It grieves me to think about the loss of those years. I do have peace knowing that the Lord could have shown us these truths earlier, but in His timing and His wisdom we learned them at just the right time according to His plan. We have big age gaps in our family. In my little brain I wish we would have filled them with other children; however, the Lord knows the reason for these gaps, and He doesn't make mistakes. I am so thankful I can put my trust in Him. Yes, regrets, but peace knowing God was and always is in control.

Sue Liesmaki *is a 45-year-old wife and mother. Married to Kelly for 25 years, they have the privilege of shepherding seven children, ranging in age from one to twenty-four. Sue enjoys busy family life on a hobby farm, home educating her children, working with her family to stage theatrical performances in their barn, welcoming foster children and adults into their home, reading, researching a variety of topics, and loving Jesus. She is a work in progress, joyfully looking to Him and thankful that the Lord's mercies are new every morning.*

Through Children's Children

By Yvonne Harink

"God will be faithful through the generations to children's children who with dedication uphold his covenant and obey his laws." (From Psalm 103, Book of Praise)

I look at my family tree; my mother, grandmother, great-grandmother, and countless generations brought children into the world. It was not unusual for them to have 8, 10, 12 children or more. When I read the stories in our community history book, I paid special attention to family size and age of motherhood, and I read of many families with mothers who bore children right into their 40s.

Yet, when I was expecting my last baby at the age of 45, I longed to relate to other women making the same journey. At this time in history, we're walking a road less traveled, and it's comforting to walk along with someone else. While my story may have been ordinary a few generations ago, today it has become extraordinary to have so many children, and to keep having them in one's 40s.

We are living in times when marriage, family, and motherhood are under intense attack. Satan has always hated children, and particularly children of believers. He uses every cunning tactic to prevent them from being born. While this has always been true, I believe a student of history will find that our age stands out as militantly anti-child. What we are witnessing today is really the death of a culture. The despair of our age is marked by addictions, abortion, euthanasia, divorce, suicide, and gender confusion. It's the time Rudyard Kipling described in his poem "The God's of the Copybook Headings": "The women had no more children, the men lost reason and faith… for the wages of sin is death."

As human beings, we are driven by our ideas, our beliefs, and our faith. History and culture flow out of our thoughts. All our life we are sorting the ideas that are thrown our way, either openly or subtlely. Are they good ideas? Are they true? Or, are they lies, couched in convincing rhetoric? We grow in courage when we know that what we are doing is right and true. The problem is, there is so much confusion out there, and it can be hard to sort through. Our feelings toward the birth of babies has a lot to do with our worldview. The most fruitful idea for us to dwell on is the knowledge that God gives us promises. These promises are held up throughout Scripture, for all believers. Isaac Watts formulates this thought in one of my parents' favorite hymns, "Thus Saith the Mercy of the Lord":

> "Thus saith the mercy of the Lord; 'I'll be a God
> to thee; I'll bless thy numerous race, and they
> shall be a seed to Me.'"

Children aren't our idea. They are God's idea. Before they are conceived in the womb, they have already been conceived in the mind of our Heavenly Father. (Romans 8:28-29) God assures us repeatedly that He will be a God to us and to our children. As believers, we are all spiritual heirs of the promises made to Abraham and confirmed throughout the Word, *"I will establish my covenant with him as an everlasting covenant for his offspring after him.*" (Genesis 17:19) This promise is confirmed in numerous places, including Peter's sermon in Acts 2:39, "*For to you is the promise, and to your children…*"

Most of my ideas about family and children were formed in my first six years of life, the years of observing and imitating; feeling secure, loved, and part of the team; and feeling that life was perfect and whole. I was a very blessed child as I grew up with the distinct privilege of having not only a mother at home but also a dad. This is a very special experience in today's society as few children have both a mom and a dad at home. I was born seventh in a family of eleven children. It was shortly after I was born when my parents made a leap of faith, buying a 100 acre piece of land to try to make a living off of it. Giving up his sawmill business, which had swallowed up all his time, my father came home, planted a large vegetable garden, raised livestock, and kept busy with numerous enterprises enabling our family to live off the land.

When I was 2 years old, my oldest sister, at age 12, drowned in the river that bordered our land. While I don't remember the event, my earliest memories include a lot of talk about Margaret, visits to the graveyard, pondering about heaven, and yearning to peek through the clouds to see her. A time of great sorrow for my parents, it was also a time where they drew near to God. I was a quiet, reflective child, taking it all in, and thinking deeply about the meaning of life.

There is so much magic and security in growing up in a big family. I remember the overwhelming feeling of being loved and cherished by older siblings, and later loving the little babies who were added to the team. Oh, the thrill of having a new little sister! I was 10 when my mom had her last child at the age of 42.

Our family was not wealthy. We didn't go on many vacations. But I have many rich memories of summer days, when everyone was working on the farm, picking berries, hauling hay, butchering chickens, feeding livestock, and building farm structures. The family discussions, read-alouds, crafting times, baking in the kitchen, meals, picnics, walks, tree huts, hay houses, hide and seek, hours of play— life was full of security, adventure, and fun.

Childhood memories are the strongest glue to form convictions. The idea of having a large family grew out of my upbringing very naturally. It was God's way of showing me love, and in later years it would be my greatest motivation to pass on His love.

My parents sent us to private Christian schools, and later I attended a private teachers college. I always hoped to have a large family but didn't think about it too much, one way or another. In the 1980s there was a lot of discussion about world overpopulation. For one of my assignments I wrote a paper on that topic. As part of my research I read the book The Population Bomb by Dr. Paul Ehrlich, who painted a dramatic picture of catastrophe heading towards societies that did not limit population growth. According to him the greatest economic threat facing every society was babies. Only by drastically reducing the world population would the next generation be saved from dismal starvation.

This project got me initially interested in the hype about world overpopulation. I admit to a little nagging doubt at one point, wondering if he just might be right. Over the years I've always been interested in reading about this issue and have been overwhelmingly convinced that Ehrlich's ideas are deceitful lies. Sadly entire nations, such as China, as well as much of the Western world are caught in the grip of these false ideas that have dehumanized millions.

Instead of world overpopulation, we are facing a demographic winter. For more on this, research the ideas of Julian Simmons, who proved Paul Ehrlich's theories completely false. (Simon wrote a book in 1977 called *The Economics of Population Growth*, in which he documents his findings. In 1997 it was republished as *The Ultimate Resource 2*. Christians who are concerned about the rhetoric of overpopulation will find his work helpful, though the author is not a Christian. Another recent book on this topic is written by Jonathan Last, *What to Expect When No One's Expecting, America's Coming Demographic Disaster*, Encounter Books, 2013.) Also, take a look at www.demographicwinter.com. Children are the world's most amazing resource. God created the entire universe, furnished the earth with every blessing, and then placed the crown of creation, a human being made in His very own image, to be the engine driver of His handiworks.

Unbelievers, who see man as a product of chance and as little more than a higher-order animal, do not comprehend what humans really are. Only Christians know man's real significance. So often we don't stand in awe enough of the potential of each human to use his mind, to think, create, and to develop all the hidden potentials in the earth. One of the most powerful ways of imparting this truth to the world is to welcome God's little ones, even when it brings us pain or inconvenience. Our world needs children. It especially needs children of believers. Every child born is God's greatest gift to parents, families, churches, and communities.

While I still had a lot of hazy questions in those days, thankfully, God directed my life so I would meet and marry a man whose heart was also open to the idea of having children. We were married in March of 1989 and had a honeymoon baby, born nine months after the wedding. Looking back, it was my worst pregnancy, the only one in which I suffered severe nausea, feeling sick most of the time. I think it must have been that I was physically not in the best shape, and that I was not eating properly. I only gained 17 pounds, but delivered a healthy 7 pound son. He was born in the hospital, as most babies are in Canada, and though I had an episiotomy, it was a classic, natural delivery.

I remember going to prenatal classes, which were helpful but also interesting in several ways. Our instructor had birthed three children and talked about her body being strained to the limit. I wondered what she would have said if I'd shared the fact that my mom had birthed 11 children. I also found it interesting that in our prenatal classes I was the only mom not planning to go back into the work force. My parents had instilled in us that a woman's place is in the home, and it would be unthinkable to go back to work and take my baby to daycare. My husband worked for a dairy farmer, and we rented a little house close to the farm. We might not have been wealthy in worldly terms, but those first years were a lot of fun.

After the birth of our son, the health nurse came to visit. Among other things she asked if we knew about birth control, gave some information, and suggested a few options. When you stand at the beginning of your marriage, after conceiving immediately, it can seem scary. How many babies could we possibly conceive in a lifetime? What if we ended up with 20 children? How would that be responsible? We found ourselves wondering what type of birth control choices we should make.

Around that time one of my sisters came across the book *The Way Home* by Mary Pride. It had just been published a couple of years earlier and had already gone through numerous printings. It must have hit a chord as the Christian community was looking for answers to the questions about birth control. Mary Pride articulated the trap that couples have fallen into— believing that it's wrong and scary to have too many babies. She lamented the fact that while communistic countries such as China have enforced a one child policy, here in the West we have willingly embraced what she called "planned barrenhood," and instead of looking at children as God's greatest blessing, we fear them and are ashamed of having too many. We've lost our willingness to take risks and have bowed down to materialism. Mary Pride also did a good job of showing the real risks involved in almost every form of birth control and gave the encouragement that maybe the healthiest choice is to let God plan our families.

I'm thankful that at that crucial time in our marriage we were exposed to books like this and could also discuss these things with friends. It helped us to see that the decision to have a baby and the ideas tied to birth control have a much broader effect than the pregnancy itself. They affect our social order, our way of life, and will have incredible impact on future generations. Ideas have consequences, and I'm so glad we were thinking about some of the best ideas in those years. It helped us to see life in terms of eternity, rather than in light of materialism.

When our son was 9 months old I became pregnant again. I remember feeling a lot better during that pregnancy than in the previous one. It was during this time that we moved across Canada to Alberta, where more of my family lived. We soon received a healthy, 9 pound daughter. After Jocelyn I experienced our first miscarriage. It was only at about nine weeks, and I quickly recuperated. In time, everything cleared up. I don't remember it as being that traumatic, but I mention it because over the years I miscarried many more times, at various stages of pregnancy.

In due time our daughter Angela was born. Looking back I believe that was one the busiest times in my life. When you have three little ones, you have very little help and can feel overwhelmed. By the time Justin was born (17 months later) the older children were able to help more. Michael was born 28 months later, after which I had my second miscarriage, at 12 weeks. Soon after came Nicole, our sixth child.

Then I had three miscarriages in a row. Two of them were at 12 weeks, and one was at 16 weeks. The 16-week-old baby may have died earlier, but it was definitely further developed than the others. It was the only one that I held in my hand, and I could see clearly that it was a little boy.

Within a month I was pregnant again, and this time I had no problems, other than a little spotting. That seemed like a long pregnancy, but it was soon forgotten when we took home another beautiful little girl, Marlissa. Looking back, these were happy times for our family, though not stress free. While we had no health issues, we did have financial trouble. We were hog farmers, and those were the years that the markets plunged, never to recover. We tried different ways of farming but found ourselves over our heads in debt and could hardly see a way out. I remember lying awake at night, planning out how we would relocate our family of nine to some little trailer, thinking we would probably lose the farm. Those were the years my husband worked a full-time job off the farm while trying all sorts of farming enterprises on the side.

As a homeschooling family we pulled through together. We managed to refinance and keep the farm. Our children were eager to help; they took on jobs at a very young age, pitched in to buy their own clothing, and lended their aid in so many ways. Our oldest son was already very busy in his own woodworking business and soon built us beautiful furniture. When he was 17 he built us a new kitchen, making our house much more attractive. All the children helped with farm chores from milking a cow to raising free-range chickens, rabbits, pigs, goats and lambs. Sometimes people have the idea that only the rich can have big families. It was obviously not true in our situation, though our children often assured us that they were making us rich.

Two years after Marlissa, Seth was born, followed by another miscarriage, and finally Elliott, our 11 pound baby, who was born when I was 39. All of our babies were born in hospitals with no complications. They were classic births: head down and 6 to12 hour deliveries. I was blessed to always have excellent health, and I never had a single complication while delivering babies.

After bearing our ninth child at 39, I sadly felt that I was probably reaching the end of my fertile years. Yet my husband and I also looked at it as the beginning of a new season. It was around this time that we started to get serious about natural birth control.

Evidently we didn't master it, as I had three more miscarriages in my early 40s, roughly one every two years.

When I was 40, my older sister Teresa got pregnant at the age of 45. While all my brothers and sisters have been blessed with large families, this was the oldest conception (to my knowledge) of any of the sisters. While her story initially contributed to my fear factor, it is really a beautiful story of trial and triumph.

My sister Teresa and her husband Len had 10 healthy children. She suffered a few miscarriages along the way, including one in her 40s, and at 45 she again found herself pregnant. A few months into the pregnancy the ultrasound showed she was expecting twins! The whole family was excited about this news, and Len and Teresa accepted it with their usual grace and calm. The next ultrasound was not as pleasant. It showed that one of the babies appeared to have a heart defect, and part of the bowel had not developed properly. This combination is clearly a sign of Down syndrome. This was a shock to our whole family because until now everyone had perfectly healthy babies.

While Teresa and her husband took it all in stride, this was not an easy time for them. Teresa shared that she suffered from a feeling of dismay, that somehow God was using them to show the world it was irresponsible to conceive a child at this age in life. The medical community stressed the fact that they were older. While not put into words, the implications were, "What were you thinking to conceive a child when you are 45? Don't you know that statistically the chances of having a genetic defect go up? And who is going to take care of the child when you are not there? You will be 70 when she is 25." These kinds of thoughts can make one feel insecure and almost guilty about the pregnancy, as if one should be ashamed to bring this new child into the world.

Teresa handled the pregnancy well and delivered two little girls. One was born with Down syndrome and needed surgery on her duodenal artresia (bowel) immediately after birth.

Because of her weak heart she was not able to suck and was tube fed through her nose for the first year. At 1 year she had heart surgery, after which she was fed with a stomach tube for another year.

Now, five years later, Teresa and Len reflect on their trials but also on their joy in this precious gift of twin girls, added to their family of two daughters and eight sons. These little girls have enriched them with so much joy, and although she is a lot of work, Teresa's family accepted the little girl with Down syndrome as truly a GIFT.

Teresa said she found encouragement from Governor Sarah Palin, who had a son with Down syndrome when she was 44. Palin articulated her thoughts beautifully as she prepared her children for the birth of their new brother:

> "This new person will help everyone put things in perspective and will get everyone focused on what really matters. Many people will express sympathy, but you don't want or need that, because Trig will be a joy. You will have to trust me on this. I know it will take time to grasp this and come to accept that I only want the best for you, and I only give my best. Remember though: *'My ways are not your ways, my thoughts are not your thoughts ... for as the heavens are higher than the earth, my ways are higher than yours!'*"(P. 184, Sarah Palin, *Going Rouge*, 2009, HarperCollins Publishers. Sarah Palin wrote a letter to her children to prepare them for the birth of their brother Trig. She decided to write it as though it were from Trig's Creator, the God in whom they put their trust.)

It always takes courage to be open to conception, at any age. But, in one's 40s, it takes special valour. In our case, my sister's story impacted our fears. I had three miscarriages in my 40s, each time at week 12. Each time emotions ranged from fear and dread to faith and elation. Each miscarriage involved extreme sorrow, followed by repentance and a feeling of unworthiness to even bear God's children.

When I found I was pregnant at 44, I braced for another miscarriage. Somehow I didn't expect to carry this child full term. As the weeks passed, I felt a mixture of elation but also of real fear.

I tried to analyze the angst. What exactly was it I was afraid of? Could I actually put it into words? While my husband always delighted in his babies and was proud of each one, was he resenting this one? Was he blaming me? Was it the feeling of being out of control, of being overwhelmed by the thought of traveling up that mountain again, of getting through the next months of pregnancy? Was it fear of medical problems? An early delivery? Birth defects?

It had been six years since we'd had a baby in the house. What was it going to be like to start all over again with baby training? What will it be like to raise this child who might not have a sibling close in age to play with? Then again, what if it is twins? Some statistics claim the chances of twins gets higher with age. Where would we put them? Would we have to build an addition to our home? What about our vehicle? Would we be faced with buying another 12-passenger van again? How would we swing this financially?

There was also fear about the older children. What would they say? Would they be embarrassed to tell their friends and co-workers? At the time our oldest son was 22 years old.

I think the sick feeling in the pit of my stomach was also partly guilt. I really was a hypocrite. I had always been vocal about the beauty of big families, but actually I was not brave enough to do it. I felt like a coward, afraid to handle all the possible challenges. The underlying fear was really the fear of man, of what people would think and say.

The only cure for fear is to confess it to the Lord and experience His power, as He really does answer prayer. Courage comes from the Lord. There is so much therapy in actually listing all the promises in the Bible of the Lord's blessings, especially those that pertain to having children. Another source of comfort to me has been the Psalms. Psalms have always been a part of my life, as we memorized them in school and sang them in church. To keep up Psalm singing in our family we try to sing a "Psalm of the week" with every meal. I usually write them out on sheets of paper, and even writing out the verses is therapy to me. We alternate between the Psalms from the Book of Praise and from the Psalter Hymnal. Some of my favorites are verses from Psalms 16, 25, 46, and 91.

As Kevin Swanson recently reminded me at a homeschooling conference, the Psalms are a special gift to us from our LORD. He gave them to us as a very special help in overcoming fear and discouragement. They represent the best poetry ever written, the deepest psychology, and the most heartfelt prayers.

If our older children had to get used to the idea of a new sibling, they sure didn't show it. The younger ones reacted with laughter and excitement. My oldest daughter shared, "Well, I know who is responsible for this one. Nicole recently told me that she is still praying every night for one more baby."

Looking back, the pregnancy went so fast. I might have been a bit tired, and the varicose veins in my right ankle flared up, but experiencing the miracle of another baby growing in the womb was such a special privilege. Pregnancy is a time of nesting, of staying at home, putting your legs up, and taking up cross stitching or knitting. It is a time to tune out other troubles in life and focus on the new life you carry.

It was bonding for our whole family to await the arrival of another little brother. We were thankful that the ultrasound showed that it was one healthy little boy. This was the only pregnancy in which we decided to find out the gender of the baby. Preparing for his birth was a family project. The girls could not resist buying baby outfits, and together we settled on a name: Kenton.

Baby Kenton was delivered with no complications. He was a healthy and vigorous boy, who grew and thrived in our home. God is so good. Looking back I really can't say it was much harder than any of the other pregnancies. Yes, I am a sinner. I was tired and had times when I suffered from a dose of self-pity and was short-tempered and irritable. But after the birth I bounced back quickly and enjoyed the help with the baby.

Nicole and Marlissa will always remember the fun they had taking turns giving their little brother his morning bath. When the older children came home, the first thing they did was to pick up the baby, or at least have a look at him.

My husband and I both feel blessed with all our children and take great delight in this last little one. Sometimes, when we tuck him in at night we marvel at him. It seems it all went so fast.

I realize that not everyone is able to have a lot of babies. It's not something that all husbands and wives agree on. Infertility is also a growing problem. In a fallen world, bodies break down, life gets overwhelming, and sometimes birth control has to be considered. I'm not writing to discourage or judge those who have had to limit their family size but only to encourage anyone who is looking for reassurance and inspiration.

In our day and age we are bombarded with the idea that babies are a burden, a hindrance, and that it is irresponsible to have too many of them. We are told that they will harm your health, your marriage, your relationships, our economy, and our ecosystem.

The ideas we believe, and the thoughts we entertain will affect the course of history. There is no greater way we can influence the future than through giving birth to God's children and raising them to reflect his image. Before babies are conceived in the womb, they are conceived in the mind. God's mind planned every detail of their existence (Psalm 139). Before the foundations of the earth

He foreknew each baby He would form. He takes great delight in knitting them together in their mother's womb and allowing them to take their first gasp of air and become real characters in His story.

The mystery of history is that although God is sovereign, He uses real men and women to fulfill His plan. History shows that giving birth can actually be God's way of growing a nation. Each new child can grow into generations of children who will inherit the earth. It's hard work to bring babies into the world. It's even harder to raise them. But, in spite of all the heartache and pain, I firmly believe there is no joy, fulfillment, or sense of accomplishment that can compare with this work.

I thought that one day

I would be a famous artist

And create great works of art

Instead, God made me a mother,

And my children are His masterpiece.

The design of their lives

Will live on after me.

What is painted on their hearts

Will last an eternity - Anonymous

Yvonne Answers the Survey Questions

1. How do you deal with the fear of increased miscarriage, infant loss, or birth defects? How can one handle that kind of pain—especially over and over again?

Fear is really the opposite of faith, and I've found the only cure for it is to ask God to take it away, to repent of it, and to experience that God answers prayers and really does turn our fear into praise. I mention in my story that I had nine miscarriages, most of them occurring around 12 weeks. We never did find out why. I think it might have had to do with hormone levels. I don't know. Usually, once I was passed the 12 week stage the danger was over. For me, the telltale spotting would almost always mean the end of the pregnancy. Only once did it prove otherwise.

I was fortunate that most of the miscarriages went smoothly at home. After a day or two of contractions the baby usually came, and things would clear up naturally. Sometimes I visited the doctor. Only once did I need a D&C.

I want to share this with other women as encouragement because a miscarriage can be such a traumatic event, especially if you have never delivered a healthy child. They can make us think that something is wrong with us. Yet, as my doctor often said, miscarriages are normal for some women, and we often won't know why.

My husband never really seemed to grieve a miscarriage. I did. To a mother, the baby is ripped out of her womb, and it doesn't matter how you paint it, it is traumatic. From the moment you know you are harboring another little person in your womb, your life unconsciously revolves around them. It's frightening, awesome, and exhilarating, all at the same time.

Miscarriages made me ponder the miracle of the other healthy children we had. It also made me think about the pro-life message that every life begins at conception, and that these little ones were also created for a purpose. Just because they never saw the light of day, doesn't mean they aren't still souls who will live for all eternity. Sometimes I sit in my nursery and look at the newborn baby pictures of our live children and wonder about the other ones who went to heaven. I know God had a purpose for their lives, and I wonder if I will know them in the new heaven and the new earth.

2. How do you balance life with older kids and babies? Do you feel this is unfair to the older children? How do they feel about having more brothers and sisters? Is it being greedy to want more babies at the risk of not being able to meet the needs of the rest of the family?

Instead of seeing it as unfair to the older ones, I believe growing up in a big family is ideal training and preparation for reality. Children who grow up in big families have fewer expectations of being served and catered to, which can be a great asset to them when they marry. They have many opportunities to learn that happiness comes from serving others, and at times they have to do their own problem solving.

Fitting our last baby into our modest home meant that we had to build a temporary bedroom in our downstairs playroom for the 6 and 8-year-old boys. The older children had to sacrifice some of their recreation and hang-out area. It's just the way it is. No one complained about it.

Actually, by the time Kenton was born, the older children enjoyed more independence and didn't need their parents to be included in all their activities. While there are times that we might go to watch a baseball or hockey game, our older children don't expect us to be at all their events. We've already experienced this with the holidays. My husband is from Holland, and travel is expensive. It is too costly to all visit together, so the children have to take turns.

When children become young adults, we have to let them go. This has been hard for me at times, but having a new baby in the house helps. The beauty is, the new baby also acts as a magnet pulling everyone home. Having a little baby in the household is also wonderful training and preparation in the arts of childcare and child training for children. We hope our children have their own families someday, so a major part of their education should include how to deal with babies. While they see his adorable sides, they also are exposed to challenges, such as a baby throwing temper tantrums, messing up their toys, and getting into their things. Sometimes I hear the comment, "Yes, life was sure easier before he was born." But then we all agree he is worth it. At times he needs to be disciplined, but we're happy he is so active, curious, and adventurous. It's a sign he is healthy and intelligent.

Our children have always delighted at the thought of having another sibling. The mystery of a family is that love grows, and the pie just gets larger. Every new member gives more opportunities to give love and also to receive it. A family's basic need is love and security, and a new baby gives another generous dose of this. The idea that it is greedy to want another baby is ludicrous. Instead, a baby is a generous gift from God to each family member. It is a gift of the husband to the wife and the wife back to the husband. It's a gift of parents to the children, and to grandparents, the church community, and society at large. A new child means a potential playmate for children in the neighborhood and a possible employee for businesses. There is no more generous gift that God can grant than another little human being.

3. What about the ethical issues of repeated miscarriages? Shouldn't I avoid conception if I know that the chances of that child living are minimal? Am I enabling death when I should be promoting life?

Life and death will always belong together. Because of the fall into sin, every creature that lives will also die. God has determined the hours we live, and we will not be able to change even one minute of this predetermined time. If God decided that some children will not live beyond three months, then that is His will.

A year ago, as we stood around the grave of a 10-year-old nephew who tragically died due to a farm accident, some of the above thoughts crossed my mind. I thought, "If only he had not been born, then no one would have to bear the sorrow of his death." Yet, talking with his family, we all agreed that we are so thankful for his birth, even though God called him home sooner than we expected. Now we have great memories, and we live in the glorious hope of the resurrection. Even though we might not understand it, God has a purpose in every life, whether lasting for a few days or 100 years.

4. Do pregnancy, childbirth, and recovery get harder in your 40s? I already feel like I'm coming apart at the seams! How will I hold out until menopause if I keep having babies? Am I acting responsibly when it comes to taking care of my health?

I can't really say that my last pregnancy was so much harder than any of the others. I may have been a little more tired, but the recovery was not much worse than with any other pregnancy. I believe in taking a good vitamin supplement, good nourishment, and getting lots of rest.

Remember the promise of 1 Timothy 2:15, *"Women shall be preserved through the bearing of children if they continue in faith and love and sanctity with self restraint."* As Nancy Campbell explains in her article "Preserved Through Childbearing," the word preserved in 1 Timothy 2:15 is the Greek word sozo. It means to be "protected, delivered, restored, saved and preserved." Nancy gives evidence that pregnancies actually bring physical healing to our bodies and help to prevent aging. The amazing hormonal functions which accompany a pregnancy are exactly what God created our bodies to need. Increasingly, research is finding that a pregnancy can help to prevent various cancers and can actually bring healing to the body. We are also preserved emotionally and spiritually since children have a way of delivering us from our self-centeredness and self-pity and help us to focus on the will of God.

5. How do I deal with extended family members, friends, and even the medical community who disapprove of our continuing to want more babies as we get older?

I don't really know how to answer because I was blessed with a very supportive doctor who was encouraging and helpful. Our church congregation also supports large families. I come from a family that has been blessed with abundant children; my parents currently have around 85 grandchildren and over 20 great-grandchildren.

The sister right under me in age has been a testimony of courage and strength to me. She is really the one who should be writing this chapter as she has an incredible story to tell. After her second child she was advised not to risk having any more. Three of her pregnancies involved lengthy bed rest, hospitalization, and premature babies, yet she and her husband have steadfastly continued having babies. Presently she is expecting baby number 13 at the age of 43.

My husband was born and raised in Holland in a family of seven children and as part of a tight-knit community that had many big families. While big family trends are decreasing somewhat over there, his family has always been supportive of us.

6. Will I have the energy I need to continue to raise children into my 50s if I have some in my 40s? Is it fair to the child to have older parents?

I am strengthened by one of God's promises given in Isaiah 40:31, "*But they who wait for the Lord shall renew their strength; they shall mount up with wings like eagles; they shall run and not be weary; they shall walk and not faint.*"

If we deliver children in our 20s, how do we know we will have energy to raise them in our 30s? We just don't know the future. I know some pretty energetic 80 year olds. I also know of some very sick 50 year olds. Just last week a 40-year-old mother of teenage children in our town died of a heart attack.

All we can do is pray God gives us energy to continue to be faithful in raising our children, at whatever age. We've often discussed with our children the fact that our youngest ones will have a very different childhood experience than our older ones. While they will have older parents, they will also have many older brothers and sisters to interact with. God knows that our birth order and place in the family has a profound effect on our development, character, and intelligence. It is His way of making us all completely unique while preparing us for the job He planned for us.

Is it fair to the child to have older parents? Is life ever fair? Every person is born to different opportunities. The miracle is that each one of us has received the gift of life. I don't know about you, but I think that every child goes through moments while growing up where the realization of what a miracle it is just to be alive is just too overwhelming. These are really awesome, spirit-quickening moments. We don't choose the gift of life. We don't choose our parents. We don't get to choose their age. We just are.

If you could choose, don't you think you would rather be born to older parents who were in a stable, loving marriage, than to be born out of wedlock, without a father in your life, as almost half of children are today? Yet nobody blinks an eye anymore at this reality. (The out of wedlock birthrate is said to be at around 42 percent today.) Also, consider the benefits of older parents who have had more life experience and more time to grow in sanctification. Besides these benefits, older parents are usually more financially stable and may possibly be able to do more traveling, visiting, and ministering.

7. How do you explain miscarriage to older children, especially if you have repeated losses?

I think it is best to just be honest. They are going to have to deal with these issues in their lives as well, and they are watching how we are dealing with our fertility. It's a great opportunity to talk about the issues surrounding birth control, and the fact that miscarriages can happen.

I've always tried not to be a drama queen about miscarriages, but instead handle them discreetly. My husband and I preferred to wait as long as possible to tell anyone that we were expecting for several reasons. First of all, it's our private secret. Secondly, it makes the pregnancy go faster if you can go through the first part privately. And thirdly, it does not give the children as much time to get excited and start counting on a new baby.

8. How does having babies in your 40s affect your relationship with your husband? Don't I owe him some of my best years?

Although we both will say that our last baby has strengthened our marriage, at times I could feel myself slipping into a pity party. My husband is a very busy man. He works hard at his job, on our farm, at his church duties, and as a volunteer fireman. At times life is overwhelming. I felt very sorry for myself when he made a trip to Holland, and I could not go along. I didn't have the energy to go with a baby, and he felt he had to visit his aging father. I was glad he went, but I did struggle with a selfish heart. Having a new baby really does tie you down again, and it is easy to feel blue.

At that time I found a good friend in Ann Voskamp's beautiful book *A Thousand Gifts*. It really is all about attitude and keeping a grateful heart. There is therapy in keeping a thankfulness journal and jotting down the very real gifts that God puts all around us, if only we have eyes to see them.

Our Christian calling is to enter into holy marriage. This means that our marriage is to be consecrated to the Lord and to his service. It is not about our own pleasure but the Lord's glory. This is the only true recipe for marital bliss. Instead of feeling that I owe my husband my best years, together we give God our best years, which brings far greater satisfaction. The quest for selfish pleasure is what makes marriages fall apart.

Having babies in our 40s has only made us feel more dependent on each other and on God. The valleys and hilltops we've traveled together have taught us patience and trust, and we both know we couldn't have done it without God's constant presence.

Christ redeemed marriage in order to return it to a Garden of Eden, the place where God's own sons are conceived and made in God's very likeness. Marriage is the holiest of places, and as Nancy Campbell says, each conception is actually a matter of God himself coming down to visit us.

The devil knows this, and his attacks have always centered on this garden. He will use any ploy to defile our sexuality, to replace it with fear, shame, and guilt. Mark Stein has made the point that the birth control movement has bred the sexual revolution and given birth to not only adultery and divorce but also homosexuality and gender confusion in general. Having children is one of the best protections for our marriages and one of the loudest pro-life statements, not only for today but for future generations.

9. Do you have any practical tips for high mileage mamas dealing with fatigue, pelvic separation, joint pain, varicose veins, etc.? In other words, what kinds of pregnancy issues did you have to deal with, and how did you deal with them?

I always had to deal with low iron and took supplements for that. In my later pregnancies varicose veins became a bit of a problem. I recommend taking an afternoon nap and sitting down when possible. Also just take it easy, stay home, and get rest. I recommend a good vitamin supplement such as Reliv. My sister swears by essential fats and has also been helped by brewers yeast.

10. Are there real statistics (not skewed to the cultural norm) available regarding having babies in one's 40s? How many mothers do you know who have had babies in their 40s? Share your thoughts regarding statistics and odds.

Initially, when I knew I was pregnant, I found myself researching online a lot about the statistics of delivering a handicapped child at the age of 45. While there are some interesting finds, I did not find it comforting or convincing. After all, what are statistics, really? I don't feel qualified to judge whether they are skewed. But do I trust them? I have to think of Mark Twain's line on statistics. He claimed that there were really only three different types of lies: "lies, damn lies, and statistics."

Even if the statistics are true, does it really make a difference? Statistics are not promises. They guarantee us nothing. We are called to trust God, not to start calculating as Ahab did. He played the game of statistics when he went into battle dressed in soldier's garb instead of in his kingly attire. Statistically there was far less chance of getting killed as a soldier than a king. However, a stray arrow found its way into his heart and killed him. Statistically he thought it had about a 0.001 percent chance of hitting him. God planned it to be 100 percent.

God ordained before the foundations of the earth what kinds of children He would give us. No amount of calculating can change that. Even if we deliver perfectly healthy children, every day of our lives we risk injuries which could cause disability. I know of children who have had strokes, developed autism, or had accidents that led to permanent brain damage.

Personally, I know of several moms who delivered children with Down syndrome or other disabilities while in their 20s and 30s. My sister is about the only one I know of who had a Down syndrome child in her 40s. I know of a lot of other normal children who were born to women in their 40s.

11. Hind sight is 20/20. Do you have any regrets? Looking back, is there anything you would have done differently?

While we are so much in the thick of our story that it's hardly hindsight, all I can say is we are both thankful for every conception. We are also thankful for the fruitful ideas that fueled our lives and for a God who keeps His promises. I'm thankful for an amazing husband who is such a faithful provider and wise father for our family.

Despite our fears and, at times, our weak faith, God continued to shower His blessings upon us. Though we weren't really trying to have babies in our 40s and were following natural fertility cycles, we are both happy we never did anything to permanently prevent babies from coming.

Yvonne Harink *is the 46-year-old mother of ten children. She has been married to her husband, Jan, for over 24 years The Harinks make their home in Northern Alberta, where their days are filled with many adventures including homeschooling, raising animals, playing, wood working, mechanics, welding, crafting and gardening. Yvonne has benefitted from following writing programs together with her children. She writes a monthly post for Visionary Womanhood, and has written articles for publications such as AHEA Magazine, Reformed Perspective, and Christian Renewal.*

A Body Built for Baby Building

By Dr. Regina Brott

What you will find in this chapter is holistic advice for naturally addressing the most common health concerns faced by women who have welcomed children for a lifetime, especially those who have either had multiple pregnancies or have been blessed with children during their later years of fertility. However, many of these concerns also apply to women in the early childbearing years. I will be addressing how to prevent, minimize, and correct physical wear and tear that pregnancy, nursing, and childrearing can take on a woman's body. Most advice will be fairly general, but I pray it would point you in the right direction as you research your own specific concerns.

I am sharing from the perspective of a chiropractor, a wife and mother, and a Christian. Most often, as is the case with myself, chiropractors tend to suggest the most natural, or least invasive, recommendations for your overall health. My particular practice is primarily women and children as well as families that come together for wellness care. My advanced training is in maternity and pediatric care through the International Chiropractic Pediatric Association.

Health Care Professionals

Whether your primary concern is fertility, pregnancy, menopause, or general health, I always recommend thoroughly evaluating your health care professionals and having a well-rounded team of providers whom you are comfortable with. With each appointment, even if you have a long standing relationship with your doctor, try to bring one or two questions in addition to your health concerns that will help you get to know his/her professional stance on issues that are important to you.

In addition to your primary physician, you may want to consider several other health care practitioners for your own care and/or your baby's. A naturopath, chiropractor, massage therapist, nutritionist, exercise coach, or doula would be a few examples. While it is not necessary to utilize every one of these practitioners, it is important to listen for recommendations and establish relationships where you see fit. It is convenient to have a trustworthy resource when a question comes up or when care is needed.

Take time to research what health issues each practitioner can help you with. For example, chiropractic can affect fertility, pregnancy related back and pelvic pain, baby position in utero, ease and duration of labor, birth trauma, breastfeeding issues, emotional health, and infantile colic, to name a few (find research at http://icpa4kids.org/Chiropractic-Research).

Try not to ignore health concerns or accept them as permanent when they may not be. Even if health care is limited due to finances, there is likely a way to get the care you need if you just ask. Most importantly, remember that no professional can take your place as the best "doctor" for yourself and your baby. Your own thorough research may be all that is necessary to find the answers you are looking for.

Preparing for Pregnancy/Basic Wellness Measures

Taking measures to improve overall wellness is important for many different reasons, but it is especially important for producing healthy babies. Focus first on those things that will most effectively boost your immune system, balance hormones, and help your body better handle stress.

Two of the most efficacious areas to focus on are nutrition and exercise. A helpful nutritional guide by Donielle Baker, author of *Naturally Knocked Up*, is included in this book. Utilize this resource and others provided in the resource appendix, as good nutrition is absolutely vital in creating health *and* babies.

When it comes to exercise, the key is consistency. For most people, this means it has to be enjoyable. Create a routine that is realistic for your stage of life and that you look forward to. Give yourself variety, and try to include some family members in the activity. Let your children have fun alongside you on their own exercise mats (blankets work well), or do things outside when the weather allows.

The three areas of fitness to include throughout the week are cardiovascular exercise, strength training, and stretching. For cardiovascular exercise, aim to have your heart rate increased for a total of 30 minutes each day. This means you should be breathing harder than normal but still able to speak sentences. The most effective way to condition your cardiovascular system, tone muscles, and burn fat is to do short bursts of intense activity (2-3 sets of 30-60 second bursts with 30-90 second recovery periods after each) throughout the day. Some simple ideas are jumping rope, jumping jacks, getting involved in a game of tag, or running in place. Make sure to push yourself for that short amount of time.

Because variety is important for your muscles as well as your brain, you may want to try alternating burst training with brisk walking, biking, swimming, or other similar activity every other day. One or two days a week should be reserved for lower intensity exercise such as a relaxing walk.

Incorporate some form of strength training several times a week. It may be helpful to find some guidance if you have any questions about strength training, whether from your doctor, a trainer, or even your own research. It is important to use good form and to exercise within the limitations of your body.

To give you some ideas for a strength training routine, there are several areas of the body that tend to need more emphasis: upper back, abdominal muscles, and buttocks (gluteus muscles). This is because the majority of us spend a fair amount of time in a seated position, carrying or holding objects in front of us (cooking, carrying children, lifting, etc.), or using poor posture. The result is that the chest (pectoralis muscles), low back, and hip flexors (or the muscles used to do an old fashioned sit-up) end up very tight. Notice that the three areas I recommended focusing on in your strength training are opposite the three areas that I said are typically too tight. When you flex one muscle group, the opposing muscle group has to relax. Your brain knows that opposing muscle groups can't be contracted at once, or you would not accomplish a given motion. Therefore, just by strengthening your abdomen you are teaching your low back to relax, for example.

A few other common misconceptions about strength training are important to mention:

- **Small, controlled motions are often more effective than large, quick motions.** This is the case with abdominal exercise. If you are bringing your chest close to your thighs, you are likely working your hip flexors (iliopsoas) rather than your abdominal muscles. Instead, think about drawing your navel toward your spine and shortening a string that connects the lowest point of your sternum to your pubic bone.

- **Don't underestimate the importance of stabilizing, or postural, muscles.** While it might seem like a waste of time to spend your workouts on the small, less noticeable muscles, those are the ones that are going to keep your body most functional in the long run. Musculoskeletal pain and injuries are often a result of muscle imbalances between postural muscles and phasic muscles (those designed for larger movements). So, to make the most of your time, look for exercises that work several areas of your body at once. Often these "functional" exercises require an element of balance. Balancing movements require your brain to quickly make slight adjustments in the stabilizing muscles, training them to do their job more effectively.
- **Strength training does not have to be fancy.** Make it as simple or complex as you'd like.

Even if you don't have time to do any other exercise during the day, try to work stretching into your routine. Regular stretching is critical to avoid the problems that come with a decreased range of motion. Maintaining a full range of motion will help you avoid pain and degenerative processes that lead to arthritis as well as make nearly every activity of life easier and more enjoyable. In addition, motion helps to keep your brain healthy as information processing is very closely linked to spacial memory. Motion is also important for balancing hormones and keeping stress levels in check— factors that are both known to influence fertility.

For stretching, one place to begin is to stretch out the common areas of chronic tightness: chest, low back, and hip flexors. A few other areas that are especially important for women include the neck, tops of the shoulders (trapezius), and upper back (levator scapulae and rhomboids). Women tend to carry stress in these areas. When stretching each of these areas, keep in mind that each muscle has fibers that run in slightly different directions. In order to stretch these various fibers, adjust your position slightly until you feel the stretch move to a new area. Make sure to be patient when you are stretching and hold each stretch for several deep breaths. Any stretch can be made more effective if you activate the opposing muscle group. For example, when stretching your rhomboids (the muscles between your shoulder blade and spine), the common approach would be to curve your shoulder forward and pull your arm toward your opposite hip. Make this stretch more effective by flexing the muscles on the other side of the scapulae (the teres muscles). You can do this by using your opposite arm to create resistance against the outside of your elbow as you push your elbow up and out (as though you were trying to elbow someone in the nose).

Another stretch/strengthening combination that is important in maintaining proper alignment and function before, during, and after pregnancy is the deep squat. Your feet and knees should be slightly wider than hip distance apart (more when you are pregnant), your knees fully flexed, and your toes pointed slightly outward. Your bottom should be near the floor. Stay in this position for several minutes at a time, if possible. Incorporate this stretch into your daily life by using it anytime you need to pick something up, reach something off a low shelf, or play with a small child. This will spare your lower back the stress of bending at the waist as well as strengthen your lower body muscles and tone your pelvic floor more effectively than kegels (see www.alignedandwell. com on pelvic floor dysfunction).

In addition to good nutrition and consistent exercise, be prepared in advance to handle challenges to your health. Keep a selection of natural first aid options and immune boosting home remedies on hand so that you can address symptoms at their onset. This will help you to avoid pharmaceuticals, which can be especially harmful while you are pregnant or nursing. Consider some of the common health challenges your family tends to face and find vitamins, herbs, and whole foods that address those issues. Vitamin D, C, A, E and B complex, zinc, echinacea, colloidal silver, probiotics, fresh garlic, and turmeric are some supplements to get you started. Having a variety of high quality essential oils on hand can also be helpful not only for contagious illness but also for everything from cuts and burns to stress reduction.

Use only the highest quality you can find for anything that you put into or onto your body. When purchasing supplements, look for those that are made from whole foods and are minimally processed or raw. Extensive reference manuals, as well as topical reference books, are widely available and can be wonderfully helpful to have on hand when determining what to use. A few thorough manuals are *Prescription for Nutritional Health* by Phyllis A. Balch, *Healthy Healing* by Page and Abernathy, or *Smart Medicine for Healthier Living* by Zand, Spreen, and LaValle.

Don't dismiss the simple advice of getting adequate rest and hydration (a minimum of half your weight in ounces of pure water each day), using good posture, and avoiding unnecessary stress. These are actually some of the most important things you can do for your body. Whether you are hoping to conceive, pregnant, nursing, or taking care of a family, these basic wellness measures can help you better fulfill the roles God has called you to.

Restructuring Goals

When addressing any health concern, especially age related concerns, patience and persistence are important. Small, consistent lifestyle changes are more likely to become habits. Over five years those changes make a world of difference. In addition, be wise about when to intentionally slow down the pace of life. Sometimes the issue is less about your body not performing the way it should and more about your own unrealistic expectations of your body. Know your limits and consider the cost of expecting more from yourself than what you are feeling up to at a particular stage in life.

Sleep and Fatigue

The first things to consider if you are dealing with fatigue are basic lifestyle issues such as sleep habits, water intake, activity level, and stress level. Next, consider nutritional deficiencies such as iron and vitamin D. Iron deficiency is a common cause of fatigue during pregnancy and postpartum and is more likely to occur in women of childbearing age due to menstruation. Dietary sources of iron include dark green leafy vegetables, legumes, lean red meats and organ meats, red raspberry leaf or nettle tea, and blackstrap molasses. Cooking in cast iron skillets also supplies dietary iron. Eating foods rich in vitamin C, such as orange or tomato juice, will aid in iron absorption. Vitamin D deficiency is also very common, especially in areas with limited sunshine during winter months. While the best food sources of vitamin D are oily fish and eggs, supplementation is usually necessary if you live in a colder climate. Discuss fatigue with your health care provider to to rule out more serious conditions and find out whether supplementation is necessary.

From a musculoskeletal standpoint, the most common problem people have regarding unrestful sleep is poor bed and pillow support. A firm bed is generally better for supporting your spine. Pillows should be small enough that your head and shoulders stay aligned in the same way they would if you were standing up straight with good posture. All too often, pillows are too large and push the head forward rather than providing only the necessary support for the natural curve in your neck. Buckwheat hull pillows can be a helpful solution to this problem and can be adjusted to body size by adding or removing hulls.

Pelvic Instability

Pelvic instability is very common during pregnancy, but it can be worse after multiple pregnancies and with increased age due to previous wear and tear on the ligaments that stabilize the pelvis. A hormone called relaxin causes pelvic ligaments to relax in preparation for labor. High levels of relaxin are beneficial during labor but can cause mild to severe discomfort in one or more areas of the pelvis, especially during pregnancy after the baby engages, or drops lower into the pelvis.

Exercises that strengthen the small postural muscles of the pelvis are important before, during, and after pregnancy, even for women without pelvic instability. Starting these exercises early, before the onset of pain, can help minimize severity. One of the best exercises for strengthening stabilizing muscles is pelvic rocking which can be done while sitting on a large exercise ball. Tilt the pelvis forward, backward, and side-to-side slowly, as far as you can without discomfort. Replace your desk or living room chair with an exercise ball so that you can do these frequently throughout the day. You can also increase pelvic stability by standing in a semi-squat position (holding onto a chair if necessary) and tapping the toes of one foot in front of you, to the side, and then behind you, repeating this motion for several minutes with each foot. Even walking is helpful to keep these muscles active. See also the above section titled "Preparing for Pregnancy/Basic Wellness Measures" for a description of deep squats that will successfully strengthen pelvic muscles and improve alignment.

Chiropractic adjustments can also help to correct misalignments that easily happen when pelvic ligaments are loose. The Webster Technique is very effective in gently reducing pelvic, low back, and round ligament pain as well as facilitating proper positioning of the baby and maximizing the size of the pelvic opening in preparation for labor. To find a chiropractor who uses this technique, visit the

International Chiropractic Pediatric Association website: www. icpa4kids.com. After pregnancy, chiropractic can ensure that the pelvis heals correctly as the pelvic ligaments begin to tighten.

In some women, a degree of pelvic instability can continue after pregnancy. This becomes more likely after having multiple pregnancies. In these cases, exercises and adjustments should be continued on a wellness basis. A pelvic stability belt can also be worn on days that require more time on your feet. If necessary, a pelvic stability belt can be helpful during pregnancy.

General Joint Pain during Pregnancy and Postpartum

General joint pain is common during and after pregnancy and can also be more pronounced after multiple pregnancies and in later years. While spinal pain is most common, pain in the joints of the extremities (hips, knees, etc.) can also be problematic.

Low back pain is often caused by the extra weight of the baby pulling forward on the spine. Consciously keeping your abdominal muscles slightly flexed throughout the day will minimize strain on, and arching of, the low back. One of the best and safest ways to strengthen abdominal muscles during pregnancy is pelvic rocking while on your hands and knees. With your arms and legs shoulder width apart, pull your abdomen up toward the ceiling and hold tight for a few slow breaths. Then lower your abdomen until your spine is again straight. It is not necessary to arch your low back toward the floor. Repeat this exercise for several minutes, several times a day. This exercise will also increase blood flow to the baby and give him or her a gentle massage even before birth.

Upper back and neck pain during pregnancy is often due to poor posture as the extra weight of increased breast size pulls the upper back forward. After pregnancy this can be even more pronounced due to poor posture during nursing. Use a pillow or two under the baby so that you don't need to slouch forward to nurse. As much as possible keep your head up while nursing, or at least stretch your neck periodically.

Using correct posture whenever you sit will not only help with spinal discomfort, but it can ensure that your baby has enough room to get into the proper position for birth. (For more information on how to gently influence baby positioning see www.spinningbabies.com.) Your sitting posture should be much more like you would sit on an exercise ball than on a soft couch. Your pelvis should be tipped slightly forward and your legs slightly apart. Allow your upper body to naturally straighten up when your pelvis is in this position. Deep squats, as described in the section titled " Preparing for Pregnancy/Basic Wellness Measures," will also help improve posture and decrease pelvic joint pain due to misalignment.

While improving posture and balancing muscles are the primary goals in removing the cause of joint pain, the following interventions can help repair damage and manage pain: chiropractic adjustments and massage can correct and prevent further musculoskeletal imbalance; natural muscle rubs like essential oils are effective for relaxation and tissue healing; and light exercise, such as walking and stretching, increases blood flow to joints. Pregnancy pillows can also give the low back a break by safely cradling the abdomen while allowing time lying face down. Supplementation with glucosamine, chondroitin, and MSM can reduce pain and minimize and repair damage to the joints, but there is limited research on its use during pregnancy. Other home remedies can be found by using a good reference manual.

Finally, ice and heat can be helpful in minimizing pain and speeding recovery. A general rule is that heat should not be used unless the problem is clearly chronic. If an injury is fresh, only ice should be used, as heat will increase swelling and pain. If the swelling stage of an injury is clearly past, heat and ice can be alternated.

Varicose Veins

Varicose veins can become a problem for some women after one or more pregnancies. The extra pressure of the uterus, along with hormonal changes that affect the veins, can make venous blood return more difficult, leading to pooling in the lower extremities. While varicose veins can be troublesome to deal with, there is much you can do to reduce and prevent further varicosities.

Exercise that increases your circulatory rate should be an important part of every day. Walking, swimming, and performing postures that elevate your legs to the level of your heart or above, such as leg lifts, are excellent choices. Pelvic tilts, pelvic rocking, and deep squats, as discussed in other sections, can also improve pelvic circulation. Whenever possible, elevate your feet above the level of your heart. If you must sit for an extended period of time, make sure to take a brisk walk at least once every hour. If you are able, sit on the floor rather than a chair. Wear support stockings throughout the day if you are on your feet a lot, especially during pregnancy.

Vitamins that strengthen the circulatory system include C (with bioflavonoids), B, and E. Good sources of vitamin C include citrus fruits (the white inner skin is high in bioflavonoids), dark green leafy vegetables, broccoli, and tomatoes. Vitamin B can be found in organ meats, whole grains, and brewer's yeast, also called nutritional yeast. Healthy intestinal flora also allows for vitamin B production in the gut. (See www.westonaprice.org for more information on the benefits of creating healthy intestinal flora through food and supplemental probiotic sources.) Good sources of Vitamin E include sunflower seeds, almonds, spinach, and dried apricots. Supplementation of these vitamins may be helpful and should be discussed with your health care provider.

Exercise During Pregnancy and Postpartum

Several of the exercises recommended in the sections titled "Pelvic Instability and Separation" and "Joint Pain during Pregnancy and Postpartum" are also recommended for general wellness during pregnancy and postpartum. These exercises include pelvic tilts while on an exercise ball, pelvic stability movements while in a semi-squat position, and pelvic rocking while on your hands and knees. In addition, it is helpful to activate your upper back muscles throughout the day by squeezing your shoulder blades together as though you were holding a pencil between them. As with any postural exercise, frequency throughout the day is the most effective way to re-train your brain to create a new "normal" posture. Exercises that strengthen your gluteus muscles (buttocks), such as squats or leg lifts while on your hands and knees, are also important to maintaining proper posture during pregnancy and afterward. Finally, daily walking, swimming, or other low impact cardio work is very important for both mother and baby.

Daily activity modifications and stretching are just as important as other types of exercise. These include proper sitting position, especially while nursing (discussed in the section on general joint pain), as well as sitting on the floor or an exercise ball rather than a chair or couch whenever possible. Thoroughly stretching pelvic, back, and leg muscles is especially important during pregnancy and in preparation for labor. Spending time in a deep squat position (as described in the section titled "Preparing for Pregnancy/Basic Wellness Measures") is a wonderful stretch to widen the pelvic outlet for birth and stretch pelvic ligaments.

Extra instruction on cardio, strength training, and stretching is also given in the section on basic wellness measures, although several modifications should be made. Burst training is generally not advised during pregnancy unless done with significantly less intensity. During pregnancy you should also avoid lying flat on your back, jogging and bouncing, increasing core temperature and pulse beyond a safe range (see your doctor to determine what is safe for you), activities requiring balance, any risk of abdominal trauma, and becoming dehydrated and/or exhausted. Pregnant or not, avoid anything that hurts. After the birth of your baby make sure to take time off from exercise until your body is fully recovered. Talk with your doctor about when you can resume regular exercise.

If you have diastasis recti (splitting of the abdominal wall along the midline of three fingers widths or more) during or after pregnancy, avoid aggressive abdominal exercise. Instead, continue the pelvic rocking while on your hands and knees, placing extra emphasis on tightening the abdomen and pulling it up toward the ceiling. You can also place your back against the wall in a semi-squat position and tighten your abdomen drawing it in toward the wall. In this position, and throughout the day, you can use your hands to pull the sides of your abdomen toward the midline, giving yourself a hug. This will encourage the tissue to knit back together.

I hope this information gives you encouragement and direction to improve your physical health. Yet keep in mind that although our physical condition is very important, our spiritual condition is infinitely more so. Therefore, I especially pray that the wisdom and Scripture shared throughout this book would bring you great comfort and confidence in the Lord.

Dr. Regina Brott *is the wife of 6 years to Lukas and the 29-year-old mother of two little ones. After receiving her Doctor of Chiropractic degree from Northwestern Health Sciences University she completed her specialty training in maternity and pediatric care through the International Chiropractic Pediatric Association. She now enjoys running a family wellness practice from their home in Farmington, MN (www.victoryfamilychiro.com) and is thankful for* *the time it allows at home with her family. She and her husband also enjoy serving the Lord in their local church.*

Nutrition for Fertility in Your 40s

By Donielle Baker

I may possibly be the only contributor to the book under the age of 40—I'll be 32 at the time of publication. I have a background in nutrition and fertility, and I'm no stranger to fertility problems and loss.

Growing up in a semi-large family myself (five children is definitely above the cultural norm), I always wanted four children. While it has not been the Lord's plan for my life, at least not yet, one of the benefits has been the realization that I do not control my fertility. Whether it's from the aspect of trying to become pregnant or by taking steps to prevent pregnancy, this is the background from which I write; I have learned over the last seven years that I am not in control of when I bring babies into this world.

However, I also believe that I should be taking care of myself nutritionally during this time. A farmer cannot will a seed to grow; yet he takes care of his soil and nurtures the land so that when the conditions are right, his crop is plentiful. Whether you are plentifully fertile or not, this chapter is for you. Taking care of yourself nutritionally can benefit your children and give them a legacy of health. It can also help you move through pregnancy with less complication and a reduced risk of pregnancy loss.

There are no guarantees, of course. We live in a fallen world where death and disease are part of our lives, and it is in those times that we cling to our Heavenly Father. He is good, and our pain is never worthless as long as we learn and grow in our faith through our experiences.

My Fertility Story

I was finally diagnosed with polycystic ovary syndrome in 2002, but only after I had spent hours upon hours researching my own medical issues. When I was 18, my doctor at the time just prescribed the birth control pill, saying many women had irregular cycles, and taking hormones through the pill would fix my problems. If and when I wanted to get pregnant, there was another little pill I could take that would force my body to ovulate.

Since I agreed with the cultural norm of waiting two to four years before starting a family, I went along with the medical treatment thinking I'd be on the pill when I was married anyway. You know, so my husband and I could have "our time" before we had children.

The problem was, the pill wasn't fixing any of my problems. In fact, in many ways, I believe it was making them worse. I was just giving my body fake hormones so that it didn't have to try to produce any natural hormones itself. I suffered everything from migraines and stomach upset to emotional instability. I was on those beastly little things for four long years while waiting for my husband to be ready to start a family, and I had come to think that what I was feeling was just my normal. Little did I know how much effect they actually had on me.

It wasn't until we started thinking about starting a family that I really started to look at the natural ways a person can increase fertility. I knew that it may take a long time for me to actually conceive, and I wanted to make sure I was eating a healthy diet.

So I ate what is medically considered a healthy diet. Skim milk, wheat bread (store-bought), high fiber cereals (store-bought), and lots of fruits and vegetables (non-organic) with very little red meat and fats. Although I was eating the best I knew how at the time, I would still go six to eight months between cycles, and I never knew when ovulation was coming. Fortunately, we were able to become pregnant just weeks before calling my doctor for help, and I now have a son who was born in August of 2006.

I consider this nothing but divine intervention as I was so sure of myself and what the medical community had to offer. I was planning on asking for prescriptions and letting my doctor figure out how to help me achieve a pregnancy. But instead, God had different plans for my life and led me down an entirely different path.

Although I was able to become pregnant once, I *knew* that my body still was not functioning properly. Since my son was born, I've spent hours and hours researching and reading about traditional, nourishing foods and natural fertility. Over the last couple of years I've even been working on my Master Herbalist Certification to learn even more and hopefully help other women walking the same journey I've walked.

I wanted to be able to regulate my body so I never had to rely on fake hormones to prevent or achieve pregnancy. Eight months after starting on my journey to better health, I was able to do just that. My body was finally receiving the nourishment it needed to regulate my hormones, and I began to have regular cycles for the very first time in my life—naturally.

With natural and regular cycles, I was able to conceive our second child, a daughter. After she weaned two years later, I again began to have regular cycles and conceived our third—a baby that was only with us for about 10 weeks before we found that he had miscarried.

Losing a baby has taught me so much, and I'm thankful that through his short life I've been able to experience my faith more fully. What I wouldn't give, of course, to be able to snuggle with him each day. However, because of him, my life and faith have changed for the better.

I've also experienced the physical symptoms of stress due to this life circumstance as again I struggle with correcting my hormones and balancing my body. Stress does matter! In this new chapter of my life, I've again realized how important nutrition is as I work to heal my body.

Nutrition and Fertility

Nourishing your body with specific nutrients will help to ensure your hormones are being produced appropriately (which gets harder with age) and will also help as you begin to enter perimenopause and menopause, easing your body into the transition. Nutrition is important if you struggle with wanting more children and can't, or if you are open to having more children but are concerned about age related risks.

Before the age of industrialism and processed foods, traditional cultures actively fed couples specific foods to help prepare their bodies for pregnancy. Dr. Weston A. Price documents many of these traditional marriage preparations in his book *Nutrition and Physical Degeneration*, a book he wrote after traveling the world in the 1930s to find out why traditional cultures, separated from modern foods, were able to experience the bounty of health compared to those in the United States.

Today we don't do much in preparation for pregnancy other than take a prenatal vitamin, leaving our bodies lacking in the nutrients that protect and build our DNA as well as grow and build our cells and the cells of our babies. And we do almost nothing to rebuild and renourish after each pregnancy, causing health to degrade further after each child. This is one reason that women are fraught with cavities, fatigue, thyroid problems, and autoimmune diseases among other health issues.

Consuming special foods for fertility can not only increase the odds of conception, but can also give your baby the best start possible by providing them with nutrients that ensure proper growth and development.

Traditional Diets

As a dentist here in the United States, Dr. Price became concerned with the growing prevalence of tooth decay in our society. So he traveled the world researching the reasons other cultures did not have the same problems. He found that people who had diets devoid of processed or refined foods had no tooth decay or need for corrective braces. They were full of vitality and health. They did not have problems with fertility and pregnancy, cancer and heart disease were unknown, and, for the most part, they were happy and mentally healthy.

He found that **what** they ate and **how** they ate it were key factors in their overall health.

He also found that eating for fertility was extremely important to them, no matter the country or tribe they came from. In some cultures it was customary for couples to refrain from getting married until after the women had been able to consume these nutrients for a certain number of months when these foods were in season. Many other cultures found it important for women to eat certain foods before marriage and traveled far distances to provide it for them. And other cultures even held special ceremonies that included many of these foods.

It is intriguing that although these people had no real scientific knowledge of why they needed certain nutrients, or even what those nutrients were, they instinctively knew from generation to generation how to build healthy bodies and healthy babies.

Nutrients For Fertility

In my book, _Naturally Knocked Up_, I talk about food as well as natural family planning, exercise, and alternative treatments, all from my perspective as a Christian. I've found that nutrition is the foundation for our health, and I devote half of the book to talking about the types of food we eat. Specifically, the nutrients listed below. While they aren't more important than other nutrients in many regards, I find it important to talk about them because they are greatly lacking in our diets.

Dairy and seafoods seemed to be prominent fertility foods for these indigenous people, and together they offer nutrients necessary for conception: vitamins A, D, E, and K2, iodine, and omega-3 fats. Most of us eating a modern American diet are basically eating ourselves into infertility, or other health issues, by not consuming the foods that nourish our bodies with these essential nutrients. All of these nutrients are also directly connected to a baby's bone structure as well as brain and neurological development.

Unfortunately, most of us no longer consume the foods that nourish our bodies. Even some of the "healthy" and "organic" foods we buy in the stores have been pasteurized and processed so all the precious vitamins and minerals are damaged. The standard American diet is now full of white sugars and flours, chemicals and preservatives, all _robbing_ our bodies of the vital nutrients we actually do consume.

Vitamin D

This important vitamin supports the production of estrogen in both men and women, is needed for insulin production, and is key in regulating cell growth. Vitamin D is also activated into an endocrine hormone within the body.

And it seems that primitive societies knew better than us on how to fulfill their daily requirements for Vitamin D as intestines, organ meats, skin and fat from certain land animals, as well as oily fish are all rich in this important nutrient. When is the last time you had intestine with your meal?

Other ways to increase your Vitamin D intake would be to include the following in your diet. (IU per 3.75 ounces or 100 grams)

- Cod liver oil—is actually the richest source of vitamin D.[2] It also contains vitamin A for better assimilation in the body.

- Lard/Tallow—from grass-fed and pastured animals, the second richest source of vitamin D.

- Pastured eggs—especially the yolks and from chickens who have had regular access to the great outdoors eating grass, worms, and other insects.

- Wild caught fish—especially fatty fish like herring.

- Butter—from grass fed cows.

- Organ meats—I know—ew, right? But they are chock full of nutrients!

- Sunlight

The way the animals are raised and fed also affects the amount of nutrients we gain from eating them. Products from animals that are allowed to be out in the pasture are recommended as the exposure to UV-B rays from the sun allow the animals body to produce more vitamin D, in turn, making more vitamin D available to us.

You'll also notice that while the above-mentioned foods are high in Vitamin D themselves, many of them are also high in cholesterol. Now, you'll have to believe me as I tell you that cholesterol is not bad for you; in fact, it's very necessary. Vitamin D is actually synthesized from the cholesterol in our body when we are exposed to the sun.

Modern RDA requirements are a measly 400 IU per day. The Weston A. Price Foundation as well as other natural and holistic doctors recommend at *least* double that amount. Many alternative health practitioners tell women to take 5000 IU per day when not pregnant and 2000 IU per day during pregnancy.

Vitamin A

Vitamin A can be classified into one of two groups: retinols, which are found in animal products, and carotenoids (beta carotene), found in plant foods. The great thing about retinols is that the body can easily convert them to a usable form of vitamin A. On the other hand, it takes a lot more beta carotene to come up with the same amount of usable vitamin A. Infants and children, as well as those in poor health (decreased thyroid function, celiac, diabetes) or on low fat diets, have an even harder time converting beta carotene.

The list of foods below are per 3.75 ounces (or 100 grams)

- Beef liver (30,000 IU)
- Butter and cream—again, levels will be higher on grass-fed cows
- High vitamin cod liver oil (230,000 IU)
- Regular cod liver oil (100,000 IU)
- Eggs—pastured chicken eggs contain two-thirds more vitamin A than conventional eggs and seven times more beta carotene.

320

The current RDA for vitamin A stands at 5000 IU even though the Weston A Price Foundation seems to think that the work of Price showed primitive diets contained almost 50,000 IU per day. As you can see, it wouldn't be hard to get well over 5000 IU by making sure you get a small amount of just one of these foods into your diet daily.

The conventional medical guidelines also list that exposure to over 10,000 IU per day may be toxic, and this is true in supplemental form. So make sure you get your vitamin A from whole foods.

Vitamin E

Again, this is a fat-soluble vitamin, but it's also an important antioxidant. An antioxidant deactivates free radicals within our bodies. Vitamin E also has a property in it known as tocopherol. The name tocopherol was given after a fertility study was done with rats in 1936 and in Greek means "to bring forth a child."

- Butter—from grass-fed cows
- Organ meats
- Grains—vitamin E is found in the wheat kernel which is removed to make white flour. It is also easily damaged during processing and can become oxidized. Freshly ground wheat is always best.
- Seeds—sunflowers contain 35 milligrams per 3.75 ounces
- Nuts—almonds contain 26 milligrams per 3.75 ounces (90 percent of which is tocopherol)
- Legumes—varies from 7 milligrams to 28 milligrams depending on variety
- Dark green leafy vegetables
- Unrefined (and unheated) oils—olive and sunflower oil
- Pastured eggs also contain three times more vitamin E than conventional eggs.

Current RDA guidelines are 15 milligrams for both adult men and women. I can't find anything else regarding how much we should consume, but it seems to me that a diet of fresh "real" foods and freshly ground grains would be *much* higher than this.

Vitamin K2

Vitamin K2 is a fat-soluble compound that assists vitamins A and D, also known as Activator X by Weston A Price. It is found in certain fatty parts of animals that feed on young green growing plants. In the process, the animals eat rapidly growing plants, which are high in vitamin K1. Part of this vitamin K1 is then converted by the animal's tissues to vitamin K2. The amounts of vitamin K2 within the animal products will then vary widely depending on what the animal eats and when they eat it, making pastured animal products especially nutrient dense in the spring and early summer. Sources include:

- Liver
- Egg yolks
- Butter
- High vitamin butter oil {natural supplement}
- Fish eggs

If you'd like to read even more about vitamin K2, I'd recommend an article written by Chris Masterjohn, "On the Trail of the Elusive X-Factor: A Sixty-Two-Year-Old Mystery Finally Solved" (http://www.westonaprice.org/fat-soluble-activators/x-factor-is-vitamin-k2).

Iodine

Iodine, a non-metallic trace element, is required by our bodies for making thyroid hormones. If you do not have enough iodine in your body you cannot make enough thyroid hormones. When our bodies are deficient in this element, it affects our thyroid, adrenals, and entire endocrine system. Not only is it important in a fertility diet, it's essential in the prenatal and nursing period as well. Infant mortality rates start to climb in areas known for iodine deficiency, and it's also been linked to higher rates of miscarriage and stillbirth. Many who live in the Midwest, especially Michigan, are deficient in iodine. It's commonly referred to as the goiter belt.

This nutrient used to be prevalent in our soil, but unfortunately, we've destroyed so many of the nutrients with bad farming practices and chemicals so that much of what we currently grow is lacking in key nutrients— iodine being one of them. While it's not found in adaquate amounts in our soil anymore, it is still prevalent in seafood. Our bodies cannot make iodine on their own; it must be consumed in our diet.

- Fruits and vegetables grown by the sea, including coconut products
- Blackstrap molasses (158 micrograms per 100 grams/3.75 ounces)
- Saltwater fish; haddock, whiting, herring (330 micrograms per 100 grams)
- Butter from cows fed on iodine rich soil
- Dried kelp (62,400 micrograms per 100 grams)
- Spinach (56 micrograms per 100 grams)
- Milk and dairy products (14 micrograms per 100 grams) (at least 20 percent of iodine is lost during pasteurization so raw is best)
- Eggs (13 micrograms per 100 grams)

The recommended RDA guideline is small: 150 micrograms for women and increase to 220 when pregnant and 290 when nursing.

On the other side of the coin, too much iodine in your body isn't a good thing either. And because iodine directly affects your thyroid and hormones, it may be something to work with a health professional on if you are deficient. Hormones are crazy things, and we don't want to supplement with this nutrient without knowing what we're doing.

Omega 3 fatty acids for Fertility

There are 3 different types of omega 3 fats; alpha-linolenic acid (ALA - plant based), eicosapentaenioc acid (EPA - animal based), and docosahexaenioc acid (DHA - animal based). Plant based ALA can be found in:

- Walnuts
- Flax seed
- Hemp

Animal based EPA and DHA can be found in:

- Egg yolks from pastured chickens {contain two to four times the amount of omega 3 as conventional eggs}
- Oily cold-water fish like salmon, herring, tuna, cod, and trout

These healthy fats have been shown to help increase a woman's fertility by regulating hormones and ovulation as well as increasing both the quantity of fertile cervical mucous and the blood flow to the reproductive organs. It is also thought that these good fats help women who are suffering from endometriosis. And a recent study done last year suggests that women suffering from infertility, on average, have lower levels of omega 3 fats (http://www.ncbi.nlm.nih.gov/pubmed/19330610?itool=EntrezSystem2.PEntrez.Pubmed.Pubmed_ResultsPanel.Pubmed_RVDocSum&ordinalpos=1). Men who do not have enough omega 3 fats in their system may have issues with sperm production since the DHA within these good fats help protect the sperm from free radicals and damage.

Vitamin B

This water-soluble vitamin is actually a group of eight vitamins that help to promote overall health within the body. Making sure you get enough B vitamins in your body can help regulate menstrual cycles and help maintain quality of both egg and sperm. Vitamin B6 is especially helpful in lengthening the luteal phase of the cycle as it can help support the production of progesterone, a hormone that many women over 35 have a difficult time maintaining.

Foods with ample amounts of this vitamin include:
- Liver
- Lentils
- Beans
- Avocados
- Kefir
- Potatoes

Vitamin C

A powerful antioxidant, vitamin C helps to protect the DNA of both egg and sperm and can help neutralize toxins within the body. It also aids in sperm and semen production, keeping the semen less sticky and allowing the sperm to move freely. (The health of our men is just as important as they age.)

Foods high in Vitamin C:

- Red peppers
- Oranges
- Broccoli
- Kiwi
- Papaya
- Strawberries

Zinc

This nutrient is an essential component of the genetic material within our bodies. A deficiency in zinc can cause chromosomal changes in both the male and female, which, in turn, causes reduced fertility and greater risk of miscarriage. In women, zinc is important in helping the body utilize reproductive hormones estrogen and progesterone. For a man, it can greatly impact the sperm count since zinc is found in high concentrations in the sperm. It is also needed to make the outer layer and the tail of the sperm.

Ways to get zinc:
- Beef, venison, and poultry
- Eggs
- Whole grains
- Whole fat dairy products
- Seeds like sunflower and pumpkin
- Molasses and maple syrup

I believe that all foods and nutrients created by God are good, but these specific nutrients have been shown, both scientifically and traditionally, to assist the body in balancing and producing hormones as well as nurture the proper growth and development of a baby. For this reason I find it important to focus on foods high in these nutrients when dealing with infertility as well as possible conception.

Unfortunately, our society has deemed many of the foods that are high in nutrients that are helpful for fertility as "bad," and we no longer eat them. **But what we need to remember is that this is the food our loving Creator has made for us, and He makes no mistakes.**

The most important thing we can do is focus on eating whole foods—foods that have not been processed or purchased off the shelves in a box. The majority of foods that Americans place in our grocery carts have already been processed so much that the nutrients are often lost or damaged, and they rob our bodies of nutrients, as they are harder to digest, leaving us well-fed but malnourished.

On my blog and in my book I discuss how to prepare whole foods in order to obtain the most nutrients from them as well as what foods may help overcome specific hormone and fertility-based health problems. There are, of course, foods that hurt our fertility; some may even be a bit more natural, but due to our over consumption of them, they are no longer healthy for our bodies until we're in a state of true health.

Foods to Avoid

Sugar

One of the anti-nutrients all health care providers, holistic health coaches, and nutritionists can agree on is sugar. This particular food can cause widespread damage throughout your body. One of the many ways it does is by causing insulin levels to rise. When you eat a sugary food, your body needs to release insulin in order bring down the levels of sugar in your blood, which then drop to low causing your adrenals to produce other hormones to return it to functioning levels. Insulin is a hormone, and when it constantly floods your system, rising and falling, it brings along all of the other hormones as well. The different parts of the endocrine system are connected, so when just one hormone cannot be regulated, it no longer performs and regulates the others – including sex hormones (testosterone, estrogen, progesterone, etc.)

Sugar may also be hard for our body to digest, especially refined sugar, taking the nutrients our body has stored in order to get rid of it. It is also hard on the liver, our bodies' natural detoxifier.

Caffeine

Studies have shown that women who drink one to one and one-half cups of coffee each day had up to a 50 percent reduction in fertility. Three cups a day has been linked to early miscarriage (new evidence shows 200 milligrams as the limit). If there is one substance, other than sugar, that moms tend to use daily, it's caffeine in the form of coffee or soda. It's hard taking care of little ones that don't let you sleep as much as you'd like, or maybe you feel stretched thin with multiple children in the home and use it to stay on top of your game. I've been there and feel like I have had to constantly break my addiction to caffeine over my years as a mother.

One of the many problems with caffeine is that the liver has to convert caffeine so that it may be passed in urine. The liver also has to deal with excreting hormones. If the liver is overworked in one area (ridding the body of toxins, including caffeine), it can't function properly. Caffeine also increases the excretion of calcium, which is important in helping your body absorb vitamin D as well as providing a baby with strong bones during pregnancy.

Most importantly, caffeine causes stress on your adrenals, which produce and maintain the proper production of hormones. When the adrenals aren't functioning properly, it becomes difficult for them to regulate your endocrine (hormone) system.

Alcohol

In women, alcohol may actually prevent the production of progesterone, a vital hormone ensuring a pregnancy is carried to term. In men, alcohol reduces the levels of sperm-making hormones which can actually wipe out a sperm count for three months after a heavy drinking session. (It takes three months for new sperm to mature.)

Low-fat Foods

It seems our bodies *need* fat in order to maintain our cellular structure. Removing the fat from milk has actually been shown to cause an imbalance of hormones throughout the body causing a failure to ovulate or produce a healthy egg. In a recent study, scientists found that women who ate full fat dairy were found to have a 27 percent lower risk of infertility (http://www.naturallyknockedup.com/is-milk-affecting-your-fertility/). Women who drank low-fat milk products twice a day were found to be *twice* as likely to not ovulate. This study shows that eating healthy fat, like that found in milk, is helpful in reproduction.

Good fats to consume are butter, coconut oil, lard, unheated extra virgin olive oil, and unheated pressed seed oils. Vegetable fats are too high in omega 6 fats and tend to cause inflammation in the body.

Soy

Soy contains phytoestrogens, and while some health practitioners (even holistic ones) think that eating soy can be healthy, I have a problem with eating something that includes plant-derived estrogens (http://www.naturallyknockedup.com/what-i-think-about-soy-milk/). While in some cases a diet that includes a small amount of soy may not be bothersome, many men and women find they have issues with this particular food and that it causes problems with their hormone balance.

Soy may also contain high amounts of phytic acid, which prevents nutrients from being absorbed and robs bodily stores of nutrients. (It may bind to nutrients like zinc and carry them out of the body.)

Lastly, a very large portion of the soy grown in the United States is genetically modified, meaning that scientists have changed the DNA of the plant by merging it with cells from other organisms.

A few studies have been done on animals that show genetically modified foods may decrease fertility.

Processed Foods

This category of foods contains many of the harmful substances we place into our bodies like MSG, trans fats, high fructose corn syrup, and soda. There really is nothing more sabotaging to healthy eating than processed foods. Not only do they place various toxins into our bodies, thereby making the liver less efficient at cleaning them out, but we, once again, use a lot of nutrient stores digesting them.

While we may never have a perfect diet, we can make a conscious effort to cut back our consumption of certain foods so that our bodies can function in the way that we were created to function. It's all about eating for nourishment.

So what does eating like this look like? The menu below is one of my own personal menus, and I share it to give you an idea of how you can incorporate healthy foods into your diet. More importantly this menu lacks refined sugars and processed foods that deplete your body of vital nutrients. The only sweeteners I use are honey, maple syrup, and very sparingly, whole cane sugar.

Monday:

Breakfast - two egg omelet with cheese and veggies, sausage

Snack - whole milk yogurt and berries, small amount of raw honey if needed

Lunch - salmon sandwich (canned wild caught Alaskan salmon with homemade mayo)on sourdough bread, steamed broccoli, cheese

Snack - cut veggies and avocado aioli

Dinner - roast chicken with gravy made from chicken broth, various steamed veggies with butter

Tuesday:

Breakfast - whole milk yogurt with berries and a touch of raw honey

Snack - cut veggies and homemade dip

Lunch - salad with red and green lettuce, baby spinach and lots of colorful veggies, chopped nuts, cubed cheese, organic ranch dressing, and steamed vegetables with butter

Snack - apple and crispy almonds

Dinner - tacos with homemade seasoning and shells. Serve with cheese, dark green lettuce, homemade guacamole, crème fraiche (like sour cream) and fresh salsa.

Wednesday:

Breakfast - 16 ounces yogurt or kefir smoothie (1/2 cup yogurt or kefir, ½ cup raw milk, 1 raw egg yolk, 1 Tablespoon melted coconut oil, 1/2 cup frozen berries)

Snack - deviled eggs

Lunch - homemade chicken noodle soup made with bone broth

Snack - cut veggies and organic dip, cubed cheese

Dinner - grilled or baked salmon, steamed vegetables, baked potato with real butter

Thursday:

Breakfast - fried eggs (optional – on whole wheat sourdough toast), smoothie

Snack - yogurt and berries

Lunch - chicken sandwich (from leftover grilled chicken) with lettuce, homemade mayo, cut veggies

Snack - apple, cubed cheese

Dinner - Meatloaf or seasoned hamburger patties, sweet potato fries, salad with homemade dressing

Friday:

Breakfast - soaked oatmeal with butter, raw cream, walnuts, and maple syrup

Snack - cut veggies

Lunch - taco salad (leftover taco meat, red and green leaf lettuce, some iceberg lettuce, cut avocado, fresh salsa, seasoned brown rice, and sharp cheddar cheese.

Snack - orange

Dinner - grilled steaks, lots of steamed vegetables with butter

Saturday:

Breakfast - scrambled eggs w/ chopped spinach and cheese

Snack - apple

Lunch - butternut squash soup

Snack - yogurt

Dinner - gluten free homemade pizza topped with lots of colorful veggies and healthy meats like sausage

Snack - homemade popcorn on the stove with real butter and coconut oil

Sunday:

Breakfast - sourdough pancakes, smoothie

Snack - hard boiled eggs

Lunch - salad with baby spinach, leftover roast chicken and lots of colorful veggies

Snack - apple, crispy nuts

Dinner - Italian Cream Cheese Casserole with steamed veggies and salad

As Christians, we are to be a light in the world, to behave differently than the masses. And it's my personal belief that this thought also lends itself well to the way we eat and take care of our bodies. In the Bible and throughout history Christians were to prepare their foods differently and were sometimes asked to avoid certain foods for a time. Daniel was instructed to avoid the king's food, and he and his friends were blessed with strong bodies and good health. The Israelites were told not eat the foods or use the same types of medicine as the Egyptians in order to maintain their health.

Just as we ask for the Lord's leading in other areas of our life, I feel that we should also be asking for wisdom in how to nourish our bodies and our families.

Problems That May Arise as We Age

As much as we would like to remain young, it's no secret that fertility decreases as we age. It is, and has been, the way of life for many thousands of years. Throughout our 30s and into our 40s our fertility gradually declines until we enter menopause.

This does not mean that pregnancy is impossible or that it may always lead to a negative outcome. I feel that the way we treat our bodies and actively work on healing and maintaining our health can help our reproductive health. It's all about nourishing the body to balance hormones no matter what our age or stage in life.

Egg Quality

We are often told that our egg quality decreases as we age and that there is nothing we can do about the risk of miscarriage or birth defects. But we can do something to better the health of our eggs. A woman's primordial eggs were developed before she was even born, but once a specific egg has been given the signal to continue development in preparation for ovulation and possible conception, there is a 90 day time period in which nutrition and lifestyle can make an impact on the quality of the egg (http://natural-fertility-info.com/increase-egg-health). So both the egg and sperm have an active lifespan of just over three months, and the way we treat our bodies now will affect the health of the egg in our cycle three months from now.

If a body is malnourished (meaning it doesn't have the proper nutrients) the egg and its DNA will also be affected. This means that it becomes even more important as we age to eat a nutrient dense diet.

Our age comes into play because we live in a fallen world. We're exposed to toxins that break down and damage our bodies, and most of us have at one time or another eaten very poorly. So the age of our cells and our bodies are based not necessarily on a number, but on our diet and lifestyle.

Are we actively building our bodies up, or are we just getting them through another day?

Thyroid Problems

After much research and talking with many different women, I have learned that many of us suffer from some sort of thyroid problem, whether it's sub-clinical or undiagnosed hypo/hyperthyroidism. Many women have also been suffering for years due to thyroid issues, and their doctors have been unable to show them how to heal their bodies.

Why am I mentioning this in a chapter about fertility? Because if the thyroid is having problems, there will also be problems with other parts of your body, especially the reproductive system. The thyroid is like an engine light telling you something is wrong, and if you can get to the root of the problem and heal it, then problems in other parts of your life begin to reverse as well.

I also think there are many women feeling like they might be depressed or anxious, overwhelmed, and constantly fatigued. Yes, having babies and small children do contribute to that, but not to the extent that most women experience it.

Women who have children are also more apt to have problems with their thyroid because these precious little bundles of joy take these important nutrients from our bodies, and we're not replacing them in sufficient amounts.

Common Symptoms of Hypothyroidism (under active thyroid):

- Depression
- Anxiety
- Low basal body temps and/or low temperatures throughout the day
- Cold hands and feet
- Morning headaches that go away throughout the day
- Infertility
- Fatigue
- Cloudy thinking
- Weight gain or inability to lose weight easily
- Sensitivity to cold weather
- Constipation
- Digestive problems

- Poor circulation
- Slow wound healing
- Need excessive amounts of sleep
- Gets sick often (colds or viral infections)
- Itchy and dry skin
- Dry hair that breaks often or thinning hair
- Thinning of the outermost part of the eyebrow
- High cholesterol

Symptoms of Hyperthyroidism (overactive thyroid):

- Heart palpitations
- Heat intolerance
- Nervousness
- Fast heart rate
- Hair loss
- Muscle weakness

The following may also indicate Hashimotos, an autoimmune thyroid disorder:

- Heart palpitations
- Inward trembling
- Increased pulse rate, even at rest
- Feelings of nervousness and emotional distress
- Night sweats
- Difficulty gaining weight
- People with Hashimoto's also tend to go back and forth between the symptoms of hypo and hyper thyroid.

I have written more in depth about thyroid conditions on my blog, so if any of these symptoms ring a bell, please look into proper testing and treatment. This is also one area of health where conventional doctors often drop the ball, so you need to be well informed.

Healing the thyroid - Learn the basics of how the thyroid functions, signs and symptoms, lab tests you need run, and how to heal it naturally (http://www.naturallyknockedup.com/healing-the-thyroid/).

Complications, Miscarriage and Loss

Miscarriage is a sensitive subject and somewhat difficult to approach. I'm so sorry if you have traveled that road of loss.

We've already discussed how our age, lifestyle, and nutrition can affect our bodies in many ways. We may be lacking in specific nutrients, or maybe our DNA is damaged, which can lead to complications in pregnancy or even the loss of our little ones. I feel both problems can be lessened with proper nutrition and taking care of other health problems we may face.

But again, we live in a fallen world, and there are many things out of our control. Health problems and death are a part of our sinful world, yet through the grace of God we can find hope in our futures.

My belief is that while the medical world looks at pregnancy complications and pregnancy loss as a normal part of aging, it doesn't have to be that way. Too often I see women who are told that their multiple miscarriages are due to their advanced maternal age (over 35), and proper testing is not done. Often our doctors fail to look into potential causes, and families suffer as a result.

In order to know what's going on with our bodies, it's important to practice natural family planning. Through the use of charting your basal (waking) temperatures and keeping track of your cervical fluid, you can not only pinpoint the day of ovulation, but you can also make sure you're ovulating each month, which doesn't always happen as we age. You can also see how long your luteal phase is (after ovulation and before your period) which may signal progesterone issues if less than 12 days. If you have a luteal phase defect, you may not produce enough progesterone to sustain a pregnancy, and this can be fixed by supplying specific nutrients to increase your own progesterone production or through the use of a bio-identical progesterone cream. There is also a simple lab test to check your progesterone levels in early pregnancy to make sure your body is producing it in the correct amount. I think every woman over 35 (and younger depending on reproductive health) should have this checked at least once within the first six to eight weeks. They can do two simple blood tests, two days apart, to make sure that it's increasing in the proper amounts. If it's not, progesterone supplementation can be used until the second trimester when the placenta takes over and produces progesterone.

Often this isn't checked until someone has multiple losses, and sometimes it isn't checked at all in women who are over 35 because age is considered the cause of the loss.

It becomes even more important as we age to find a doctor that is willing to work within our beliefs on family size and who will help keep us healthy without using our age as an excuse.

Enzymes

Something I'll touch on briefly, because age also affects this area of health, are the enzymes our bodies naturally produce. Over time we can gradually stop producing enzymes that help us digest our foods and rid the body of cellular waste, and this happens more often when we eat a diet high in sugar and processed foods. This can often show up in the form of nutrient deficiencies when our bodies can't absorb the nutrients we're consuming, or as blood clotting disorders when our blood becomes "gummed up" by not expelling cellular waste.

Nutrient deficiencies are problematic, because if we don't have enough essential fertility nutrients, our bodies cannot reproduce effectively or produce the correct level of hormones. Clotting disorders can develop and cause miscarriage as the blood supply through the placenta is reduced, resulting in pregnancy loss.

There are many different enzymes the body needs, and I'm just beginning my research on them, but if you struggle with health issues or problems with fertility and/or pregnancy loss, it will be well worth your time to look into it.

Resources:

1. Systematic Enzyme Support - http://www. systemicenzymesupport.org/faq/hormones.htm

2. What Are Systemic Proteolytic Enzymes - http://www. losethebackpain.com/proteolyticenzymes.html

3. Fertility Enzyme Therapies - http://natural-fertility-info. com/fertility-enzyme-therapy

Being over 40 doesn't mean that your ability to grow your family is over, and it also doesn't mean that complications and pregnancy loss are inevitable. It simply means that you need to pay special attention to your health and nourish it to the best of your ability and God-given resources. It may be harder to weed through health information and keep our bodies healthy as we age, but it's not impossible.

I pray that this information has been helpful, but not overwhelming, as you journey into opening your hearts and growing your families. May the Lord bless you and your family.

Donielle Baker *is an amateur herbalist and mama to two little ones. She writes to inspire people to work with their bodies holistically to balance hormones and heal their reproductive system. Donielle has a passion for nutrition, natural living, and spreading the word on how food truly affects our health. Her blog, Naturally Knocked Up, focuses on fertility, hormone balance, and reproductive health, and her book on natural fertility (of the same name) is a great resource on how to make natural fertility treatments work for you.*

Recommended Resources

Fertility, Cycles and Nutrition 4th edition by Marilyn M. Shannon

The Way Home, Beyond Feminism Back to Reality by Mary Pride

Lies Women Believe: And the Truth that Sets Them Free by Nancy Leigh DeMoss

Stepping Heavenward by Elizabeth Prentiss

A Woman After God's Own Heart by Elizabeth George

Loving God with All Your Mind by Elizabeth George

Large Family Logistics by Kim Brenneman

A Love that Multiplies by Jim Bob and Michelle Duggar

Love in the House by Chris Jeub

Natural Family Planning: The Complete Approach by John and Sheila Kippley

Be Fruitful and Multiply by Nancy Campbell

Children: Blessing or Burden, Exploding the Myth of the Small Family by Max Heine

Naturally Knocked Up by Donielle Baker

Standing on the Promises, A Handbook of Biblical Childrearing by Douglas Wilson

What Your Doctor May Not Tell You About Pre-Menopause by John R. Lee M.D.

What Your Doctor May Not Tell You About Menopause by John R. Lee M.D.

Trim Healthy Mama by Serene Allison and Pearl Barrett

Loving and Little Years by Rachel Jankovic

Fit to Burst by Rachel Jankovic

When People Are Big and God is Small by Edward T. Welch

A Mom Just Like You by Vickie and Jayme Farris

I Will Carry You, The Sacred Dance of Grief and Joy by Angie Smith

The Call to Wonder by R.C. Sproul, Jr.

Without Moral Limits: Women, Reproduction and Medical Technology by Debra Evans

What is a Family? by Edith Schaeffer

Passionate Housewives Desperate for God by Jennie Chancey and Stacy McDonald

www.fertilityflower.com

"The Baby Conference" by Vision Forum

"The Hopeful Theology of Miscarriage" by Doug Phillips (DVD)

"The Birth Control Movie: How Did We Get Here" (DVD)

"Rescued: The Heart of Adoption and Caring for Orphans" (DVD)

Would you like to expand your vision beyond the walls of your home and the confines of your time in history? Do you long to see things from a different perspective than the world around you?

A higher one?

Come and visit us at VisionaryWomanhood.com where you will get rich, meaty articles written by several of the writers who contributed to this book. Discover a biblical worldview on the topics of motherhood, wifehood, home education, missions, homemaking and more!

To introduce you to all the Visionary Womanhood blog has to offer, I'd like to give you a PDF download of *The Best of Visionary Womanhood Volume One* **FREE**. It's packed with 35 of the most beloved articles from the 2011-2012 archives. (Regular price $5)

Not only will you get a PDF download of this book, but you will also get *Visionary Womanhood Gatherings: A Titus 2 Mentorship Tool for Women and Maidens* AND the first chapter of *The Heart of Simplicity* also **FREE.**

Coupon code: NEWREADER

Go here to redeem your coupon code: http://www. visionarywomanhood.com/the-best-of-visionary-womanhood-volume-one/

Made in the USA
San Bernardino, CA
06 December 2013